LIVING WITH DREAMS

LIVING WITH DREAMS

Dr Roderick Peters

ANDRE DEUTSCH

First published 1990 by
André Deutsch Limited
105 – 106 Great Russell Street, London WC1B 3LJ

ISBN 0 233 98583 2

Printed and bound in Great Britain by
St Edmundsbury Press, Bury St Edmunds, Suffolk

*for Elsa and Fuschia and
Dylan*

CONTENTS

Dreams and the sex of the dreamer * Experience and theory * The nature of dreams and dreaming * Natural phenomena * Mind and psyche * Interpreting * The structure of dreams * A model of the psyche * Conscious and unconscious * Ego * Ego nucleus * Ego functions * Persona * Unconscious psyche * Self * Archetypes * Shadow * Collective shadow * Anima and animus * Other archetypes

The dream-ego * The dream-ego in relation to its setting * The dream-ego in relation to other dream figures * The dream-ego in relation to the drama * The dream-ego in relation to the self

Definition * Representing the immaterial * Past, present and future * Tapestries of symbol * Conventional relation * Collective symbols * Engaging with symbol * Known and unknown * Symbol and propaganda * Figures of speech * Two halves * Inside and outside and archetypal image * Symbols, archetypes and fate * Soul, spirit and symbol * Symbolic attitude * Learning about symbols

Mare of the night * Nightmare and childhood * Nightmares and talion law * Recurrent nightmares * Nightmare and self-reflection * The purpose of nightmares * Personal and collective * Good and evil: love and hate

12 ANXIETY DREAMS

Failing in duty and expectations * The examination * God and the parents in early life * Guilt * Shame * Loss and abandonment * Engulfment and disintegration * Aggression * Envy and jealousy

13 EROTIC DREAMS

Libido * Male and female * The young * The lonely * The adult * The orgasm * The two loves * The two women * Keeping Eros in the dark * Sex and religion

14 DREAMS, DAYDREAMS, FANTASIES AND VISIONS

15 COMMON TO ALL

The four elements * Points of the compass * Time *Colours * Overworld, world, underworld * Supernatural * Home * The Royal Family * Forests and animals * Dress and undress * The wound * The way * Living with dreams

ACKNOWLEDGEMENTS

Discretion makes it impossible for me to thank by name all those who have given me permission to use their dreams, daydreams, fantasies, and visions. Namelessly, then, I thank you; not only for the material but for all that we have experienced together.

I am grateful to André Deutsch, Andrew Franklin, and Tom Rosenthal for their belief and encouragement; to Alex Stitt for his enthusiastic and stimulating editorial help; to my wife, for help with many tiresome tasks; to my children for their encouragement and understanding; to my friends − Francine Winham, Martin and Corinna Perry, Chris Blackwell, Joe and Meike Blackwell, Desmond and Jo Corcoran, Philip and Wendy Haworth, Andrew Samuels, and Christopher Perry − all of whom have helped me, one way or another, to write this book. And I am grateful to Mavis Fleming for her cheerful spirit and steady self-effacing work.

INTRODUCTION

THERE WAS A TIME when dreams were held in high regard; believing that they contained clues about the hidden shaping of events, about destiny, many people valued dreams because they might help with the ever-doubtful matter of survival. Actually, this is still true for many parts of our world; I place it in the past only because I belong to the technological and scientific 'first world'. Most likely, dear reader, you do too.

Perhaps it has something to do with how much control we have acquired over our environment, and perhaps other reasons come into it too, but one has to admit that dreams are no longer held in high regard by our complex civilization. Certain specialized groups take a particular interest in dreams: psychiatrists and analysts, clinicians and researchers in sleep and dream laboratories; and artists, especially film-makers whose moving picture medium is well-suited for using dream experience. But outside the realms of science fiction it is hard to imagine the President of the United States, or his counterpart in the USSR, appointing a dream-interpreter to high office as the Pharaoh did with Joseph!

Belonging to one of the groups that *do* take an unusual interest in dreams — I am an analyst in the tradition of Carl Jung — I might be accused of an understandable bias when I say that our culture as a whole has lost sight too much of the value of dreams. Leaders used to dream for their tribes or nations (and still do in certain places where the tribe is well-unified and small enough) but this no longer happens in our huge and powerful nations; perhaps they are too big and too internally disparate. Nowadays dreams belong to the individual, the private citizen. It is at this personal level that I mean that dreams are undervalued.

They are given little time in our busy Western way of life, and so much value is attached to applied consciousness that many are actually ashamed of admitting an interest in their dream-life.

Dreaming, whatever else it may be, is a part of our healthy functioning; it makes just as much sense to pay heed to our dreams as it does to our weight; more, in all probability, because dreams are active communications. An interest in dreams which is not unbalanced — that is to say, not being used as a retreat or escape from the waking world of reality, but rather as a complement to it — is both healthy and wise.

1

If you do not keep it out with armour-plated scepticism, the content of this book will probably change the way you live with your dreams. Because this is a potent matter, and not an innocuous pastime, my sense of responsibility requires me to make a few introductory remarks.

Your dreams are *you* too. Paying heed to your dreams is like bringing known and unknown parts of yourself into contact. Do you choose to go this way? From these pages dream — a state of the psyche different from waking — will reach out and touch you. Streaming along the very channels created by your interest, dream will bring its shadows and strange lights to the super-structures of your consciousness. The 'you' you have known will not remain quite the same. You will change. Dream can see you where you cannot see yourself. The walls you have built (not just you; we have all built them, more or less, from our earliest childhood) to keep away dream will weaken. Like a mist rising from the dark earth dream will enter the glass of your self-reflection.

Of course dreams are going on whether we remember them or not, and they influence us unconsciously even when we don't remember them. Actually to direct some portion of conscious attention to dreams that are remembered is, however, a different matter. Entering into a participating dialogue, or relationship, with your dreams; being prepared to recognize things about yourself which you did not know, and may feel you would have preferred not to know; and engaging in the moral dilemmas which will necessarily appear ... all this will challenge you. But you will know, and be, more of yourself.

Bear in mind, finally, that dreams have to be *lived with* to know their value; dreams whose meaning may have been wholly obscure when first remembered often begin to be understood as time passes and developments take place; instant analysis or interpretation may be a beginning, but it will never be the last word.

Writing about dreams presents a peculiar difficulty; the dream itself is experiential and visual, usually wordless; its translation into words and concepts could be a lengthy business in itself, were one to try to capture every shade of meaning and allusion. But that is only the beginning; each of the images within a dream, so subtle and many-sided, has a number of associative connections with the dreamer's life, not only in regard to the current situation but to the past as well. So something, at least, of the dreamer's life has to be described if the meaning of the dream is to become visible. A single substantial dream, exhaustively described, and with every associative link pursued, could easily make a book in itself.

As if this were not difficult enough, the fact is that single dreams cannot provide a real understanding of the wonderful way in which psyche works through dreams. Only by following through a dream-series of some months can one begin truly to see the urge within psyche to communicate with consciousness, see how certain themes are repeated and represented in a variety of forms until consciously grasped, see developments taking place.

My difficulty, then, has lain in the need to provide a long-enough dream sequence and the problems of balance and book-length which necessarily arise. The only solution I have found has been to gather into two successive chapters most of the dreams from the series, together with all the commentary, but to use certain dreams from the series to double up as illustrations for the particular themes being dealt with in other chapters.

The book as a whole contains the texts (usually condensed) of 145 dreams. Fifty-nine of these come from the one person whose series of dreams we follow. The criticism might be made that this places too much reliance on the dreams of a single individual. Such a criticism would find a familiar home in the already half-century long debate between psychiatry and analysis: psychiatrists, especially those with a physical (or 'organic') leaning, mistrust the sweeping theories which analysts derive from deep study of a few individuals. Analysts, on the other hand, believe that psychiatrists spend so little time with so many different individuals that understanding can go little further than diagnostic categorization.

Their differing attitudes belong in turn to a more general pair of irreconcilable opposites: whether knowledge is better gained through deep immersion in the particular, or broad survey of the generality. Both, obviously, have their place.

A further criticism might be levelled at the overall gender imbalance. Since a dream-series can only have come from either a male or a female it is bound to create a disproportion. In the event I have used a dream-series from a man and so the book as a whole has more men's dreams than women's dreams. But there are eighty-six dreams outside the series, drawn from some sixty individuals; to go some way towards restoring the sex ratio, fifty-three of these were dreamed by women and the remaining thirty-three by men. Although the sex of the dreamer is naturally of the highest importance in understanding a dream, there is so very much in common between the dreams of either sex that I hope women readers will not only understand the reason for there being fewer women's dreams in my book but also appreciate that almost as much can be learned from the dreams of either sex.

There is, finally, the inevitable inconvenience of having to turn to other parts of the book (page numbers are given) in order to read the text for some dreams.

All in all, though, I believe the advantages of having a dream-series outweigh the disadvantages, and I hope you will bear with me.

3

A last remark concerning sources and references: *Living with Dreams* is not a specialist nor a scholarly work and detailed references to sources, which would be numerous and cumbersome, are not given. Some chapters end with a short list of relevant further reading.

I would not like it to be thought that the absence of references is in any way a failure to acknowledge the work of others; the research, ideas, and influence of many has gone into this book, and I know it. The one individual whose influence is so comprehensive that I must acknowledge it in gratitude, is C.G.Jung.

Roderick Peters
London, 1990

One

DREAMS AND REALITY

DAY IS DONE and kitchen creaks to slow silence; in the faintest green haze from the oven's digital display, a cat delicately picks its way across the clutter of washing up on the draining-board.

In the front bedroom the woman reaches across her sleeping husband to set the alarm-clock and switch off the light. Moments later the crash of splintering crockery from downstairs is instantly followed by terrified screams. They pierce straight to the centre of her being, as they always do; but she thrusts away the faint quiverings of her own panic and rises swiftly from her bed to hurry down the corridor to her boy's room, glancing anxiously into the darkness of the hall as she passes the stairs.

Turning on the globe lamp at the head of his bed she sees his arms raised as if to ward something off, and his head turning from side to side. She kneels and lays her hand on his forehead; his three-year-old face is pale and damp; tiny beads of sweat glisten from the tip of his nose and his fair hair clings to his forehead in wet strands. His eyes are wide open but they have the lightlessness of unawake eyes.

'Never mind, darling. It's all right, Tombalino,' she says softly as she strokes the hair back from his forehead in slow rhythmic movements. 'It's all right now.'

He becomes soothed and lies still; awareness drifts slowly into his eyes. He knows she is there without ever fully waking up. After a moment he turns his head and stares at the window.

'She was trying to open the window. She was breaking it in,' he trembled.

She gazed down at her little son; it hurt her cruelly to see his suffering and be able to do so little to stop it.

'What was she like?'

'The witch-woman ... she wants to kill me. She's got black and white spots all over. Her nose ...' Even as he spoke his eyes began to search as if for a moment he felt again her evil presence.

'It's just a bad dream, Little One,' she told him. 'Just a bad dream. She's not Real. See ... here I am. I'm Real ... see.' She moved closer to him and the little boy nuzzled into her. Very soon he was asleep.

5

Is his witch real or unreal? This mother, like so many mothers and fathers through the generations, is helping her little one to distinguish between dreams and reality. Being awake, knowing himself and his mother and his room, is one thing, she says, and dreaming is something else. What he knows when he is awake is real; what he experiences when he is dreaming is not real.

To know the difference is essential for sanity; one might almost say that sanity *is* knowing the difference. But whether the difference is truly between real and unreal begs the question 'what is real?' Perhaps our being told, when we are little, that waking experience is real and dreams are not real is an appropriate way of helping us to know the difference; but perhaps when we are older and know the difference better we can find less blunt a tool to divide the two. This is necessary because the fact is that dreams do have their own reality. If, as adults, we dismiss dreams as unreal then we actually lose sight of a valuable part of our overall reality.

EMOTIONAL REALITY

There are times when one wakes up, having slept a good eight hours and expecting to feel refreshed, only to find one is actually limp as a dead fish. It can feel as if one has done continuous hard work for those eight hours, or been through a prolonged emotional ordeal. This is precisely right of course, and it brings us to the emotional reality of dream.

Occasionally there is awareness of dreaming within the dream; one says to oneself, as it were, 'I know this is a dream'. Far more often, though, the dreamer is wholly immersed within the dream, involved in a drama the scenes of which are the animated images of a complex tapestry of emotions. Consider the following dream:

21.4.77 I enter a dark forest, passing an old man on the way; I know he will watch which way I go. Then I am on a rocky outcrop, alone, deep in the forest; suddenly I see a naked woman bring a baby onto a stone shelf above an abysmal drop; she puts the baby right next to the edge and even dangles it over while she postures in various orgiastic positions with her genitals thrust forward. I'm torn between lustful fascination of watching her and the wish to save the baby; other children appear and one little girl asks me to help. I get up to do so but the vertiginous height and proximity of the edge make me sick to my stomach and wavery in mind; other women come and pick up the baby.*

*All dreams *preceded by a date* are from the person whose series of dreams appears in Chapters 6 and 7. See the Introduction now, if you haven't already.

6

So long as he was *within* the dream, the dreamer experienced himself, his surroundings and the other figures no less vividly or intensely than a waking experience. In fact from the viewpoint of emotional awareness had he lived through the same feelings while awake he would have felt he'd had quite a day! What felt less real than waking experience was his orientation in space and time; he couldn't have said where the forest was exactly, nor when all this was taking place; it was unclear whether the old man was 'on his side' or against him; he could not have said where the children appeared from.

But even without knowing anything about the dreamer, nor what he himself said about the dream, it is not hard to imagine the intense emotions of lust, anxiety, even terror, which evidently were experienced in the dream, and perhaps gave rise to it.

One may reasonably assume that the dreamer's waking reality is not actually like that. But it is a reality that emotions such as these, which have found dramatic portrayal within the dream, do exist within the dreamer and are being brought into contact with consciousness at this particular time and in this particular way.

The simple fact is that dreams are often powerful subjective experiences. We may grind our teeth (a woman broke five teeth so grimly did she grind them), weep, cry out, laugh, be paralyzed with deadly fear, feel rage and murderous anger, experience the profoundest love for a person, sacred awe, sadness for some beauty lost, or sexual arousal and orgasm; our hearts beat furiously and our minds race. More than a few people will admit that the emotional experiences most secretly influential throughout their lives have been in dreams. Indeed most of us probably feel more emotion while we are dreaming, whether we remember the dreams or not, than we do in our waking hours.

Emotions are rather more than strong feelings; not all feelings are accompanied by sensations of physiological changes such as the heart beating faster, or difficulty in breathing. In other words, emotions involve bodily sensations. Given the undeniable emotional reality of dreams one would expect them to be accompanied by detectable physiological changes. The work of the last forty years in sleep and dream laboratories (of which there are some 200 in the USA alone) has shown this to be so.

Remembering one's dreams, living with them, understanding them more or less well, is a process full of uncertainties; one is constantly attempting to assess oneself and one's dream images and experiences in a way that is necessarily subjective. The reassuring certainties of scientifically established facts scarcely enter into it, which makes it all too easy for idealistic or unrealistic views of dreams to be advanced.

Before setting out into these uncertain waters of the role of dreams in our lives, and leaving the relatively certain shores of scientific fact behind, then, it is well worthwhile to have a look at what science *has* established about sleep and dream. These parts of our lives have only received co-ordinated study for the last half century, and like every area that science begins to explore, more questions come to light than answers; nevertheless the little that is established can provide us with some solid ground from which to begin our journey and upon which we may touch down from time to time.

SLEEP

The circadian rhythm, an immensely complex and sensitive symphony of physiological changes, governs our bodily state from one rising of the sun to the next. Co-ordinated by some inner timekeeping, our entire physiologies are subtly altered according to the hour of day or night.

Just how much this timekeeping is linked to the light of the sun has been confirmed by the discovery of the *suprachiasmatic nuclei*; these are tiny groups of cells situated above the place where the optic nerves cross over as they leave the eyeballs and sweep towards the back of the brain. They play some important role in setting the clock of the circadian rhythm. This rhythm, as we all know from jet travel, takes quite some time to reset itself when we travel to a place with very different hours of daylight from those to which we have been accustomed. It has been shown that stimulating the suprachiasmatic nuclei by exposing people to bright lights at certain times can reset the internal clock faster than would normally be the case.

Recognizing that our physiology is set for sleep in the hours of darkness highlights the problem that shift-workers have; they have to try to sleep when their physiology is not set for it, and try to work when they are physiologically prepared for sleep. The many accidents, mistakes, and lapses of concentration to which shift-workers are prone are a part of the price we pay for our compulsive drive towards 24-hour productivity.

Sleep is, of course, a natural part of the circadian rhythm; to most of us the purpose of sleep seems obvious enough; sleep restores our energy, and 'knits up the ravelled sleave of care' as Shakespeare put it. It is not surprising, perhaps, that sleeping habits have a statistical relation to length of life: those who sleep between seven to eight hours a night live longest; either more or less and you are likely to die younger. But the scientists who study sleep cannot be satisfied with such true but imprecise answers to questions about the purpose of sleep; they want to find out all the intricacies of the how and the why of sleep. Most investigators would say this remains a mystery, but it is safe to say that whatever else we need from sleep, we certainly need to have our dreams.

We can tolerate being deprived of our non-dream sleep more readily than our dream-sleep. Although this has long been intuitively understood by some, it was only established scientifically once scientists were able to determine exactly when dreaming takes place during sleep. By and large, dreaming does not occur just randomly during sleep; all of us dream, every night, in a number of quite well-defined cycles.

REM SLEEP

Up until the late 1940s there had been a vague assumption in scientific circles that the brain closed up shop during sleep, switched itself off, as it were. Then Nathaniel Kleitman, a physiologist at the University of Chicago, directed a postgraduate student of his, Eugene Aserinsky, to look into the question of eye movements during sleep; Aserinsky's studies led, in 1951, to the discovery of certain periods during sleep when the eyes move in a very rapid and characteristic manner. This phenomenon has now become widely known as REM sleep ('Rapid Eye Movement' sleep), and subsequently been shown beyond all doubt to have a special connection with dreaming. By making simultaneous recordings with the electroencephalogram (the EEG, which records electrical brain waves) and the electro-oculogram (the EOG which records the movements of the eyes), the relationship of eye movements to phases of sleep could be studied.

It turns out that we begin our nights with about an hour and a half of sleep during which there are a few slow rolling movements of the eyes, but none of the rapid eye movements associated with dream. During this time the brain waves are gradually lengthening. The changing rhythms of the brain waves in sleep fall into four stages, clearly discernible to a practised eye (see diagram overleaf). The last, stage 4, corresponds with deepest sleep.

Shortly after the sleeper has entered stage-4 sleep, at a moment which is typically marked by a change in sleeping posture, the first REM period of the night begins. Eye movements take on a characteristic darting quality and are very frequent, while the brain-wave pattern alters, rising through the lighter stages of sleep towards stage 1. The rapid eye movements go on for about twenty to thirty minutes and then stop, this transition also being marked by a change in posture. This first REM period comes from the deepest level of sleep; the dreams it has brought tend to have a different quality from those of later REM periods (of which more in later chapters).

Once the first REM period is over, the next cycle begins. The sleeper sinks into nearly as deep a level of sleep as before, and then, once more, the rapid eye movements begin.

Each REM/non-REM cycle lasts about ninety minutes. The sleeper rises close to stage-1 sleep during each REM period, but as the night proceeds

9

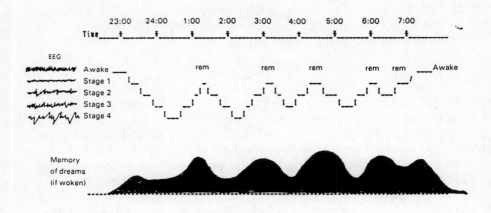

Stages of sleep and pattern of dreaming

the subsequent descent is shallower. There are usually four or five cycles each night, and by the time the last cycle has been reached the depth of sleep before and after the REM is no more than stage 2 (see diagram).

The lighter sleep of the last REM cycle, together with the fact that dreams are being experienced closer to waking-up time, are doubtless the main reasons why dreams are more easily remembered from these periods. But another factor is that the dreams themselves are unmistakably closer in character to waking consciousness than the dreams of earlier REM cycles. The rapidity and frequency of eye movements are greatest in the later REM cycles.

So far we have only been considering the adult's pattern of sleep. But sleep is not quite the same bedfellow from the cradle to the grave. Infants sleep a great deal and the elderly do not sleep much. Not only does the duration of sleep change, there is also change in the proportion spent in REM.

Infants sleep about sixteen hours a day, but a good six hours of this is REM sleep. In adulthood through middle age sleep occupies some six to eight hours a day, of which one to one-and-a-half hours is REM, a drop from the 40 per cent of infancy to about 20 per cent. The elderly sleep little more than three to four hours, and REM sleep is reduced to only half an hour, which is, however, still the same 20 per cent proportion as in earlier adulthood. These changing proportions have prompted hypotheses that REM sleep may be involved in the maturation and development of the neuronal system. In other words, if our brains are to grow optimally they perhaps need dreams.

In summary, then, the outward pattern of a night's sleep consists of four or five cycles of non-REM/REM; changes in sleeping posture occur about ten times per night: one before each REM phase, and one after.

DREAM

But what is happening inside, both inside the mind and inside the body?

By waking people up at every stage of sleep and getting them to describe what they have been experiencing, a reasonably consistent picture has emerged of the mind's activity throughout sleep; and this can be matched with the objective evidence of physiological changes.*

In stage 1, which is 'falling asleep', thoughts lose clear consciousness and begin to wander, often becoming conscious only if something occurs to disturb the descent into sleep; even then they are fleeting and difficult to catch. Hypnagogic images may be experienced during this stage; they are startlingly vivid images, almost hallucinatory, which appear completely unexpectedly as one falls asleep, persist for a moment or two and then vanish. A man who was dropping off to sleep, for instance, was abruptly jerked back to consciousness by the shocking sight of a rotting skull which had his father's face looking at him with a knowing sneer. It is hard, and perhaps pointless, in this early stage of going to sleep to distinguish between thoughts-with-images and dreams.

Stage 2, in which the subject appears definitely asleep to the observer, and which the subject himself describes as sleep if he is awoken from it,† is not devoid of dreams either. Vivid dreams are occasionally reported from this level but more commonly the awakened sleeper describes the subjective mind activity as 'thought-like'. This, in fact, holds true for all non-REM sleep: vivid dreams in the form of images *do* occur but usually there are no

---

*Incidentally, for those who doubt the existence of an unconscious component of the psyche, believing that our minds begin and end with what we are conscious of, there could hardly be clearer proof of the existence of unconscious psyche. Very often it happens that individuals woken in the small hours describe vivid dreams, and yet have no memory of them the following day. Surely the memory of them must be there, but unconsciously?

†Although it is a characteristic of many who consider themselves insomniacs to feel they have *not been asleep* when woken from stage 2, or even deeper stages of sleep.

dreams in the ordinary sense of the word but rather a process of thought-like activity.

Stages 3 and 4 see the blood pressure and heart rate, both of which have been falling steadily since sleep began, reach their lowest level; respiration has slowed, the pupils are constricted, and flow of blood through the brain has diminished; the body's thermoregulatory system is functioning, i.e. sweating and shivering will happen as and when necessary for the maintenance of normal body temperature. Shortly after the sleeper has apparently settled into stage-4 slumber, the rapid eye movements begin.

At this point the EEG alters dramatically (see diagram p.10), climbing from the stage-4 trace back through the lighter stages and soon showing a trace more like that of wakefulness than sleep (which is why REM is also known as 'paradoxical sleep'). Thermoregulation is now suspended, i.e. sweating and shivering temporarily cease; engorgement of the penis and clitoris occurs, and uterine contractions increase.

Needless to say, these bodily sexual manifestations have been speculatively linked with the sexual images frequently seen in dreams. It certainly seems to fit very well, but against it one must bear in mind that the same erectile changes accompany dreams which are not sexual. Furthermore, as the following physiological changes suggest, it is truer to the overall picture to see the sexual excitement as one part of a total arousal of the autonomic nervous system.

Our physiologies are, in fact, in the most intensely powerful and amazing state of excitation. Dr Frederick Snyder of the National Institute of Mental Health in the USA has described it as 'a third state of earthly existence'. Breathing becomes erratic, often held in as if in suspense, only to change suddenly to a furious panting as if the most gruelling activity is taking place; similarly, the heart speeds up and slows down to remarkable extremes; the kidneys make more concentrated urine; and the blood pressure can rise to heights which would cause alarm in a hypertension clinic and then fall with great rapidity. Not surprisingly, in view of all this body work, the metabolic rate rises steeply. Many brain regions reveal electrical activity beyond that of waking, and blood flow through the brain increases by some 40 per cent.

All this is happening while we're dreaming. Subjects aroused from REM sleep regularly report vivid images and dramas in which they have been emotionally involved in one way or another. Considering all that is going on in our bodies while we are dreaming it is hardly surprising that we sometimes wake up from a night's sleep feeling totally exhausted; we may have been through something like a massive firework display of our nervous systems.

Dreams may not be real in the sense that they are not the same reality as waking experience, but they are as real as real can be in themselves; the subjective conviction that dreaming is often an intense emotional experience is fully backed up by the physiological evidence of remarkable emotional activity.

ACTING-OUT DREAMS

Given that in many of our dreams we are running, walking, climbing, making love, hitting out, struggling furiously, swimming, etc., the question arises, How come we do not actually perform these physical movements while we dream them? How is it that we do not strangle our bedfellows once a week and regularly wreak havoc in the bedroom?

A few people do; it is rare, but the physical acting out of dreams does happen, and *has* led to bedfellows being strangled and even to charges of murder.

Very many people have been to sleep laboratories, for a wide variety of disorders, among the commonest of which are insomnia, excessive somnolence, narcolepsy, bruxism (teeth grinding), head banging, sleep paralysis, sleep myoclonus (which is usually an involuntary kicking out of the legs), nightmares, sleepwalking, sleep apnoea (periods of suspended breathing during sleep), and Ondine's curse (an irrational but gripping terror that one will not be able to breathe automatically if one falls asleep). Among this grisly list there are a few, usually middle-aged or elderly men, who come because they have acted out their dreams, or some of them, and have been horrified to discover the fact when they awoke. Extraordinary strength and agility may be manifested, to a degree which amazes witnesses.

Clearly there must be some natural mechanism usually preventing the muscles from executing the movements taking place in the dream. What happens, it seems, is that when dreams are most vivid, certain neurons in the brain stem switch off impulses from reaching down into the muscles of the body, thereby effectively paralyzing action. Struggling against this, especially as one rises towards wakefulness from a frightening dream, almost certainly accounts for that feeling in a dream of trying to walk through sand, struggling for effective movement, or trying to shout or scream and being unable to manage anything more than a squeak. It is an important natural safeguard that enough self-awareness and consciousness has returned before muscles are connected up again, especially when one has the muscular power of an adult body. The paralysis preventing bodily action seems more easily overcome in young children.*

*In the illustration at the beginning of this chapter (p.5), for instance, the little boy was 'pushing away' with his arms.

In later chapters we shall see that the content of dreams often appears to compensate for what is absent from consciousness; reports indicate that the men, and occasionally women, who act out their violent dreams are characteristically *compliant and gentle* in their waking-conscious lives.

Whether or not one believes that dreams have meaning, there can be no doubt that we need our REM sleep, and this is effectively the same as saying we need our dreams. Experiments have proved what all of us know from personal experience — that deprivation of REM sleep has to be made good; if too much has been lost, attacks of extreme sleepiness will occur with instant dreaming. If sleep is impossible, either for internal reasons (e.g. the intense angers and anxieties of psychotic illness) or for external reasons, the REM state will eventually erupt through into waking consciousness — which is a terrifying experience, effectively a nightmare from which one cannot awake because one is awake. This can also happen with the prolonged and heavy use of certain drugs which seem to interfere with the dreaming process, such as Diazepam (Valium) and related tranquillizers.

FURTHER READING

Colqhoun, W.P. (ed.), *Biological Rhythms and Human Performance*, London: Academic Press.
Kleitman, N., *Sleep and Wakefulness*, Chicago: University of Chicago Press.
William Dement, 'The effect of dream deprivation', *Science*, vol. 131.

Two

THE MYSTERY OF DREAMS

WE HAVE ESTABLISHED that we do dream, several times every night; that we need to dream if we are to remain sane; and found out just how much our bodies participate in the dreaming process. All of this is interesting, and helps one to appreciate that dreams have an extremely powerful inner reality, different though it is from outer reality.

But the fact remains that physiological knowledge is about as much use for understanding the *personal meaning* of a dream as it would be for understanding the personal meaning of falling in love. Objectively it provides much food for thought, but that is hardly the most important aspect of the experience. For each of us today, whether we know the science or not, just as for man since the dawn of our species, dreams are immediate complex experiences of the subjective psyche.

DREAMS ARE PRIVATE

Dreams are the most private of our complex experiences; even if you were hooked up to all the laboratory apparatus, and every happening in your body lay exposed to the most intelligent and knowledgeable observers, they could never know the actual content of your dream — how you in your uniqueness experienced it — unless you told them.

Dreams unquestionably involve our bodies; they may even be rooted in our matter; but their flowering and their fruiting is in our psyche. In our mind, our psyche, our soul, dream is an immediate datum of experience. The experience may be very deep and moving; occasionally it can be seen to be the immediate cause of profound changes:

A woman dreamed she was walking through autumn woods with her husband and another couple. It was beautiful. They came to a hilltop overlooking wild moorland to the sea beyond. The other man, who seemed like her brother, pointed to a tent some distance away; it was made of skins and before it sat two men carving fairground horses. The four of them approached the tent and her brother wanted to buy one of the horses. Then three identical women appeared; they were triplets with flawless skin, auburn hair and beautiful hazel eyes; all wore linen shifts of olive-green but each with slight differences in design.

One of the triplets stood directly before the dreamer, who caught a look that passed between her husband and her. It was a look of deepest intimacy, of a tender, deep and rich love that existed between them beyond the need for words. Alarmed and instantly filled with a violent frightened fury she caught the string around the neck of the woman's dress and pulled as if to strangle her.

'Don't you ever dare to look like that at him again!' she hissed.

Then she was trying to expel the woman through a door that had appeared; try as she might she could not get the door to close shut. All the while the woman was attempting to explain that the dreamer was misunderstanding something and asking her to come with her through the door so she could make everything clear. Eventually the dreamer followed the woman and was given a printed sheet of paper which she read. The printing seemed like an illustrated manuscript and she had the impression that the text was Buddhist. Then the woman told her how she and the dreamer's husband had met in the past when they were very young; as is often the way with dreams, the dreamer saw what the woman described as if she were there herself. She saw the two of them meet on clifftops above the sea, saw them fall in love with each other, each for the first time, saw them make love to one another. Within the dreamer something changed, like a melting; she was touched to the depth of her soul. Suddenly, she knew and felt their love. She told the woman and her husband that she understood and it was all right.

The woman who dreamed this dream was well-advanced in her first pregnancy. It was a late child in a late marriage; early experience in her life had led to a defensive walling-off from deep love relationship.

She was awoken by this dream in the middle of the night. As she retraced it in her memory she realized there was something rather mystical about the three identical women who appeared so magically. She began to weep as she thought of that love revealed to her. It had, in fact, awakened within her. Suddenly, and for the first time in her life, she said, she knew what it was to love and, with the knowing of that love, to fear loss; she knew now what it meant to be a hostage to fortune and fate. Off and on throughout the night she wept, with joy in her heart but also poignant piercing pain and that fear of betrayal which is truly mortal.

16

THE INNER WORLD

Dreams are experiences of our souls. They are the most intimate and subtle of private experiences, often so inward and so subtle that words cannot do them justice. No attempt to comprehend dreams objectively will ever approach the true mystery of dream because it is the dreamer and the dreamer alone for whom the dream has been woven. The threads of each dreamer's uniqueness of inheritance, of experience, of imagination, of thought and feeling, intuition and sensation, are woven together with that which is eternal and universal in the mind.

Between dreaming and remembering dreams a movement of simplicity and beauty takes place; when I dream I am swallowed up into the numberless chambers of the house of dream; when I awake and remember my dream, my dream is swallowed up inside me. Asleep and I am inside the dream: awake and the dream is inside me.

What can one call the inside of dream? Not the inside of one particular dream, but the inside of dream as a state of mind which, like an ocean, is always there below our conscious surface. I have called it a realm, a house with numberless chambers, an ocean ... but I might call it a world, a universe, a multiverse. No one knows the limits. We know them even less than we know the limits of our waking material universe.

No one can tell for sure, as they fall asleep, where they will find themselves in dream, nor who will be with them, nor what they will be doing, or what may happen to them. The possibilities are infinite; and, most strange of all, this infinite realm exists first and foremost for *you the dreamer*. It is centred around your self, not anyone else's.

In our dreams we have revealed to us this inner universe, our 'Self' – self in a sense which is immeasurably greater than the limited self of our conscious self-knowledge; and yet that limited self, the I of the dreamer, is evidently important enough for dreams to seek to be understood by it. I am aware this places an intentionality in dreams; but it is hard to know how else to understand the way that dreams will repeat themselves again and again until consciousness has understood something we have needed to understand. A fearful instance of this, or rather the failure of this in the sense of a failure of understanding, is reported by Truman Capote in his book *In Cold Blood*. The subject, who had slaughtered everyone in an isolated Kansas farmhouse, had had this dream, which recurred with minor variations, ever since childhood:

I'm in Africa, a jungle. I'm moving through trees toward a tree standing all alone. Jesus, it smells bad, that tree; it kind of makes me sick, the way it stinks. Only, it's beautiful to look at – it has blue leaves and

17

diamonds hanging everywhere. Diamonds like oranges, that's why I'm there − to pick a bushel of diamonds. But I know the minute I try to, the minute I reach up, a snake's gonna fall on me. A snake that guards the tree . . . I figure, well, I'll take my chances. What it comes down to is I want the diamonds more than I'm afraid of the snake. So I go to pick one, I have the diamond in my hand, I'm pulling at it, when the snake lands on top of me. . . . He is crushing me, you can hear my legs cracking. Now comes the part it makes me sweat even to think about. See he starts to swallow me. Feet first. Like going down in quicksand.

His desire for those diamond fruits was so overpowering that he could never heed the warning. Although one might say that his destiny was revealed in the dream and he could do nothing but live it out as he did, one could also say that he failed to understand what his dreams tried to show him. It is as if his conscious self never engaged morally or imaginatively with the situation revealed to him by the dream, but always went its own regardless way until the forewarned end where he is swallowed up and destroyed by evil.

DREAM AND MYTH

This murderer's recurrent dream of greed contained unmistakable allusions to the Paradise myth, with the forbidden fruit and the serpent.* The dreamer found himself as the protagonist within a dramatic situation which would surely have made him think about the collectively known mythic story when he woke from it.

This is a common and characteristic feature of dreams; our ego, or those components of it constituting the 'I' of the dream, is drawn down into that realm of our psyche where the mythic dramas weave their endless ways. There we find ourselves embroiled within exactly those mythic patterns of idea and emotion which are the ones most deeply governing our conscious waking lives at the time. Given waking co-operation, they make it possible for us to gain insights which deepen and enrich our self-awareness and our world-awareness.

Not all our dreams are like this, of course; many may appear thoroughly banal, and perhaps some are; but to a greater or lesser degree most dreams reveal surprising depths if all the allusions and associations are diligently followed through. I hear many dreams, some five thousand each year; and I have very many dreams recorded. As I listen to the flow of dream from

*Sometimes the dream continued with the dreamer being rescued by Jesus, who appeared as a gigantic sun-yellow parrot.

my patients, or read through dreams I was told (or dreamed myself) years ago, I am brought to a helpless silence by the infinite variety of dream. It beggars all description, not only in terms of the images and stories, but equally in manifesting the noblest and basest feelings, the most passionate emotions, and the wisest and stupidest thoughts.

DREAMS FROM ANTIQUITY

In all the oldest literature in the world dreams play a significant part. More often than not the gods seemed to have chosen dream as the medium through which to communicate with human individuals:

> ...the Sun God appeared to Karna in a dream and warned him that Indra would try to deceive him by putting on the garb of a brahmana ...*

or,

> God came to Abimelech in a dream by night, and said to him, Behold, thou art but a dead man, for the woman which thou hast taken; for she is a man's wife.†

or,

> ...a prince was one day hunting and he sat down to rest under the shadow of the Sphinx and fell asleep and dreamed a dream. In it the god appeared to him, and, having declared he was the god Harmachis-Khepera-Ra-temu, promised him that if he would clear away the sand from thse Sphinx (which was the god's image) he would make him King of all Egypt.
>
> The prince later became King Thothmes IV, king of Egypt *circa* 1450 BC.‡

Sometimes, it seems, the gods used dreams to destroy those they did not favour:

> The thirteenth man whom Tydeides came upon was King Rhesus, who was breathing heavily when he robbed him of his sweet life. He was

---

*From the Indian epic, the *Mahābhārata*.
†The Bible; Genesis 20:3.
‡Mention of this story, which comes originally from a very ancient Egyptian text, can be found in *Egyptian Magic* by Sir E.A. Wallis Budge. He also deals with the Egyptian arts of procuring dreams and their magical uses.

under the influence of an evil dream which had come to him that night and, through the machinations of Athene, had taken the form of Diomedes son of Tydeus.*

DREAM AND REVELATION

In most of these dreams from antiquity the deity is not described in terms of his (or her or its) appearance. It does not seem to have been the visual appearance of the deity which mattered − or even appeared in the dream; what mattered was the revealing of something which could not otherwise have been known by the consciousness of the dreamer. One might almost think that the source was described as a divinity because nothing else could explain the origin of the revelation.

If there is one perennial view of dreams across all time and all mankind, it is this: that *dreams can reveal to us that which is not consciously known.*

This broadest of views can contain the ideas of both East and West, Freud and Jung, classical past and scientific present.† In Freud's famous words, dreams are the 'Royal road to the unconscious', where unconscious effectively means unknown.

TEMPERAMENT AND THE USE OF DREAMS

The revelatory nature of dreams may have been the universal experience of mankind, but revelation *per se* has not always and everywhere been the first consideration. Dreams have been, and still are, used in differing ways by differing temperaments; the will to power, both secular and sacred, makes for a different use of dreams than the will to knowledge.

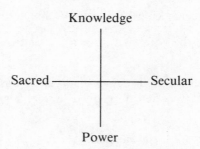

*The *Iliad* of Homer.
†With the exception of a small minority of dream researchers who, apparently oblivious to the subjective experience of dream, explain dreams as the random firings-off of brain cells.

This diagram abstracts and separates four temperamental differences into two axes. It does so for the purpose of grasping quite different views of dream. 'Sacred' refers to those with a strongly religious temperament, and 'secular' to those with a markedly materialist, rationalist temperament. Either of these temperaments may incline more towards the acquisition of power or knowledge.

In reality, of course, and in the majority of individuals, all four temperaments are likely to overlap in some measure; one who understands dreams in a secular way, for example, and uses them for power, will probably have some sense of the sacred in dreams, and will find some knowledge in them which he sees as an end in itself rather than as a means to power. The same, in reverse, will be true for someone who understands dreams in a sacred way, and who uses them primarily for ends of knowledge. But there are always a few who constitutionally (and to some extent culturally) lie toward the extremes, and they are convenient to use as examples of types.

The four figures described below have an archetypal quality; that is to say, they come across as types rather more than as individuals; they may be found in all cultures the world over, and in all essentials they recur endlessly through time. They are archetypal images of certain fundamental attitudes which exist towards life in general (and dreams in particular) and can − more or less − possess an individual so that his life becomes an expression of the archetype.

SECULAR POWER

This is the figure of the wazir, or the prime minister in ancient courts, the wise and trusted adviser to the monarch, the dream interpreter who holds important state office. He or she seeks power over other people and employs his gift at an individual or tribal level in such a way that he rises to high office. Dreams are understood as revealing previously unknown factors in the present situation, or events yet to unfold; they are interpreted in the worldly and practical terms which shape policies of government, taxes, foreign relations and so on. The legend of Joseph from the Old Testament must be one of the most celebrated examples.

Although Joseph* carefully explains that God interprets dreams (through Joseph), the way he asks the butler and baker to recommend him to the Pharaoh as a skilled dream interpreter, and his subsequent appointment to the post he himself had advised in his interpretation of Pharaoh's dreams, a position second only to the Pharaoh's throne, reveals him as a man whose temperament sought secular power.

*Genesis 40−2.

In every 'developed' country this figure is all but invisible today. One might think of Laurens van der Post and his role with Prince Charles, heir to the British throne, but van der Post has at least as much of the 'sacred knowledge' figure about him as he does of the 'secular power'. Perhaps one may see some trace of him in the astrologer advising Mrs Reagan who, one must presume, had some influence on her husband, the President.

Ever since the Age of Reason, around the seventeenth century, rational scientific consciousness has been the ideal aspired to for the management of affairs; the old dream-interpreters, astrologers, and like 'readers of signs', were relegated from public importance to dubious back-street practice.

In much of the 'undeveloped' third world, though, village and tribal leaders still take dreams into consideration just as Joseph did. Dreams continue to be deployed for secular power far more than most city-dwellers might imagine.

SACRED POWER

This is the figure of the sorcerer, magician, witch, wizard, shaman. Their temperament attracts them to the acquisition of sacred or magical power; they do not appear in secular office. They are the weird men and women of power, usually detached from the corporate identity of the community, using their gifts to good or evil ends. They are little known in the West of today − although they do exist there − but they continue to be one of the most important life-influences for rural people in the third world. I know this from immediate experience, having worked for ten years among people who lived in apprehensive awe of the Juju man, witch-doctor, medicine man, shaman, etc.

In West Africa, for instance, I spoke with a witch-doctor who had put a spell upon one of my patients. He was a small wizened man with the blackest of black skin, yellow eyes, and an edgy, nasty sort of presence. He neither admitted nor denied this particular spell, but explained how the juju had taught him how to take on the form of a large cat in his dreams. As cat he had the power to move and act both in the waking world and the dream-world; he could travel to great distances; he could make attacks upon the sleeping bodies of other people, or enter their dreams and attack them in their souls. He was approached regularly by people from many villages in the neighbourhood who paid him to defend them from other sorcerers, or to revenge them for received injuries in the ever-present web of spell and counterspell.

Victims of the sorcerer or magician often consulted me in the hope that my immunity to the spells (as a European, and especially as a scientific doctor, I was always assumed to be immune) might protect them. Unfortunately, this was often not so; at least one man, who was admitted into the hospital, died eight days later without my being able to find any physical disease.

Although there are local cultural variations, such sorcery is little different from the accounts of Carlos Castaneda, in which he describes his apprenticeship to the Yaqui Indian Don Juan (whether Don Juan has real or legendary existence does not alter the accuracy of the sorcery described).*

Both the way sorcerers use dreams in West Africa and the Far East, and the Don Juan accounts, are remarkably similar in many respects to the practice of magic described in ancient Egyptian texts.† In our own scientific West, where even orthodox religion is dying of anaemia, and magic is almost universally dismissed as primitive fantasy, there still exists a small but vigorous body of tradition derived from Egyptian magic.‡ I was consulted not so long ago by a painter who had dabbled with magic; although he had withdrawn, he was still too terrified to go to sleep because 'he was being attacked in his aura while he was asleep'. He described how he experienced the attack in a dream:

> He was in his house, which had been devastated; all the plants had been poisoned and his pets savagely mutilated and crucified. Entering his bedroom he felt a malign but invisible presence which terrified him to the point of paralysis; he tried to shout but was unable to utter a sound; then his sight was 'sucked away' until he was blind.

SECULAR KNOWLEDGE

This is the figure of the man of science, the philosophic evaluator of down-to-earth knowledge, the reasonable man temperamentally devoted to truth and discovery, sceptical of religion, mysticism, or anything demanding a more than natural explanation.

Dreams are used as a means to further self-knowledge when this is useful for successful adaptation to society, or for the relief of psychic suffering; they are also used, less personally, in the study of the psyche as a proper field of scientific enquiry in its own right. Although this figure has, like all the others, walked through the centuries, he is especially characteristic of modern times. The best-known example of this century must surely be Sigmund Freud.

*See, e.g., *An Alternative Reality* by Carlos Castaneda.
†Fascinating accounts of this are given in *Egyptian Magic* by Sir Wallis Budge.
‡I am referring to the writings of relatively recent magicians such as Aleister Crowley and Israel Regardie. See also W.E. Butler's *The Magician: his training and work*.

He devoted himself to the task of trying to understand his own and his patient's dreams at a time when this was not only scientifically un-fashionable, it was almost unthinkable. He looked at the strange jumble of seeming non-sense and part-sense and began to work away at it method-ically. Gradually he found that he could arrive at a rational and meaningful sense in it all which, so it seemed to him, had been cunningly disguised through a mass of symbolism, condensation of various images into one, displacement, over-determination, and sundry other mechanisms. He decided that the rational and meaningful 'sub-text', which he called the 'latent' content, had been disguised into the 'manifest' content of the dream (i.e. the dream as it is actually experienced) by a 'dream-censor'.

He explained the inferred existence of the 'dream-censor' by conceiving firstly, that dreams exist in order to protect the need for sleep; and secondly, that the unconscious psyche consisted predominantly of our ancestral instinctual nature which has to be repressed in civilized society. These repressed energies, which he understood to be primarily sexual appetites and desires, appear in dreams because they seek fulfilment. There they find it, albeit disguised with symbolism so as not to affront and awaken the civilized consciousness.

Dream contents of a supernatural or religious nature he interpreted as primitive wish fulfilment or sublimation of the real-but-unacceptable sexual instinct. His unveiling of the sexuality rampant in our nature provoked a furore throughout Europe, particularly because he ended the illusion of the sexless innocence of children.

SACRED KNOWLEDGE

This is the figure of the mystic, the wise old man, the hermeneut, the prophet, the poet, the alchemist, the priest. Temperamentally inclined to see the divine hand in all things, to see eternity as the backdrop behind time's arrow, this figure also uses dreams for self-knowledge and to acquire philosophic understanding of the psyche. But the priorities are different; outward adaptation to society and waking reality is not disregarded of course, but the truest and deepest desire concerns the soul's relationship with God, the mystery of the individual soul's participation in the world soul, the struggle to feel 'at one' with one's own nature (particularly involving the struggle between good and evil).

Just as Freud exemplified the temperament of 'secular knowledge' so Carl Jung must be the outstanding individual of this century to exemplify the temperament of 'sacred knowledge'. At first agreeing with Freud, and supporting his work on dreams and psychoanalysis, he later came to view dreams somewhat differently.

Naturally enough, he saw the same almost incomprehensible and seemingly irrational dream as it actually appears, and he agreed that it was possible to interpret this 'manifest' dream into something that made rational sense.

But he turned things the other way round. Rather than assuming the 'latent' text was there all the time below the surface, and then disguised by the censor, he came to think that the dream as it was experienced was entirely natural and undisguised. It appeared as it did because that is the natural expression of the ancient and collective level of psyche from which it comes. Rational consciousness found it hard to understand in somewhat the same way as you or I might find it hard to understand Chaucer in Middle English. This is not because he deliberately disguised what he meant to say, but because language has changed and moved on, and if we are to understand what he meant we have to make an effort to interpret into our own familiar language.

So Jung saw dreams as natural products of the psyche (and soma, because, for Jung, psyche and soma were ultimately one and the same thing). And he did not agree with Freud that dreams were wish-fulfilments of repressed sexuality. They may be, and quite often are; but Jung was convinced there was more to the unconscious than bottled-up sex. The attitude he took towards dreams was always to remind himself that he *did not know* what it meant; to try to allow its meaning to surface as he and the dreamer worked with it. In this approach dreams are infinitely varied in their meaning.

Among the endless variety of dreams, some were, he believed, genuinely religious. Nature itself, in Jung's view, is intrinsically mystical; religious thoughts, feelings, symbols, and images are not arrangements of a psyche defending itself from an unpalatable reality; they are a natural ingredient of psyche, in fact a central reality for some people.

The 'Self', a term he carried over from the ancient Indian religious texts, is conceived to be the centre (and, paradoxically, the circumference) of the total personality. This total personality comprises not only all that we know ourselves to be, but also all that we are but do not know ourselves to be. Images of the Self, appearing in dreams or other products of the psyche such as visions, are indistinguishable from images of God. In other words, Jung saw the image of God as central to our being.

Understandably, then, while Jung agreed with Freud that dreams were the 'Royal road to the unconscious', he was more inclined to see dreams as having something valuable to offer consciousness; it seemed to him that they often provided the natural compensation for attitudes of consciousness that had become too one-sided.

These four figures – the minister with secular power, the sorcerer with sacred power, the scientist with secular knowledge, and the mystic with sacred knowledge – summarize quite different attitudes to, and use of, dreams. Most people incline towards one or another but can also recognize the other types within themselves.

There is one other use of dreams which perhaps needs a different type to describe it, although it may also belong to one or another of the above figures. It is the use of dreams for creative inspiration, whether the creativity is expressed artistically, scientifically, mathematically, or in any other way. Many examples of this are mentioned in biographies and auto-biographies of creative people; composers who have dreamed of tunes, writers who have dreamed of stories or characters, and so on. Two well-known examples are Coleridge's dream which became his poem 'Kubla Khan', and Kekulé's dream of the six dancing figures which gave him the ring structure of the chemical Benzene and ushered in the era of organic chemistry.

It is easy to say that it must be intolerant and arrogant for any one view to claim possession of the one and only truth. After all, anyone who has thought about dreams for any length of time will have realized they are very mysterious things; quite mysterious enough, one would think, to allow for the co-existence of differing beliefs. But convictions arising from one's own temperament tend to be strongly felt and their fieriness makes it hard to be even-handed.

One cannot help but wonder, if one works with dreams a good deal, where they 'come from'. Somewhere, somehow, there must be a 'centre' creating the dream images, all loaded with their emotional and feeling potential, weaving them together with a knowingness old as the hills and new as the dawning day. That is the central mystery of dream.

FURTHER READING

Artemidorus, *The Oneirocritica* (trans. R.J. White), New Jersey: Noyes Press.

Budge, Sir E.A. Wallis, *Egyptian Magic*, London: Routledge & Kegan Paul.

Butler, W.E., *The Magician: his training and work*, London: The Aquarian Press.

Castaneda, Carlos, *The Teachings of Don Juan*, London: Penguin.

Freud, S., *The Interpretation of Dreams*, London: George Allen & Unwin Ltd.

Freud, S., *Introductory Lectures on Psychoanalysis*, part 2, London: George Allen & Unwin Ltd.

Jung, C.G., *Dreams*, London: Routledge & Kegan Paul.

Three

REMEMBERING DREAMS

FOR MOST PEOPLE in the west life seems too busy to give any time to dreams. Many say that they never remember their dreams, and feel quite satisfied with that state of affairs. Apart from psychotherapy there is no form of work in the West that brings true familiarity with the role dreams play in our lives. But in many parts of the world, where life is not so hectic, dreams are enjoyed and shared with family and friends.

SHARING DREAMS

When I was walking in the Himalaya I was delighted to discover that the four local men who were looking after us told each other their dreams every morning while they brewed tea and slapped chapatis for breakfast. Sitting cross-legged around the fire, they hooted with laughter, sometimes rolling right over in merriment.

I wondered if their dream-sharing was no more than close friendship while on a journey, but they told me that village life was no different in this respect, except that dreams were more plentiful and vivid at these high altitudes (we were moving between 12,000 and 18,000 feet).

They were not surprised to hear that my work involved hearing other people's dreams; they explained to me that if someone dreamed a dream which felt unusually important to their spiritual growth, or seemed ominous, or particularly troubling, then they would take it to the gompa (monastery) where there was a Tibetan priest skilled in the understanding of dreams.

Among peoples such as these, dreams are remembered simply because they are a part of oneself. They find amusement and delight in the things they get up to in their dreams which they would never do when awake. They accept without question that their dreams will help them to know things they need to know, like risks of avalanche, changes in the weather, or evil spirits haunting a particular pass. And they take it for granted that dreams not only reflect what is wrong when they are ill, but also bring healing.

DREAMS AND THE DOCTOR

When I was doctoring in the Middle East, and later in West Africa and the Far East, I was intrigued to find that my patients frequently told me their dreams; they were presented with no special emphasis, simply as a part of their description to me of how things were with them. A villager, for instance, might come into my room, sit down, and tell me that for the past week he has felt dizzy spells, that his belly is stiff and uncomfortable, and that for the past three nights he has dreamed he was flying over a big river.

This unquestioning assumption that dreams are one symptom among others to be presented when consulting one's doctor never came into my medical training; but it is actually built into the very foundations of Western medical practice. The logo of the Medical Defence Union depicts an elderly bearded man, seated in a throne-like chair, with a branch or herb in his right hand and a chalice in his left; a snake is spiralling up the chair leg below his left hand, its head close to the chalice.

He is Asklepios (known to the Romans as Aesculapius), the Greek god of medicine. His cult spread throughout the ancient Mediterranean and remnants of the temples of Asklepios can still be found on the outskirts of most sizeable towns. Ailments of every kind were treated at major sites such as Epidaurus; the priests administered medicines and performed operations, but the core of the healing was believed to take place through the patient's dreams. Asklepios came to his believers in their dreams; he mixed medicines and summoned sacred serpents to lick the diseased area. If Asklepios visited you in your dreams you would be healed.

To be accessible for us today this needs some interpretation into modern psychological language because we no longer consciously think in god-language.

Asklepios was a god, son of Apollo; in terms of psychological facts that is to say he was not any specific person; whatever his metaphysical existence might have been (or be) his existence as it was actually known by real people was an image (or potential image) within their minds. This image had that quality called 'divinity' – i.e. part of its essence was that it possessed powers and knowledge beyond those comprehensible to mortal consciousness. So far this would hold true for images of any of the gods, but each divine image had a different character.

The character of the Asklepios god-image was infinitely benevolent, caring deeply for the physical and mental miseries of mankind. In some ways (certainly not all) the image within the human psyche of Asklepios overlaps with the later image of the Christ God. Christians who truly believe in Christ, or know Christ, will take what help is available from doctors of course; but they know in their heart of hearts that the deepest healing comes from Christ.

Even the most sceptical medical scientists have to admit that belief plays a part in cure; not necessarily belief in Christ, of course, but belief in something – in the doctor himself, in modern science, in the Buddha, etc. To be able to feel connected with the more-than-mortal healer, to feel one can lay oneself, as it were, in his (or her, or its) hands is also to feel trust in the profound healing capacities unconsciously within us.

To explain this we can use theological language and say the image of the divine healer *is* the image of the real god; or we can use psychological language and say the healing resources innately and unconsciously latent in the depths of our physical and mental being (which are, at bottom, just as much of a mystery) tend to be represented to consciousness in the image of a healing god. Either way one is dealing with a mystery, and the psychological formulation does not deny the metaphysical reality of the god – it leaves it an open question.

For the great majority of contemporary Westerners any awareness of the divine healer is, at most, a dim background sensation, all too liable to be squashed by accusations of superstition. Nevertheless it will always be there in the back of one's mind as one is wheeled down the corridor to the operating theatre.

The problem is that between people like my companions on the mountains and modern scientific medicine an ever-widening gulf has opened up. The more scientific we get about health and disease the more most illnesses are rationally understood in terms of physical happenings quite extraneous

29

to the mind. Focusing on causation we discover that, say, meningitis is caused by the bacterium meningococcus; certain social, seasonal or geographical factors have predisposed this person to be infected by the meningococcus; the treatment is clearly to kill the meningococcus; all this appears to have nothing, or next to nothing, to do with that person's mind or soul. It's just bad luck that they happened to get it rather than someone else.

People like my walking companions would readily accept the fact of the meningococcus and gratefully take the antibiotic (if they could get it), but they would never accept that the illness had nothing to do with the state of their soul. Mind and body are one, they would say, and disease in the body is also distress and dis-ease somewhere in the soul. Together with the healing medicaments for the body must go a healing of the soul's distress or else the same illness, or another, will return.

My years of hospital medicine brought me face to face with the great pool of chronically sick. I discovered the obvious: that the great majority of people rarely go to hospital until they are old; nevertheless this healthy majority is so numerous that their rare visits still account for about three-quarters of the patients in or visiting a hospital; the other quarter of 'hospital population', however, are the persistently sick; they either have the same disease which goes on year after year, or one disease followed by another and another. Seeing these people month after month for years, I came to sense that whereas some were fatefully afflicted with a poor physical structure, there were many with whom I often felt that somehow (and I did not know how) I should be treating some deep affliction in their souls rather than tinkering month after month with tiny changes in medication. And I know many of my colleagues felt the same way.

Working now as an analyst, and seeing some patients with chronic disease in the body, I know what an immense task it is to reach the often very deep level of psyche where the dis-ease written in body language can begin to find its expression in psyche language. Certainly it cannot always be achieved; but certainly sometimes it can.

In acute illnesses, though, the connection between what is going on in mind and in body is much easier to find and understand. Acute illness in children often marks the transition from a stage which has been outgrown to the next; in adulthood, acute illnesses often come when we have been continuing to 'be' in a way which has become increasingly out of tune with ourselves. The illness, which forces us to retreat from the working world for some time, and the fever which draws the mind down to the depths where we re-encounter our own myth patterns, can very sensibly be seen as serving us well. It is as if the deep core of ourselves, when it cannot reach us in our workaday persona, has to drag us down through illness so we can be immersed in its power in order to make necessary changes in our conscious attitude and behaviour.

DREAMS AND ILLNESS

When we do become ill, especially if there is a high fever, there comes a distinct moment when we *let go* of our everyday working persona, sink out of the hurly-burly of life, creep into the sickbed and hug the covers around us. From that moment we can allow our selves to be drawn down into an intensely personal experience of ourselves, a swirling phantasmagoric confusing and confused realm in which the customary boundaries between reality and fantasy become blurred; past, present and future are intermingled, bodily sensations weave their way through lurid dreams which frequently involve mythological imagery, and our sense of the passage of time is wholly out of step with the clock time of the working day going on 'out there'. The more we can allow ourselves to 'go with' the illness rather than fighting it all the way, the more we will get out of it.

Surfacing from such an illness, one often returns to the everyday and healthy world with one special composite dream-fantasy-bodily-emotional-intellectual experience which seems to crystallize the meaning of what we have been through, and which is held as a precious thing — with good reason as it is the summation of the necessary change.

A boy of 15 knew his mother was dying of cancer. While working for 'O' levels he tried to shut out all thoughts and feelings about it. Once the exams were over he came down with a really nasty tonsillitis. In a feverish delirium he suffered a horrible experience: each time he closed his eyes he felt himself, with almost hallucinatory vividness, endlessly falling, spinning violently into a void of blackness. The sense of imminent disintegration made him want to vomit. Eventually he became so tired he could no longer keep his eyes open. He fell and fell ... and fell into a dreamworld:

I was alone in a dark desolate place where I wandered in misery, and time was not.

I found myself drawing near to a high hedge; in a light like the light before the dawn I saw the leaves were stiff and glossy, laurel or holly. I wanted to see what lay beyond and searched for a way through. Then, somehow, I saw within.

I saw that the high hedge enclosed a house and garden. All lay basking in a warm sunlight that was both summer morning and yet timeless, like a day from the dawning of the world. It was a great country house, at once rich, homely, and mysterious. French windows opened onto a terrace where a figure was seated, reading a book. Flowerbeds surrounded a square lawn in the centre of which a four-streamed fountain played into a round pool. The water was no ordinary water: it glistened and scintillated with life, it was wonderful, awful, beautiful stuff and it affected the pit of my stomach as I gazed at it. A movement from the terrace distracted me; I saw the person had risen. Amazement was followed instantly by excitement and the intimation of meaning when I saw that the figure was both man and woman: he/she was naked, golden-haired, with the full breasts of a young woman and the genitals of a man. As the hermaphrodite moved gracefully down the steps and toward the fountain I felt the movements as if I myself were the one walking.

Soon he was well again. This dream experience, or rather the whole composite experience, remained with him like a jewel brought back from a deep dark mine. Now, thirty years later, it is still within him like an indestructible light, a seed of meaning. Even at 15 he knew it was more than a matter of his sexual identity; it was a holy dream, a revelation of the sacred; he had no words to explain it but he knew it gave him some basis for coming to terms with his mother's impending death. Consciously he had learned nothing of the hermaphrodite as a symbol of conjoined opposites, nor of the enclosed garden as the sacred, safe, place of transformation, nor that the Mercurial fountain symbolizes the eternal welling-up of creative mind. His intellect was unlearned, but his soul knew these images wordlessly, and their promise was healing.

So, our dreams are at least as interesting, entertaining, and amusing as any other part of our being; furthermore, dreams can not only help us to know what is wrong when we have strayed from ourself; they also may bring healing and health. By 'health' I mean ease of body and mind, enjoyment of life and human relationships, depth of experience and meaning, and the capacity to have glimmerings of the sacred eternal existence simultaneously with a practical and effective grasp of the secular temporal existence.

PROCESSED AND PACKAGED DREAMS

Engaging with one's own dreams is surprisingly hard to do. It takes courage and determination to face up totally to the inner mirror that shows us what we are so exactly and individually. It is easier to gaze into the pool of fantasy when it is more collective, less uniquely our own.

This is what we do when we read novels, but at least it is our own imagination fired by the author's skill; films, however, provide ready-made visual images. Something I have noticed in my years of travel is that people who cannot or do not see films at all often, tend to dream more (i.e. remember their dreams more). Of course this could easily be a false impression; so far as I know no one has studied the question. Even if the impression is valid, there may be no more causal connection than there would be in saying that people without washing machines dream more. But it does bring into focus the closeness that exists between dreams and films.

The box-office is a teacher highly respected by film producers, directors, and script-writers; it has taught them to stay close to the material of myth and dream. *The Hero with a Thousand Faces** has become a standard work for the industry. Films set fairly and squarely in the waking world of everyday reality need to be exceptionally good to win box-office success, whereas films which take us into nightmare-land, or mystical vision, or heroic fantasy, can still make a fortune even when they are atrociously crafted.†

Horror films have always been popular, but they have become more so since the arrival of the video. This has to do with *control*. To have control of the tape in one's own machine, to be able to turn it off and on, fast-forward it or reverse it; to be able to leave the room if one wants to, have the lights on or off, seems to encourage people to follow that fascination that leads them into the depths of their own horror.

Perhaps films are a safer substitute for one's own dreams; safer because one can watch a film wide-awake, fully conscious and orientated. In every way one has more control over the fantasy material. Packaged dreams for those who cannot, or will not, consciously experience their own dreams.

But something is lost. In one's own dreams the very nakedness of one's sleeping ego, at least partially stripped of defences and strengths, makes for involvement in the dream drama more deeply than any film, save perhaps for the best-directed moments of crisis. Even more importantly, your dreams are woven uniquely for you; what you see and do and feel and fear is custom-made for you alone. That perhaps is why horror films seem to be addictive; the satisfaction feels close ... but never quite there.

Psychiatrists and directors, critics, and assorted others, who theorize on the popularity of horror (and other genres of fantasy) films, seem to focus mostly on how people feel braver and readier to face up to waking life after having faced and survived encounters with their innermost fears and monsters. Even more so is this true for people who watch their dreams. But this only becomes possible if dreams can be remembered, and that requires more effort than hiring a video.

*One of a number of books on mythology by Joseph Campbell.
†*Evil Dead 2*, for instance.

A CAUTIOUS APPROACH TO REMEMBERING DREAMS

The main question is why most dreams are not remembered, and whether it is wise to interfere with this state of affairs. We have seen* that the four or five cycles of REM sleep each night add up to about 60–90 minutes of dream-time, and some dreams occur in non-REM sleep too. Without doubt most of our dreaming is never remembered, and perhaps that is the way it is meant to be.

We do not have to know things consciously for them to influence us; our experiences in early infancy, for instance, profoundly influence the way we feel about ourselves and our attitudes to others, but we have no conscious memory of what they were. Dreams subtly adjust us to ourselves and to life as a whole, all the time, whether we remember them or not. Gradual changes in awareness filter through from dreams that lie just beyond the fringes of full consciousness; often one can feel them come close for an instant and then, before one can grasp them and know them ... they are gone again. But we know their presence if not their exact content.

I have never met anyone who has not remembered a single dream all their life. So some dreams are remembered naturally, without there being any particular intention to do so and without any special steps being taken. One must ask oneself whether things are best left in this natural state. We know, some of us all too well, that the depths of the mind can be exceedingly frightening, and few people have never known the fear of madness.

Might it be that deliberately raising consciousness of dreams will bring more risks than benefits? We may indeed take it as certain that dreams are vital for our well-being; but if they perform their function in an invisible way each night, then why not let them get on with it and be content with the occasional dream that spontaneously sticks in the memory?

This laissez-faire attitude is probably best for some people, and for some stages of life. Unlike films, which have only an approximate 'fit' because they are for everyone, dreams have an exact 'fit' because they are for the dreamer alone. This makes them, at least potentially, more powerful and disturbing. They are a living mirror in which the dreamer sees, and more or less wholly experiences, the state of his or her inner world.

The question that arises, then, is ... when is it a good thing, and when is it not a good thing, deliberately to turn attention toward this inner world?

There are times in life, such as early adulthood, when the demands of life make it important that energy and attention are directed primarily toward the outer world. At such times it is really best for the inner world to look after itself so long as there are no major problems. The occasional dream

*In Chapter 1.

will be remembered, providing food for thought about one's inner world and exerting more or less pressure on the dreamer to adjust in some way.

But there are also times in life, such as adolescence and middle age, when enormous changes are taking place in identity, attitudes, relationships, aims and ambitions, and body shape. Dreams play a major part in readjustment of the self-image; if the relationship to the inner world is healthy there will be many remembered dreams and a good deal of attention will naturally flow in that direction.

In most people who enjoy a reasonable state of mental and physical health, then, the remembrance of dreams will ebb and flow according to need; special efforts to remember are simply irrelevant because few either desire or need to attain an unusual degree of self-knowledge.

There are, however, a number of reasons why dreams are not remembered even in this ordinary and natural way. The most general reason is also the most influential; that is to say, the whole cultural attitude is unfavourable to dreams. Our Western civilization values applied consciousness and extroverted achievement. Not only is there little collective interest in dreams (witness the fact that dreams did not come into my medical training at all) but to speak publicly about one's dreams is to invite sidelong looks. It is hardly surprising, then, that the great majority of the population soon forget the few dreams which force themselves through to consciousness.

To counter such an all-pervasive attitude of devaluing dreams, it may well be necessary and advantageous to make some special efforts to remember dreams.

A specific instance is when people have 'identified with the personas'. The mask worn by actors in classical drama was called the persona; Jung used this term to connote the social mask which we wear in our various roles. The lawyer, the doctor, the builder, the society hostess, we all have recognizable uniforms, manners, ways of speaking, and so on; these are our 'personas'. To identify with one's persona is to become stuck in that role all the time, and consequently to lose touch with many other parts of oneself.

This may have come about as a function of psychic defences (see below), but often it is no more than habit and inertia. In the latter case (and, with care, the former), it can be very beneficial to remember more dreams, and to think about them.

However, there are also more individual and personal reasons for not remembering dreams, and these need to be considered because interfering with them may destabilize a person.

DEFENCES OF EGO AND SELF

There are generally understood to be two distinct categories of defence which operate in the psyche. The first comprise the defences of the ego, and the second, defences of the self.

In common usage the word 'ego' tends to mean something rather undesirable such as boastfulness, vanity, pushiness, or being overfull of oneself. This is unfortunate because the ego, the 'I', is an absolutely indispensable structure of the psyche. Its disintegration means temporary or permanent insanity. What is actually being referred to when 'ego' is used in this disparaging way, is an ego, often 'young' for its age, which is inflated with the self and usually not yet sufficiently distinguished from it. I am aware this statement may have confused you and I will try to explain what is, admittedly, a difficult concept to grasp in the abstract.

The 'self' is best thought of as being the centre for the whole person — not just the person you are conscious of being, but including all of the parts of you that you-as-ego do not know about. If you think of a little baby, or an animal such as a dog or cat, there is a wholeness of personality there; the creature is quite clearly something more than a bundle of disparate impulses; something is directing operations, giving purpose. But whatever that something is (which is called the 'self') it does not know itself, or if it does, only to a very slight degree; in other words it is unconsciously itself, and unconscious of itself.

From this primal self develops (in the human) the ego, the 'I'; it is a conscious structure and it *knows* ; it knows the presence of the self, so that it can say, 'I know my-self' or, when it is puzzled by dreams or thoughts or feelings or some behaviour, it may say, 'I cannot understand my-self'. The self is like a star, and the ego like a planet orbiting that star; as the simile suggests, the self has intrinsically 'star-like' being. Those times when we feel we are the most special, the most wonderful, the most creative and lovable thing in the world, the centre of the universe ... these are feelings arising from and revealing the qualities of centrality and godlikeness natural to the self.

To be able to feel such feelings about oneself is vitally important; they are, of course, the foundation for self-confidence and self-love (that self-love which is healthy and without which one cannot love another). But the older one gets the more important it is to *know* the feelings, not just feel them. For the relatively undeveloped ego of a three- or four-year-old child to feel 'I am all these wonderful things' — in other words, for the ego to feel *it is* the self (some of the time) — is still healthy because it is normal for the stage of development. But an adult's ego, appropriately mature for its years,

36

must know the outer reality as well as the inner; must simultaneously know the inner wonderful self and the outer reality of being insignificant to all but a handful of family, friends and colleagues, all of whom have their own 'wonderful self' too.

So when the ego is commonly referred to in a disparaging way, such as 'He's got an ego-problem' or 'I can't stand her, she's too full of herself, she's all ego', the truth of these observations lies in the fact that the ego of the person being described *is* too full; it is too filled up with the feelings of the self; it has not separated from the self enough to be able to see that the inner wonderfulness does not correspond with the outer reality. But the way ahead does not lie in getting rid of some ego; quite the reverse; what is needed is further ego development so that the ego, the 'I', *knows* the self instead of *be's* the self.

To return to the question of defences with some idea of the difference between ego and self: the self is extremely powerful compared to the ego and everyone, to a greater or lesser extent, has defences of the ego which have arisen to protect the ego from energies of the self that are (or once were) experienced as overwhelmingly powerful, hence threateningly dangerous. This situation is often depicted in dreams:

A businessman in his late twenties, who *was* very full of himself, felt 'rattled' by news of disasters such as train and plane crashes. Although his reason told him he could not be held responsible, he felt so omnipotently powerful within himself that he was in fact troubled as if his own destructiveness had brought about these disasters. Dreams and fantasies came in profusion; in many of them the sun was so fierce and glaring and burningly hot that he could not face it.

The sun makes a natural symbol of the self, being the source of all energy for life and the centre around which Earth orbits; but the self may be portrayed in dreams in an endless variety of symbols, each of which will convey something special about how it is being experienced by the ego:

From time to time over a period of many years a woman who was constantly trying to be as good as the nuns who had brought her up had made her feel she should be, dreamed that she was in a small room which had no door and only one window, which was set high in the wall. Through the window she could see an enormous tidal wave which seemed about to break through the window and sweep her and the room away.

or,

A very troubled young woman who made her living from prostitution repeatedly dreamed (and sometimes hallucinated) that a huge ball of throbbing light and energy appeared in her room while she was sleeping and came towards her, threatening to engulf her. She felt it was extraterrestrial; sometimes she tried to ward it off with a crucifix, sometimes she saved herself by turning into a huge magical queen.

The common theme is some natural, usually wild, form of energy which threatens to engulf the dreamer. Very often the defences being employed to protect the ego from the threatening self, are also revealed in the dream. In the second example, the woman has evidently sought safety by trying to shut everything out; in the third, the young woman has had to resort to supernatural defences, religious or magical fantasy. Both found it easy to see that what they did in their dreams corresponded with what they did in their waking lives.

Where the self appears so threatening (for the wonderfulness of the self that I used to try to explain the difference between ego and self is only one facet of the many-faceted self, which can be terrible as well as wonderful, and many other things too) and the defences appear to be stretched to the limit, one must consider very carefully before doing anything to remember more dreams. They may help in the process of distinguishing ego from self, but they may do the reverse: the ego may be engulfed. This is not necessarily a catastrophe; indeed it may have to happen for a better relationship between ego and self to develop; but it can be tremendously difficult to deal with the practicalities of life for quite some while.

THE DREAM CENSOR

Freud believed that manifest dreams were disguised by a 'dream censor' which hid naked instinctual wishes in obscure symbols; this notion is no longer widely believed, and I am sure it is wrong in the way Freud conceived it. But there *is,* in effect, a dream censor of a different sort. It operates *in the remembering of dreams*: if a dream is too threatening for the ego defences, its disturbing influence is diminished by not remembering it. Obviously we cannot know much about unremembered dreams, but the times when some pattern of events during the day suddenly reawakens a dream from the previous night (or even longer ago) do provide hints about dreams which might have been remembered on waking but were not.

More reliably, experience with people in analysis regularly demonstrates that as conflicts become less intense and defences less rigid, then more dreams, and more disturbing dreams, are remembered. A young physicist from a fiercely Catholic background, for instance, knew she was having 'bad dreams' but could not remember what they were for a long time; then she remembered a dream in which:

She was sitting in the confessional, confessing to the unseen priest; after a while she realized she was naked from the waist down and she felt mortified with shame. When she got up to leave she discovered to her horror that her menstrual blood was on the seat.

This dream released a heavy flow of dreams, many of which circled around the theme of incest with her father.

It was immediately clear to both of us that this theme had been going on inside her for ages, and that although she had been unconscious of it, it had nevertheless produced inner turmoil and disturbance which had appeared in a variety of symptoms. But it was only when, in the course of her analysis, a softening had taken place in her inner experience of the Church's and God the Father's moral hostility towards women, that her defences could allow the dreams to become conscious.

From what I have said of the 'self' it may seem strange that it should ever need defences to protect it. But as little babies, we need a very sensitive matching to our 'self'; the environment, mainly through the figure of the mother, must adapt very closely to the needs of 'his majesty the baby', allowing the majestic self enough confirmation of its majesty.

If this fails to happen, in any one way or combination of ways, then the infant's true self may become hidden within a set of responses and behaviours which do not arise from the true self; they are false in that they do not express what is truly felt, but are produced because to do otherwise seems to threaten survival.

If, for instance, a mother is seriously depressed and cannot bear the crying of her baby, then that baby may hide the crying and what the crying is about, and instead become compliant and eager to please the mother. What is often called a 'false self' develops.

Because this happens very early in life, during those years when we have no conscious memory, and because the true self that is hidden away has not had the opportunity to develop normally beyond the very intense and global experiences of early infancy, it is a situation hard to remedy. People with a false self organization feel empty and isolated in a terribly painful way, but cannot understand it. Usually without knowing it they are continuing to block out everything from the true self, and this includes dreams. If a dream does reach consciousness it is likely to be dealt with by dismissal; the defences of the true self may no longer be necessary in the way they once were, but the false self has been there for so long that nothing else is known or trusted.

RETREATING FROM LIFE INTO DREAMS

Lastly there is one other situation in which people should reflect carefully before taking steps to remember dreams. Some people, especially in late adolescence or early adulthood, retreat from the necessary involvement with the outside world and tend to sit in their rooms thinking their philosophy and immersed in their dreams, becoming ever-more isolated and alienated. Usually there is something seriously wrong in the psyche, but it needs help and relationship from other people; it does not need dreams in isolation. This can be a very risky time, especially if there has been over-use of the 'mind-manifesting' substances such as cannabis or lysergic acid diethylamide (LSD).

TECHNIQUES FOR REMEMBERING DREAMS

Establishing a relationship with one's dreams is the key to remembering them better and more often. Like any other relationship, this means giving time and effort, and like most relationships it means being steadfast when times are difficult and resistances have to be overcome. The rewards may not come immediately, but they will come.

The first and most obvious thing to do is to take the trouble to keep a notepad and pencil beside your bed. Once you are looking for dreams you will find that most mornings the trailing skirts of a dream are just vanishing from sight as you awake.

Hold onto any images you can, and begin to jot them down; very likely you will find other parts of the dream drawn back into consciousness as you do so.

However you will also immediately find resistances within you; something will say, 'There's no point in writing this down, it's completely banal. I'll wait until tomorrow and see if something interesting comes up.'

Write it down anyway. First of all, it will probably not seem banal when you look at it again later; and secondly, the very act of converting a dream from the inner world to the outer world by writing it out on physical paper with a physical pencil is a strangely effective part of developing the relationship between ego and unconscious. By doing it you give the dream tangible connection with outside reality; your ego has employed its executive power over the body to make that connection. When the ego offers a hand toward the dreams, the dreams will respond positively too. It reminds me of those fairy-tales or legends where the hero sees an animal in trouble, or a beautiful spirit-woman struggling below the surface of water; he reaches out a helping hand, only to find later on that the thing he helped has become a marvellous helper to him.

Noting down key elements first thing on waking — e.g. 'in boat with blond man; sea raging; shark swimming circle' — fixes the dream (or dream fragment) in memory. But you will probably find yourself unable to reflect on it much. Although you are awake enough to lean on an elbow and write, you will still be within the spell of the dream to a considerable extent; not yet sufficiently detached from it to be able to reflect on it.

So it is necessary to arrange things in such a way that you can give some time for reflection. This should be regular if possible, and before you begin your working day, and you should be alone. Somewhere between getting out of bed and leaving for work you need to allow just five or ten minutes in which you can write the dream out as fully as time allows, thinking about it as you write, further fixing it in your mind, and perhaps beginning to allow associations to connect up.

Once you have done this, the dream will stay with you; at odd times during the day it will momentarily reappear in your mind, often as connections are being made. Very commonly it reappears quite vividly, but for the merest instant, when you lay your head on your pillow again that night.

Perhaps you are just realizing that all this will mean setting your alarm fifteen minutes earlier. Whether it is that or having less time for breakfast or a delay in reading the paper, it does mean sacrifice. As I have said, if you want to get something, you have to give something to the relationship.

If taking these simple but surprisingly difficult steps produces no results, there is more that can be done but it requires more effort. The first step is to try to make use of moments of near-consciousness during the night. Most adults are aware of being half-awake several times in the night; these moments correspond, in fact, to the posture changes which occur after each REM period (see diagram, p.10). During these half-awake moments the dream-state within which one has just been immersed is usually quite powerfully present in the mind and if one can summon up a bit more conscious will, rather than succumbing to the temptation to drift back down into sleep, then grasping the dream and writing it down there and then will provide rich material, although it may irritate the bedpartner. It is quite easy, in fact, to learn to write in the dark.

If you have a bedpartner, and he or she is accommodating, another possibility is to ask them to wake you up whenever you wake *them* up by laughing or crying or shouting, etc. This will certainly be in the middle of a dream; it is not very nice being woken out of a dream, but it is one way to bring them into conscious connection.

41

LAST RESORTS FOR THE VERY DETERMINED

Finally, if dreams stubbornly refuse to be remembered, and if your sense of purpose has heroic dimensions, you can use the alarm-clock. From the diagram in Chapter 1 you can work out roughly when your REM sleep periods will come and you can wake yourself out of them abruptly, as they do in sleep and dream laboratories. Even if you have to resort to these measures to begin with, once you have remembered a few dreams, written them down, reflected on them and lived with them, you will find that you begin to wake most mornings with dream memories. Sometimes they will vanish for a few days or longer, but if you maintain your attitude, they will return.

It is always tempting to stop writing them down, believing you will remember them anyway. If you have someone with whom you can regularly discuss them, this will be better still than writing out; but most of us do not in our culture. If you cannot talk them through, and do not write them down, they will fade and be lost because of insufficient threads binding them to the waking world of conscious reality.

CYCLES OF DREAMING

Most people who have worked with their dreams for a period of years come to know something of a rhythmic cycle in their dreaming. Times will come when they simply cannot remember any dreams; this state may persist from a few days to a month or more; sooner or later it changes into a phase of dimly remembered and almost ungraspable fragments, then intermittently some more complete dreams, but still frustratingly incomprehensible; and finally a rush of many dreams accompanied by an increase in understanding.

It is as if something stirs in the dark depths, first gathering all energy into its unseen struggle to break free from the soft clasp of eternal unconsciousness; then, as it begins to detach, clusters of tiny glistening bubbles rise ahead of it, bursting on the surface as intriguing but incomprehensible dream fragments; as it rises from the everlasting dark toward the light regions its shape, wavering and strange, is faintly visible, looming mysteriously through tantalizing dreams; finally it surfaces . . . and after all this work of the psyche, it can be almost wholly lost if waking consciousness has eyes only for speedboats, bank balances and sexual conquests.

FURTHER READING

Campbell, Joseph, *The Hero with a Thousand Faces*, London: Souvenir Press.

Emmon, W.H. and Simon, C.W., 'The non-recall of material presented during sleep', *American Journal of Psychology.*

Kerenyi, C., *Asklepios: Archetypal Image of the Physician's Existence*, New York: Pantheon Books.

Four

TAKING DREAMS SERIOUSLY

DREAMS MAY BE WITTY, preposterous, irreverent, and outrageously sexy; taking them seriously does not mean ignoring these aspects, as one might try to do in some solemn gathering. And if I say it is beneficial to pay attention to one's dreams religiously each morning, I mean a religiousness more of constancy than of holiness. That hushed and holy sincerity which descends upon churchgoers, smoothing their faces as they enter the precinct sacred to the God who is all-good, would hardly be appropriate for your dreams.

Nevertheless, some quality of respect tinged with an intermittent and gnostic sense of the holy, is not wholly out of place in our relationship with dreams. It is owed to that knowledge and understanding and amazing creativity which goes into the making of dreams, the source of which is a mystery beyond understanding. Dreams not only have the potential to show us what we are and where we are and where we have come from, but also urge us to become what we could be, and are not yet. For those who can bear to look, the human soul is reflected in the living mirror of dream.

THE LOOKING-GLASS

The glass mirror reflects our physical appearance. We use it occasionally, and usually unsatisfactorily, to try and see who or what we really are. Mainly, though, we use it to assemble our persona; we paint and pat and brush our outsides into the best we can manage to look the part we are playing; during the day we steal glances into glass mirrors to make sure nothing has slipped too disastrously, or to reassure ourselves how fine we are.

The people around us, families and friends first and foremost, but colleagues, and acquaintances too, provide us with a deeper and richer reflection of what we are. Through their facial expressions, by the look in their eye, by their actions and behaviour, and in what they say, we may see our selves as we are seen by them, at least partially and according to how much we can bear and how true we feel their mirroring to be.

44

Far more than physical appearance is mirrored by people; certainly we see through their eyes how more or less attractive we are, but it goes deeper than face, form and figure. We discover also when we are being kind or unkind, mean or generous, greedy or selfless, lovable or unlovable. And because we need people far more than we need glass mirrors, the mirroring of people is an immensely powerful influence upon us; as much unconsciously as consciously we shape our nature into an outward form which brings us the most positive mirroring from those close or important to us.

Powerful and deep though our mirroring is from other people, there are nevertheless limitations to it. No living soul can have escaped completely the pain of distorted reflections, or the state of confusion that can sap self-confidence when one cannot discern whether the other person is right or wrong in the way they are reflecting us. Children, especially, look to their parents for loving, caring, and considerate reflections of their being and their doing; when the parental mirror is itself distorted so too will be the child's reflection in it, and this is a grievous wound, particularly because of the child's lesser freedom to turn to other adults for that special parental function.

So the first limitation lies in the difficulty in trusting that the reflection given back to you is honest, valid, and caring. Once bitten, twice shy; people wounded deeply will be slow to trust the mirroring of fellow human-beings again.

The second limitation is that even the most loving and sensitive companion cannot know much about the depths of your soul, be they deliberately hidden or undeveloped as yet, and unknown. The way we see ourselves in the mirror of others *does* show us something of our essence, but it tends to show us mostly what we have done with our essence, especially what we have made of ourselves socially.

Years ago I knew a man fairly well; we were colleagues at work and occasionally met socially. I always found him kind and thoughtful, hard-working and conscientious, and, as the years passed, a good father and husband. Then one day I heard on the news that he had been charged by the police with operating a child-pornography ring. Like so many people who believe they have known someone well, I thought at first there must be some mistake. But there was not, and when I read of his activities stretching back for years I was amazed at how well-hidden a whole side of his life must have been.

In other words, the mirror of other people, though far deeper than the mirror on the wall, still reflects mainly what we show of ourselves. It does not reflect our whole complex, and often contradictory, soul.

Dreams do exactly this. We may find reflected within them the totality

45

of our soul. Some living mirror shows us, not only what we are and how we appear on the outside but also all the strange impulses (strange, that is, to our consciousness — not strange to the dream), all the wishes and fears, holy and unholy, all the hopes and horrors that are hidden within.

No man knows where dreams come from; or, to be more accurate, most people do not know, any more than most people know what happens after death. A few seem to have their own certain knowledge; but their certainty has never altered the uncertain wonderings of the majority.

True though this undoubtedly is, anyone who has worked with dreams long and well, and who asks themselves what in the world can be so all-seeing, so fertile and creative, so sordid and sublime as this unknown source of dreams, must surely find themselves wondering, just occasionally, if the mirroring eye of dream can usefully be differentiated from the eye of some 'proto-god', a divinity apparently embedded in nature within whose unconscious 'seeing' lie heaven and hell and all things between.

Respect for dreams, and even a touch of reverence, has no need to come from anything except experience. Indeed, unless you know what I am saying from your own experience, I hope you have contemplated these words with healthy scepticism. There is nothing to be gained from assuming a respect you do not feel; quite the reverse: it will only get in the way of serious interest.

An appropriate attitude with which to approach one's dreams has something of the more-or-less loving duty to oneself which accompanies care of the body, together with the sort of serious curiosity one might give to a hobby. This sounds easy enough but it can be remarkably, and persistently, difficult to maintain.

WELCOME DREAMS

Some dreams, of course, are so delightful, or beautiful, or reassuring, that we wake gratefully and hold the memory of them like a treasure. They come less frequently than any of us would wish, but at least they tend to come when we have been suffering for what feels like a long time; or when we have been grieving a loss; or have been lost and confused in our inner darkness.

An outwardly happy man had been inwardly distressed for a long time because he felt no love for his wife despite their having a good sexual relationship. He became infatuated with Anna, a younger woman with whom he felt both sexual desire and soul-love. After their first few meetings he dreamed:

46

10.11.76   I am with Anna in a mountain cave; we both have cameras. From further inside the mountain a curiously shaped black mare appears, followed by a magnificent golden unicorn; as they trot out into the sunlight upon a ledge above an immense gorge I try to capture them on film; but at the moment of pressing the button they appear as two Alsatian dogs; when I take the camera from my eye, they are again mare and unicorn.

He woke with the dream fresh and bright in his mind's eye. To see the unicorn within made him feel rich and special; for days he carried it around like a precious possession; it was the symbol of his noble 'higher' love, which had now come out into the light.

Good and lovely dreams which we do not want to forget are no problem, although there may be a temptation to cherish them as they are and not risk spoiling them by serious reflective thought. Had this man reflected it might have occurred to him that the meaning of the camera was that he was trying to capture something, and that this was not possible. Some time was to pass before he painfully accepted that he could not realistically hold onto Anna.

Strange as it may seem, dreams that reveal to the dreamer the very image of their deepest suffering also tend to be readily remembered, and taken very seriously. It comes as a relief, actually, to see it in a visual image. A young woman had been getting more and more panicky over a period of months; her appearance and behaviour were beginning to alarm people, she was sleeping very poorly, scarcely eating, smoking and drinking heavily. But she didn't know what was wrong or why. One night when there was a strong wind blowing she drank herself to sleep, and woke in the small hours from a nightmare; it was the first dream she had remembered in years:

She was in a tall thin house. A hurricane was buffeting the house which began to sway; she realized that it had no foundations. Then the walls began to crack and crumble; holes appeared and the dark furious night came rushing in. She realized the house was going to fall apart and there was nothing she could do to stop it. As chunks of masonry and rotten timbers crashed about her she scrambled desperately towards some way out.

The dream shows a complete and inevitable breakdown of the conscious personality – a mental breakdown. She knew this immediately; but it came as a relief; it was like receiving permission to have a breakdown, and understanding that she had no choice because her entire conscious personality lacked the essential foundations. With many years of analysis she regrew into a stronger person.

Dreams that bring an awareness of destiny are also gratefully received. Nothing so engenders despair as meaninglessness. Even a grim destiny is at least a destiny, bringing meaning and purpose; and that is more valuable by far than meaninglessness:

> 12.1.77 I am with a woman who is both young girl and also an equal and a lover; she is guiding me through the world; we have been many places but now we are coming to a terrible dark grimy place, which is London. Air of tragedy and doom. I have the choice not to go on, but I will because it is 'high art' to do so, even though it may mean losing something precious, perhaps our love. Destiny demands we play our parts and it may be that the doom of losing our love in this centre of darkness is part of an even more exciting whole.

But most dreams, which are less welcome, or less overarching in their meaning, tend to be received with mixed feelings (or worse). Even assuming the presence of a good will to work seriously with one's dreams, there remain many difficulties and discouragements.

EGO RESISTANCES

From the most comprehensive point of view the problems arise because the ego is no more than partly willing to undertake the work of remembering dreams, writing them down, and seriously engaging with them. I do want to work with my dreams . . . but at the same time, I don't. This ambivalence of the ego has a number of underlying reasons.

For one thing, the ego (i.e. my 'I', your 'I', everyone's 'I') never likes to undertake any work unless it can plainly see and appreciate the rewards to be gained from it. Not only are the rewards from dream-work singularly hard to see in advance, but the nature of the work itself is singularly difficult. Most people find work easier when they are dealing with 'things'; shuffling a pile of papers into order, switching the computer on and tapping the keys, sawing and screwing a plank of wood — in all these activities one can really feel one is getting on with something.

Wholly reflective work upon oneself with the aid of a dream demands complete imaginative concentration without having any external object to concentrate upon (one reason for *writing out* dreams is to give them some status as an external object). Dreaming itself is natural; remembering dreams is semi-natural; but working on dreams is, in fact, essentially creative work. Although this must ultimately be natural, there is something about it which always feels like wrestling with nature.

Partial imaginative concentration will produce partial results, but it is often the best one can do. If one is going to work on a dream at all, though, imagination must be used because one must re-enter the atmosphere of the dream, but now with ego in the waking state.

One can draw an analogy with films: when one has seen a film one really likes, the mind will often go through it again, reliving certain parts, working out the connections which were implicit, seeing it one moment in detail, the next as a whole in which all the parts fit together, and so on. In this process, a part of consciousness reimmerses itself in the film-fantasy while a part 'stays above' as it were, looking down on the whole, thinking about it, gathering meaning, puzzling away at contradictions, finding satisfaction.

Exactly the same process is the way to engage with one's dreams. Only by finding one's way back, as much as possible, into the way it felt in the dream, will it begin to become clear that 'when the man in the dream gave you that meaningful half-smile, it reminds you of the way your father used to smile from the bedroom door, and also reminds you of that man who flirted with you at the dinner party last week.'

A film, however, is an objective work of art, i.e. shaped consciously by its makers and seen consciously by its viewers; by contrast a dream is a work of nature in which subjectivity and objectivity are blended inseparably. The 'I' of the dream is usually (but not always) an actively participating subject to whom events happen and in relation to whom other people appear and disappear somewhat as in waking reality − i.e. other people, animals, objects, etc., in the dream appear objective to the dreamer. But the same dream, when viewed from another person's point of view, is entirely subjective to the dreamer.

Moreover the dreaming 'I' may both *be* itself (i.e. immersed in active participation) and *yet also see* itself (i.e. part of the dream 'I' is watching the other part as it participates). And sometimes one looks directly upon oneself in dreams. For instance:

A young actress dreamed she was watching herself from behind as she walked along the pavement. From nowhere an axe appeared and split her (this herself she was seeing) in half from head to toe. She was aghast to see her bleeding halves lying on the stone slabs.

She had, as many people seem to, the notion that schizophrenia means a 'split personality', and so she was frightened that this dream meant she had schizophrenia. She did not have schizophrenia, and although the dream dramatically shows her to be split, many people have divisions in their personality such that the right hand does not know what the left hand is doing.*

*A state of disunity actually advocated in the New Testament; Matthew 6: 1−4.

49

Compared with films, dreams are very confusing, and often harder to re-enter and reflect upon. A sense of vagueness and uncertainty hangs about them like a mist; it almost always feels as if there was more of the dream than one can remember; shifts in location and time are bewildering; there is the maddening feeling you can nearly remember what was said ... but not quite, or that you *know* that person ... but can't quite remember who it was; several people may be combined into one person, or one person seems to change into a succession of different people. It is no easy matter to *will* your imaginative concentration, to keep one eye immersed in the dream and one eye outside it and looking down upon it.

Doing the best one can, though, one relives one's way through the dream, noting the associations which disembed themselves, as it were, from the dream material, and float to the surface. This work will flesh out the initial dream material and begin the process of making conscious the connections between dream-world and waking-ego-world. Once one has done that, then, as with the film, the functions of consciousness − thinking, feeling, intuition, and sensation − have to be directed onto the material, seeing inferences, making deductions, drawing conclusions, and so on.

All the time, attention will tend to wander; any interruption, like the post arriving, or someone else coming into the room, will seem like a good excuse to put off the dream-work until another time (which is usually the end of it).

RUBBISHING DREAMS

The commonest way this process is destroyed comes into effect before the work has had a chance to begin. It takes the form of an involuntary and immediate devaluation of the dream-memory − Boring! No use bothering with that, I'll wait for something worthwhile. Unless dreams come with a strongly positive or negative charge, the tendency to rubbish them can almost be expected. A middle-aged television producer (in analysis) told me a dream:

> I saw a small dog running across a field. It tripped up an old man with a stick.

He said the dream meant nothing whatever to him. He dismissed it, saying he'd only mentioned it because he had nothing else to say. Since he often sat silently if he really had nothing to say, I remarked that perhaps the dream did have relevance, and asked him what the little dog was like.

'Just a little dog,' he said, but after a pause added, 'but there was something odd in the way it ran.'

I pressed him to continue.

'It was like the hindlegs couldn't move properly ... it reminds me of something, but I can't think what.'

Suddenly it came to him. When he was a boy the family owned a dog which frequently had erections, and it used to run in just that way when it was sexually excited.

'Oh shit!' he said suddenly. 'I know what this dream's about.' He went on to tell me about a girl he had met at a party the week before; he had found her very sexy and arranged to meet her again. The problem with all this (and he had told me he had nothing to say!) was that he was a forty-year-old married man with a wife he loved and two children who meant a great deal to him.

I asked him about the old man with the stick.

'Well,' he said, participating more readily now, 'he was quite a long way off ... my father used to lean on his stick like that when we went shooting.'

Once he stopped dismissing the dream and began to give himself to it, he soon found it brought him food for thought. What he saw of himself, reflected in the dream, was his sexual appetite, unconscious as a dog, racing around and tripping up the 'good father'. He thought about the whole situation more soberly, still wanted to meet the girl, met her the once, but told her he was married and did not want to take it further.

PROTECTING CHERISHED IMAGES

The ego's resistance to work is a part of the problem, but only a part and usually the lesser part. Less visible, but all the harder to deal with for that, is the fact that the ego has an image of the self (or in other words — I have an image of myself) which is often both cherished and defended.

The ego is far from wholly transparent to itself; it has a number of murky areas in the sense that it can both know something and pretend it does not. The ego *knows,* as it were, that taking serious note of the dreams is going to change the cherished self-image. But faced with the majority intention to work with the dream, the part that wants to keep the self-image eternally unchanging does not openly dissent but, Puck-like, goes darting off after every distraction and tries to pull the rest with it:'

An actor seemed to take it for granted that he was heterosexual, despite having minimal and unsatisfactory sexual relations with women, knowing few women and not liking them much, and being among a group of friends many of whom were homosexual. He dreamed that his father was lying beside him in bed and masturbating him.

Although he usually worked with dreams rather well, on this occasion he found it extraordinarily hard to acknowledge that there was a homosexual wish within him.

Only when he had, slowly and reluctantly, accepted this change in his self-image, could it eventually become clear that the homosexuality in his outer and inner life was a symptom, as it were, of his not yet having separated psychologically from his father. As he did so, his heterosexuality (which he had rightly believed was his true orientation) emerged properly.

His difficulty in accepting an aspect of his inner reality was mainly to do with seeing himself in a way he was not used to, and did not like. He felt that were he to acknowledge the homosexuality in the dream, he would then have to think of himself as homosexual.

This is a very common anxiety involved in the protection of the self-image: that if anything shameful, like lying or stealing for instance, should appear in a dream then the *whole self* seems to be tainted or branded. Only gradually can it be accepted that the wholeness of oneself contains many velleities; without them one would neither be human nor oneself. To know the presence of the velleities does not have to mean they must be acted out. Recognizing this is the beginning of self-acceptance.

The self-image is not the only inner image so cherished and protected; images of the parents, of hero-figures, and of children or grandchildren if there are any, are cherished too, and dreams which bring unwanted alterations to these images may be soon forgotten, or rubbished as much as possible:

2.1.77 In a big hospital I examine a boy. He is not my case, but I want to help because I hear he is Beatrice's son. His father enters; he is short and dull; then Beatrice comes in and there is instant unspoken love between us. She wants sex but in special ways, 'not like a cow', she says. I feel love rather than sex desire but say I'll give her whatever she wants because I have dreamed of her for years; she says that is my responsibility ... nothing to do with her. Then we are in a garret with a few ballet teachers led by a Lapplander and his son; Beatrice leads me into a small room and undresses me unromantically; I now see she's a bit raddled and loose, with stains in her pants.

In this young doctor's dreams the figure of Beatrice frequently appeared, and always as the object of his fervently spiritual love. Invariably, it seemed, he wants to worship her, not bed her. Every time the dreams brought in sex he protested he did not want it. In this dream her spiritual image is quite powerfully brought down to earth (or shit), and as a consequence the dreamer strongly resisted thinking about it, putting it off again and again.

When he did at last force himself to work on it, the memory which came (and was the cause of his resistance) was of the one occasion when he saw his mother's soiled pants while she was having a bath. His mother, who had died when he was quite young, was an idealized and sacred image within him, and this memory was deeply repugnant. Precisely because of this, it was important that his memory of her become more human and real.

FEAR OF MADNESS

In the following example the fear of madness combines with the powerful resistance to seeing the cherished parental image in a different light:

> A middle-aged therapist dreamed she was at a mental hospital, seeing her mother who was completely crazy, and wondering why she was not dead as she should be.

This was a nightmare dream, which is to say that she awoke in terror and had no choice but to remember it. The resistance and repudiation was enormous, though; the mother-image she cherished was of a wonderful, kind, loving, and completely sane mother.

The facts were that her mother had never been in a mental hospital nor suffered mental illness, whereas the dreamer herself had experienced more than one severe depression. The cause of these depressions had always been a mystery to her.

With this dream the beginnings of some understanding of her depressions began to emerge. Very early in her life she had experienced her mother as mad. This terrible experience later seemed to have no congruity with the evident sanity of her mother, so she forced the dreadful image out of consciousness.* The split image of the mother (consciously idealized on the one hand, unconsciously mad on the other) was unstable and untenable; dreams of the mad mother began to appear (she had them before the depressions). But previously she had not been able to allow them to damage the idealized image, and because she could allow no change she became mentally paralysed, caught between two opposites of equal intensity.

*The image of the mad mother was kept out of consciousness more by repression than suppression. Suppression means a deliberately chosen process of forgetting awkward contents by putting them 'out of mind'; while repression refers to an involuntary process by means of which contents which might be conscious are in fact kept out of consciousness. Our syntax does not yet reflect the recently understood complexity of the psyche: if 'she' refers to the conscious person then 'she' can suppress, but not repress; but if 'she' refers to the whole person, conscious and unconscious, then 'she' can both suppress and repress.

53

In this state of weakness she was overpowered (or possessed) by the mad-mother image and fell again into that state she had known in her infancy, mute and terrified and experiencing the whole world around her (for when one is very little, mother *is* the whole world around one) as mad and violating.

Fear of madness, not surprisingly, is a potent hindrance to taking dreams seriously. An aristocrat, from a European country still quite feudal in its ways, really could not say whether he had had a very happy or unhappy childhood; he had been brought up in a castle where there were only women, very powerful women. These women had groomed him to be a courtier-prince, but given him neither money nor freedom. He felt pitifully insecure, and totally at a loss trying to earn a living in the world at large. He dreamed:

He was sitting at the dinner table with his grandmother, manacled to her. He wanted to go down from the castle because there was a fair in the village; he wanted to join all the people and have a go on the roundabouts.

Somehow the chain must have been broken because he next found himself walking on the cobbles in the dark village street, high houses on either side. Far off he heard the sound of a wildly galloping horse.

The sound got closer and closer, hammering the hard cobbles and booming between the high walls of the buildings. Around the corner tears a white horse, out of control.

It is terrified, skidding and rearing; he can see it will probably kill itself. He steps into its path with upraised hands to try and save it, but it rears up so high its hooves touch the power cables and electricity courses through it.

He thinks it will die, but in fact it frantically runs to the beach and there gets cornered between two walls, one red and one black. A young hippy stands with whip upraised to strike the horse. Angry and sad, he tries to stop him.

As he woke up he realized that he was doing both the striking and the stopping.

It is plain enough that the dream has much to tell him about himself. But the fear of out-of-control self-destructive madness is in the dream, and that very fear made it impossible for him to work with the dream at that time. He was consciously willing, indeed he chose, to talk about it; but his fear was such that his voice shook with the quivering inner tension in his body and his words came out jerkily until he dried up. It was a brave attempt, but the fear won.

54

RELIGIOUS THEMES

Recognizably religious themes can often be seen in dreams, though they may be no more than half-visible behind the foreground of the dreamer's mundane life. Many people seem to find it difficult to take them seriously; it is as if they have come to believe that anything 'really religious' comes from outside: from the Bible, the Church, the priest, TV, nature ... but never from inside oneself.

A single teacher, chronically serious and sorrowful, frequently tearful, had a dream which made a deep impression upon her. While actually dreaming she took everything as it was, but the first thing that struck her when she awoke was that the time-setting of the dream had been a past age, long, long ago. Also she had not been *herself* in the dream; she had been a Jewish woman with black hair, attired in exotic robes. So vivid and yet so strange had it all been that she found herself wondering about previous-incarnation experiences:

A ritual ceremony was taking place, at the centre of which she was prostrate on the floor before an altar upon which was laid out the corpse of her dead son, a grown man. All around her Jewish folk mourn and try to comfort her. She is weeping in an extremity of bitterness and anguished pain; the depth of the grief in her heart was the strongest memory of the dream after she woke up. There, looking into her dead son's face, she understood as if he had told her, that he had *had to die*; only so could it have been for him to be what he was. This softened her grief slightly. In fantasies continued in the days after the dream, she saw him being taken and buried in a place of great beauty with a spring-like sense of life renewing itself.

I felt it could hardly have been clearer that the dream showed her deep, unconscious identification with the Virgin Mary, that archetypal mother who weeps over the death of what she has born into life. The dreamer was not Jewish, and although she had been brought up a Christian she had not considered it important to her any longer. Certainly the dream was unforgettable, and certainly she took all the feelings to heart and in this way it helped to change her; but intellectually there was a reluctance thoroughly to think through the implications. At that time she could not seem to allow that the Christian myth was actually a living thing within her and that the dream showed her where and what she was in that collective story of the drama of life.

To see the mighty Christian myth appearing so obviously in a dream is relatively unusual. Far more commonly there are echoes, hints, allusions, which can be equally helpful in their potential to reveal to the dreamer the mythic backdrop against which he or she plays their part. But they can only help if the dreamer is able to pick them up and then is willing to take them seriously.

A doctor dreamed:

15.10.76
(a) Dick and I are exploring a monastery, going through old cloisters and a sunken garden; we see a weird machine used by the monks to transcribe dance music from record to sheet music.
(b) With Dick and a woman, I steal some fruit, an apple/cherry; later, at the opera, Dick stupidly talks in earshot of the Chief of Police. Then the man and woman from whom we stole the fruit approach us and I think we're done for. Escape somehow, then I am eating the apple/cherry. I save some for W.
(c) Staying in mansion; walking steep hillside grounds with the owner's kids, my kids and Betsy; woodcock and pheasant have no fear and approach us trustingly. I'm dressed as a gentleman farmer, standing beside a train, carriage full of goats going for sacrifice; stationmaster tells me to take my dogs/kids off ledge 'in case the hospital gets a whisper'.

The companion known as Dick in the dream represents, or personifies, a particular part-attitude of the dreamer: a sceptical, materialistic, intellectual attitude combined with a penetrating and conquering approach (more of this in Chapters 6 and 7). In the first scene the dreamer, 'characterized' by this attitude, discovers that the holy monks, who should have forsworn the desires of the flesh, are cheating.

In the next, the dreamer, still in this 'Dick' attitude, has, together with a woman, stolen a fruit; this is an allusion to the fruit of the Paradise myth. The dreamer's personal associations linked the apple/cherry with incestuous sexual desires.

Now a division appears between the dreamer and his 'Dick' attitude: 'Dick' cares nothing for the irrationalities of myth and religion and so does not think twice of talking about their 'sin' in front of the Chief of Police (an allusion to the authoritative and prohibiting, potentially punishing, God-image).

In the third scene the 'Dick' attitude has gone; the dreamer is 'dressed as a gentleman farmer'; he is trying to appear very proper and conventional, all innocence. The game birds without fear are an allusion to the innocence of the lion and lamb that lie down together; paradise intact, before the sin and the Fall. But things are not really all above board; expiatory sacrifice has to be made, and something has to be kept secret although it is now expressed in terms of his real personal life — the secret must be kept from his hospital where he has to have the publicly-expected persona of the doctor.

Because it is appropriate in the context of this chapter, I have focused on the allusions to the Judeo-Christian myth within this dream, rather than attending to the many associations to his daily circumstances.

I have gone into it in some detail because the principle of what takes place here is so tremendously important. People's inner conflicts, which we may not see much of as we meet them going about their daily business, are nevertheless always present, and lie at the root of much of their suffering and symptoms of dis-ease. Quite naturally, these conflicts appear in our dreams, and this is probably well-enough understood by most people.

What is insufficiently appreciated, however, is the way in which dreams weave our individually experienced conflicts (which can seem so terribly personal and private) into the mythic tapestry which is common to all.

This is one of the great functions of the religions: the personal, which can feel so isolated, so alone, so awful to bear, becomes known and understood as being also universal, common to all, our collective destiny and fate.

Dreams offer this possibility. They do it naturally; it arises out of our nature, regardless of age or learning or outward piety. Indeed the outward form of religions is, in truth, no more than a formalization and concretization of this ever-present inner reality.

If only one can receive this offering from the mysterious depth of one's being, much healing will result. The two levels, personal and collective, each help in the understanding of the other: we can understand more of our personal conflicts by seeing them in the light of the collective; and we gain deeper and richer insight into the collective myth by seeing how it crystallizes uniquely in our personal anguish.

Furthermore, there is the enormously important experience of *belonging*; to feel one is suffering alone, all unknown to our fellow man, is terrible, whereas to know it as one's own participation in the common lot of humanity is to enable one to accept oneself, to forgive oneself, and to know true sympathy with others, which also means one is in a position to help others.

MORAL DEMANDS

Yet another obstacle to taking dreams seriously, and one of the hardest truly to face up to, arises from their ethical and moral demands. Putting it like this implies an inner morality we may not be conscious of, but which can appear in dreams. Many people *are* unconscious of their own morality and if, as often happens, they behave in a way which may seem adapted to their social circle but conflicts with their own inner morality, then they will suffer with conscience and guilt.

But I do not mean that intentional ethical and moral demands are necessarily made by the dream itself. Far more often dreams reflect to us what we are doing in a way which makes us more conscious, and a consequence of this greater consciousness is less innocence and more recognition of responsibility.

Not only imagination, concentration, honesty, feeling, intuition, sensation and thinking are required of you if you would work with your dreams; as the alchemists used to say, '*Ars totum requirit hominem*', *the art requires the whole man.* If we do not try to make changes in accordance with what we believe to be right and wrong, then dreamwork remains a mere pastime.

Every dream involves conscious moral thought in some measure, but certain dreams confront one directly. A middle-aged designer dreamed:

Wherever I go in my house, this woman (Miss A) is there too, always draping herself around me and demanding declarations of love and affection. I find it all sugary and sickening and feel I'm being false to myself. Suddenly I loathe myself so much I decide I must get things straight.

In waking reality this rather insecure man worked for Miss A, and had done for years. She behaved much as she did in the dream, but he had always put up with it, and in fact deceived her that he felt the same, because he was afraid of losing his job and not being able to find another. The dream confronted him with how ashamed he was of himself.

That very day, scared but determined, he went to work and put the record straight; to his great surprise it eventually led to a relationship of real mutual respect between them.

REMOTE DREAMS

A common difficulty, even for someone accustomed to engaging with their dreams, is the extraordinarily *remote* quality of some dreams; there may seem to be no point of application, no possible connection with waking consciousness:

A doctor dreamed he was standing with his wife upon a bank overlooking a huge swamp through which dinosaurs with a rather man-like shape were striding towards the right. He wasn't anxious, just detached.

His work and home life were regular and so far as he could see nothing unusual was going on. He could not make any associations at all and did not have the slightest idea why he should have dreamed it.

It is quite usual for people to have periods of time during which their dreams are obscure.* All one can do is write them down and wonder what they might be about. Eventually, if persisted with, something begins to become clear. Such a pattern is characteristic of the very nature of becoming conscious of oneself. Essentially this is a gradual process, although it may peak in moments which are experienced as the dawning of the light.

The man who dreamed of the dinosaurs went on to have other dinosaur dreams. Gradually some connections appeared. One of the dreams reminded him of being taken to the Natural History Museum by his father; another made him reflect on the ruthlessness of dinosaurs and reptiles, which he then linked with a ruthlessness he felt was developing in himself after decades of treating the sick. Other dreams of swamps and bogs made him think of how he felt when his emotions were swirling about and he felt stuck in them. Finally there was a dream concerning his son, who was unwell at his boarding school.

Now everything began to come together for him: he realized that if he allowed himself to think of his son, he got sucked into the swamp of his own unhappiness which he had felt when *he* was a boy, at which time he had felt hopelessly distant from his father. The dinosaur images were a combination of meanings: they were both his ancient 'prehistoric' emotions from childhood, and simultaneously the unemotional ruthlessness of his defences against those emotions.

He began to see that he had been keeping his son at arm's length because of an unconscious assumption that the boy was as unhappy as he himself had been at that age. To have let himself get close to his boy would have meant being close to those old and painful feelings in his own 'inner boy'.

Realizing now that the feelings were in him, and not necessarily in his son, he began to allow a closer relationship to develop. This was advantageous to both of them, and healing for him.

---

*See the section dealing with rhythm of remembered dreams in Chapter 3.

Five

BIG DREAMS AND LITTLE DREAMS*

ALMOST EVERYONE HAS had the occasional dream which has made a great impression upon them. Unlike the never-ending flow of dreams which come night after night, most of which are never remembered at all, while the few that do reach waking memory are forgotten within days, these 'big' dreams remain available to memory for decades, often for a whole lifetime. They become, in fact, a mysterious and fascinating part of one's self-image.

Over the years, being a doctor, I have sat and talked with dying people of all ages. It is remarkable how often they find these big dreams from years past coming to mind as they approach the mystery of death. A writer in late middle-age, dying of breast cancer and in what was to be the last week of her life, found herself drawn back to a dream she had had in her twenties; she told me it was as vivid to her now as it had been when she first dreamed it. More than anything, she said, it helped her to accept death because it brought her the certainty she was on the right path:

> She was in a forest of trees so huge that the trunks stood far apart, disappearing into the dimly lit distance like cathedral columns. She was following the throb of an immense heartbeat which was everywhere − within herself, in the atmosphere, but most of all in the ground itself. With her head she could not tell which direction to follow, but her feet knew the way because her heart told them. As she walked towards the great heart of all things, she felt her own small heart swelling inside her chest until it seemed as if it would burst with unbearable joy; tears ran freely down her face and milk flowed from her breasts.

*When Jung was travelling in East Africa, among the Elgonqui tribe, he was told that formerly the chief had been the only one to dream − and that his dreams had been the 'big' dreams, giving guidance for all the community. Since the arrival of the white man, however, and the transition to colonial administration, the chief no longer had 'big' dreams; instead, everyone in the tribe now had 'little' dreams.

Although I am borrowing this designation of 'big' and 'little' dreams, I am using it in the context of the individual, not the leader and the tribe.

She could remember exactly where she was and what she did when the dream came; the previous night she had felt a culminating emptiness that came of dissatisfaction with her life and her work. She had got drunk on a bottle and a half of wine and tumbled into bed at midnight.

At half past two in the morning she had woken abruptly and completely, feeling wonderful (which she would not normally have expected) because she was filled with her dream. She went into the sitting room and wrote it down, lovingly, gratefully, and sat there until dawn, letting its implications filter through her.

THE LONGING FOR MEANING

So long as death seems far off and life has us by the scruff of the neck, our deep longing for meaning and purpose is less easily known than our desires for wealth, success, power, human love and sensual gratification. But it is in fact so immensely powerful and deep-rooted a human need that it will outweigh all the others; no matter how wealthy and successful, an individual denied any revelation of meaning and never shown any hint of the purpose of their life, will, in their core, feel unsatisfied and deprived. Whereas one who has been granted a vision of meaning and shown, no matter how obscurely, a purpose to their life, can cheerfully accept great limitations in the lesser desires. We see this most clearly in those drawn to the religious life, but it is there, more or less, in all of us.

This longing, unconscious though it often may be, takes us to the essence of 'big' dreams: they are big because, in one way or another (not always happy, sometimes terrifying or sad), they reveal us within that framework of meaning and purpose which is usually invisible to all but the mystic.

More often than not they wake one from sleep in the small hours of the night and so grip one with the sense of having been shown something profoundly important that it is impossible to get back to sleep until one has gone through the dream again and again; a process which, of course, serves to fix it in consciousness and ensure the ego's involvement.

The timing of these impressive dreams is significant; they tend to come from the deepest sleep, from the first or second of the REM cycles, and they are characteristically woven with unmistakably collective symbolism which has a power more profound than the increasingly personal symbolism from lighter dream levels.

Both the setting of the dream and the drama which unfolds have a quality about them far removed from everyday waking reality, often having an 'other worldly' feel to them. The symbols which appear, and have such gripping fascination, are the symbols one finds in religion, myth, and legend (such as the 'world heart' in the woman's dream) and they appear

61

not just as an idea but as a fully experienced dream-reality.

Inasmuch as these symbols are innately within us, so too is the capacity to understand them innate within us; but they are so remote from contemporary rational consciousness that the innate, wordless, understanding of them often needs to be assisted by an historical knowledge of how these symbols have been understood over the millennia.

This collective stratum of the psyche from which they arise, called the 'collective unconscious' by Jung, is experienced by the dreaming ego with a paradoxical sense of weird strangeness and yet familiarity, as if one is seeing it for the very first time ... and yet one has known it for ever and ever. It is as if a part of our soul lives all the time (eternally, it would be more accurate to say) in this collective realm so different from our daily experience.

Sometimes the transition from 'natural world' to 'supernatural world' takes place within the dream itself.

A doctor in his mid-thirties had gradually become aware that much was not right in his life. He was beginning to notice things about himself that he could no longer comfortably ignore; he loved his wife but when she disappointed him he tended to become violent with huge infantile sulks; and self-consciousness was stirring over his tendency to show off and flirt with others.

He enjoyed his work and was promised great success in it, but inwardly knew that he was coasting, not putting all of himself into it; something was lacking though he could not say what it was. He had begun to realize he was not as 'good' a person as he had always taken it for granted he was. He had begun to take serious notice of his *shadow*.

He was woken one night at one-fifteen with a dream that was to change his life. It began quite ordinarily – that is to say, the dream-world felt like the ordinary world he knew:

25.3.75 I'm walking my dog along a path behind a terrace of houses, peeking into the bedrooms in the hope of seeing a naked woman. I feel depressed and seedy like the narrow littered path and the uncared-for back gardens. Unexpectedly, the nasty little path leads into a common and joins up with a sandy track which runs downhill between gorse bushes ablaze with yellow flowers.

Feeling weary I sit down. Along the track comes a soldier on horseback, very upright, dressed in a smart blue uniform with bright brass buttons. He asks me where something is. I direct him to a pond some way down the track.

Then I'm close to the sandy shore of a circular pond. A golfer, teeing off near the water, strikes his ball. At the very same instant 'a voice', not coming from anyone but from everywhere and nowhere asks me, 'What is the time?'*

I glance up at the sun which is directly overhead, midway through its course. The realization hits me that I'm halfway through my life. Still in that same one instant, the very moment my eyes alight on the sun, I see the golf ball disappear into the sun's centre. From this moment everything changed! The world is no longer the ordinary world I know. This is a world where the rules are different, where magic still lives. I'm seized with intense excitement and the certainty that I'm about to have sacred mysteries revealed to me. As the ball, a shrinking black dot, disappears into the sun's heart, the sun dramatically changes colour, darkening from a daffodil yellow through several shades until it is old gold; it shrinks in size but seems to gather in power, which has something menacing within it. From its centre, black lines appear, writhing outwards and dividing it into four. Around the rim, and in the centre of each quarter, strange archaic letters appear; they look like Hebrew. Then, from the centre, a black dot reappears, quickly becoming larger until I suddenly realize it is a large black bird like a raven flying straight at me.

Again 'the voice' speaks: 'Now is the moment of the great Double Eclipse.'

I know what I have to do. To my left, a path spirals up the sheer side of a mountain, eventually disappearing behind its shoulder. I run up it as fast as I can. As I round the bend I see what I somehow knew I was going to see: the path is now high above a valley of lambent beauty and there in the sky, on a level with my eyes and so close that they seem suspended in the liquid air of the valley, the sun and the moon stand side by side, gold and silver, equal and heavenly bodies of man and woman.

Unutterable joy and contentment fill me. I realize now that until this

---

*This 'voice' is particularly characteristic of 'big' dreams, although not restricted to them. It is imbued with authority, not so much in the sense of discipline but authority as creative, knowing, authorship. It may seem to speak from the sky or the earth or from everywhere, and it is important to notice which. In men's dreams it is more often a man's voice, in women's more often a woman's voice. Often it has some tones in it reminiscent of a parent, and something of one's own voice as well. Frequently it uses a rather old-fashioned style of language.

Things said by other people in a dream are usually taken by the dreamer with much the same range of trust/suspicion as we take things said by others in waking life. The 'voice', however, is taken as gospel (which comes from 'godspell', meaning god-talk); its truth is not doubted. Rarely (for Westerners, that is), the source of the 'voice' may be an animal, or a tree, or stone, etc, in which case it still has great authority, but proportionately less than in its global, heavenly, or chthonic sources.

moment I had been anxious that despite everything this wonder might have been withheld from me at the last minute.

I have someone with me now, though I could not say whether man or woman. I know there is more yet to come. The joy and relaxation of inner tension that have come from witnessing and participating in this wondrous marriage, which is called the great Double Eclipse, is the foundation upon which I will now be helped to build myself with hard and painful work; but I welcome it. I walk slowly and peacefully on up the path until I come to a platform of rock. The huge discs of sun and moon, so very close, shine upon a sheer cliff of smooth rock. Their rays, golden and silver, strike the rockface and create their images upon it. But, because the rays cross, these earthbound images of sun and moon are transposed, rather as the optic nerves cross in their journey from eye to brain. An old man, wise and noble, with long white hair and a white cloak (I felt he must be the 'eternal' Goethe or Bach) stands like a teacher before the images of sun and moon.

He explains to me and to my companion the complex nature and influence of the heavenly bodies as they are manifested on earth. Most of his instruction is beyond my comprehension but I know I will slowly understand it as the years pass.

As he concludes his teaching there comes the sound of hooves clopping up the rocky path. Once again 'the voice' speaks, while around the corner appears a black youth on horseback:

'Now begins the battle between the black boy and the white boy, and the white boy will discover that the black boy possesses great strength.'

With this the black youth leaps down from his mount and I close with him and we begin to struggle and fight.

One can understand that this dream made a great impression; it was dreamed by Dr M about a year and a half before the series of dreams which constitute the bulk of the next two chapters. While this 'big' dream tears open the curtain between the worlds and reveals something like a god's-eye view of his present situation and tasks which are to occupy him for decades to come, its value would be negligible if he failed to get down to the promised and foreshadowed work.

But, fired with a sense of destiny and purpose by this dream, he did not fail. The three-month dream sequence in the following chapters, although no more than a tiny part of his years of inner work, show us what that work is really like. We shall see the themes of the 'heavenly' marriage of masculine and feminine, and the struggle with the shadow, no longer as a grand overall vision, but inching their way into reality through the slow, painstaking, confusing and laborious work of psychological development.

GRASPING THE TREASURE

The big dream is a natural happening in the sense that it comes 'out of the blue' and impresses itself upon consciousness without the need for voluntary effort. Beyond this point, though, the ego has choices to make: the dream can be acted upon, or it can be put on ice — which usually means it is remembered but not permitted to engage with waking reality.

Dr M engaged with his big dream, and the woman who told me her dream when she was dying *had* engaged with her dream: she told me how, shortly after the dream, she had left her well-paid job and given herself wholly to writing the poetry and novels which had so far been her leisure-time passion. But the man who dreamed the following dream found himself unable to do what he knew he should:

> He is standing on an endless plain. He sees it is divided by a vast fault which splits the land like the Grand Canyon. The side he is on is gloomy, grey and quiet. The other side, though, is bright and sunny with people chattering and laughing like a cageful of birds. A rope bridge joins the two, but he is too scared to use it. He knows, with inward and certain knowledge, that the only way he will get across is by stripping off all his outer protective layers, right down to his nucleus, which he sees is black, and then joining with someone else who will help him over. To do so they will have to accept his blackness with love.

He understood that to bridge this chasmic split in the ground of his being it was essential that he bare his soul to another; he tried, but could not sustain the experience.

There is a theme which appears in a number of fairy tales; it tells of a treasure which, upon a certain night, rises from the deepest ocean-bed to the surface; it remains there but briefly and if it is not seized it sinks back down into the depths, not to rise again for another seven (or however many) years. Perhaps this is an unconscious metaphor describing the phenomenology of 'big' dreams. Governed by some agency beyond rational understanding, big dreams rise to the surface from the depths of psyche bringing a treasure unique to the dreamer. The treasure is unique to each, but it also has typical features:

1. With a force that can be likened to a religious conversion it shows the ego that there is meaning in life. Henceforth, in the ding-dong battle between meaning and meaninglessness that we all must endure, the dream-experience will stand one in good stead, like a bedrock that remains firm while the storms blow.

2. Sometimes clearly, sometimes obscurely, it provides an answer to that nagging question, Why am I here? What is the purpose of my being alive? The conscious individual, the ego, has revealed to it its role within a greater drama, as if an actor, hitherto unaware of his role in a play, were shown a glimpse of the whole play so he could understand his part within it.
3. As a natural consequence of (1) and (2) the ego knows itself to be a player of importance in the drama ... but also knows itself not to be the author; in other words 'I' knows itself to be within the hands of a higher authority, a supra-ordinate Self.
4. Lastly, and if these inward treasures are grasped as fully as may be, then the growth toward inner coherence and harmony with oneself (at-one-ment) will lead to outer success in whatever terms that might mean for the individual.

I should point out, although it stands to reason, that not everyone is revealed in a happy and 'good' role. 'It takes all sorts to make the world', we say, and so it does; fortunately, the capacity to accept one's role and one's mythic backdrop comes with the capacity to grasp the treasure in the first place. A middle-aged woman who had suffered a very unhappy marriage throughout her reproductive life, and was now divorced, menopausal, angry and bitter, dreamed:

> It is the dawn of history. She is living in a farming settlement near the Bristol Channel. She knows her mother is somewhere nearby, but unseen. She is with her father who is showing her suitor around the farm as if it is to be her dowry.
>
> The beasts are primitive and shaggy-haired, the buildings are those of early human settlements, she and her father are clothed in shaggy skins, but her suitor is dressed in a pin-stripe suit and a bowler-hat.
>
> Then sea-raiders attack, overrunning the farm. The pirate leader comes for her; she throws a stone fish at his head, but cannot save herself. She is grabbed from behind and taken as a slave.
>
> She finds herself on a ship at sea, dressed only in a short leather apron. The coarse foreign sailors keep lifting her apron to look at her genitals; they poke and jeer and disparage.
>
> Years and years pass by while she is taken helplessly on many voyages; always she is abused, used as a sex-object with no notice taken of her as a person.
>
> At the last she is sitting on a cliff on the island of Ithaca, howling desperately from her solar plexus.

It is a grievously unhappy résumé but, by casting her personal experience within legend and myth so that she is linked with Penelope awaiting the return of her Odysseus, it brought her meaning and hope and a way to begin acceptance of what had been and could not be changed.

A SPECTRUM OF IMPRESSIVENESS

Having spoken so far of 'big' dreams as if they were in a class of their own, it is time to admit that big dreams and little dreams are not really two separate classes at all.

Such a simple division would suggest a dream that is not big must be little, and implies that 'little' dreams are unimportant. This simply does not correspond with general experience. If you ask someone, out of the blue, whether they can remember any dreams they have ever had, they will probably remember one or two from the past few weeks, three or four from the past few years, and another three or four from long ago – probably childhood. Those from childhood clearly made a deep impression, while the most recent dreams will have been remembered because they were relatively impressive but may well be forgotten in a month or so.

The title 'big dreams and little dreams' is only useful to emphasize the variations in importance and impressiveness which dreams carry as one of their intrinsic qualities. But the facts of the matter are that dreams have a spectrum of impressiveness; at one end are those very few dreams whose significance can change patterns of a lifetime, and perhaps not everyone is destined to have such dreams, while at the other end are the relatively greater number of dreams which have minimal importance. The vast bulk of dreams lie between these two extremes.

The littlest dreams bring little that is not, or might perfectly easily have been, already conscious:

> A woman with managerial responsibility was worried because the busiest time of year was approaching and several of her staff were off sick. Just before waking she dreamed she was talking to the remaining staff and trying to divide up the work between them.

Unless there was something more to the dream than she remembered, it seems clear enough that this dream was preparing the day ahead – as dreams often do.* But it might just as well have been a waking pattern of forethought.

*The notion that dreams process remnants of the previous day that have received insufficient attention is a common one, and often true of course; what is less well appreciated is the extent to which dreams set one up for the coming day by making one start it in a certain mood and with certain patterns of thought and expectation.

By far the majority of dreams do confront the dreamer with impressions that have the potential genuinely to add something to consciousness. The dreamer of the following dream was a married man who had become infatuated with a younger woman. He knew no good would come of pursuing her but he was finding it very difficult to let go. His first comment about the dream was that it hardly differed from his waking thoughts; later he came to see there was more in it:

> 12.11.76 I am staying with W (his wife) in a big house; an intelligent thickset girl with big breasts joins us and says she is going to become my second wife; as we tumble around on the bed she tells me her story, which is a sorry tale of dispossessions nationally and personally. W is also pleased and excited that she is joining us; then two more girls come and want to join; now I'm beginning to feel doubtful whether I can satisfy them all. I feel too hot and go out of the bedroom to turn down the heating; Regina appears; in fact it's her house. She looks sad, and I know it's because she would like to marry me too but cannot ask.

The girl with big breasts looked very like the woman with whom he was infatuated (Anna), and he had consciously toyed with the idea of a ménage-à-trois. So far the dream is indeed little different from his waking thoughts, feelings and wishes. But when he began to ask himself why the dream-girl had not been Anna herself, he suddenly realized that she combined various features of Anna and Rachel, his sister. A theme of incest had appeared.

Furthermore, the 'dispossessions' had no connection with Anna, but both the dreamer and his sister had lost their mother while they were children, and his sister had suffered subsequent tragedies. Regina, who appears at the end, is a wealthy woman friend of the dreamer, one who has been a maternal figure for him.

All in all, the dreamer is not simply being treated to a dream experience of his wish to bed Anna without losing his wife; he is being shown something of the nature of his infatuation with Anna: there is an incestuous urge playing a part in it.

Although everything that happened in this dream was extremely unlikely to happen in waking reality, it all *could* have happened. In other words nothing supernatural or intrinsically impossible happened in the dream. Very often, though, the dream-world does present the dreamer with appearances or experiences which are simply impossible in the world of waking reality. And yet these are rarely accompanied by that tingling sense of having crossed the threshold into the magic world. Far more commonly they seem to be taken for granted:

26.10.76 On the hill where I work and live, a man is building a dizzyingly high metal structure which has a globe at the top. He drives me very fast in his E-type Jaguar, telling me to hold on and not worry; but when he hears that my car is parked at the hospital he puts on his siren and emergency lights because he is afraid of bugging by the security forces.

Then I am at a breakfast feast with the same man; he is Japanese now. I think he's happy and balanced but I'm told he actually has many conflicts, secret fears and tensions.

Time has passed; the police have tracked him down; now he is French, his name is Emperor and his work is described as 'Ingenieur'. Having been discovered he suddenly falls down the steps of the metal structure, breaks his bottle of wine, and dies. Dick appears, as if from the Emperor, and immediately decides to enter the globe and fly away into the space of Universe because 'things have fallen apart on Earth'. He gets in alright, but I find it very hard and the height frightening and only manage to get into a basket hanging below the globe itself, from which I fear falling at any moment. Then I am floating up over a mountain, above a monastic school for girls; at first it is dark and they are all asleep, but then I am closer to ground-level and looking down upon many masculinized women playing sex games; I have a violent orgasm which sprays up into the stars.

I am out of the flying thing and now in a tropical garden in which a woman lives; all very beautiful but I see a Russell's viper upon a tree trunk; then nearly tread on two thin brown snakes which slip into a stream; I meet the woman and ask for a machete to kill the snakes but she only has a spade; we look closely at the Russell viper.

The *content* of the dream — some illegitimate construction by a Mephistophelian character, an emergency escape from Earth into space, a conflict between monastic spirituality and orgasmic sexuality, a descent into a garden with allusions to the Garden of Eden — might seem grand enough to have been experienced as a 'big' dream. But in fact the dreamer, although interested and moderately impressed by the dream, did not feel it was anything exceptional.

Sometimes the appearance of the supernatural in dreams has its potentiality for meaning actively blocked for fear of what it might do to deeply held allegiances:

A young priest, struggling to bring his sexuality under control, dreamed he was in his church. A whirling dervish in flowing robes and wearing a tricorner hat rushed up the aisle, picked him up bodily, and swept him through the air to a window set high in the church wall, pressing him violently against the glass so that he feared it would burst and he would fall out. Then he found himself in his car, driving his father through a maze of London sewers.

Consciously, this man was always hungry for immediate and dramatic experiences of a religious nature and one might have guessed this dream, with its evidently powerful spiritual energy, would have impressed him greatly. In fact it did not, or perhaps he would not admit it; he was interested in it for a brief while, and rather alarmed by it, feeling that it represented a threat to his Christian faith. He felt he should respond to it not by exploring the symbol of the whirling dervish but by trying harder to be good.

ONLY THE DREAMER CAN TELL

It is quite impossible for anyone but the dreamer to know how 'big' or 'little' a dream may be. Dreams are not 'big' simply because of what might seem to be 'big' dream content. The powerful collective symbols and the weaving of mythic themes, which are characteristic of big dreams, probably occur most nights in dreams from early REM cycles. Usually they do not wake one up, nor are they remembered in the morning. Even if they are recalled, they are more likely to seem strange and far-off than to be enormously impressive. If one is not ready for Beethoven's ninth symphony, or for *King Lear,* then they too seem remote and irrelevant.

What matters for an individual is not meaning and beauty which others can see, but the profound effect of receiving something because one is ready for it. If one listens to nothing but pop music and reads nothing but newspapers one is less likely to be ready to receive the treasures that Beethoven and Shakespeare have to offer than if one tries to learn the language of classical music and literature. It is the same with dreams. People who have paid no attention to their dreams *may* remember big dreams, but they are less likely to because they will be less ready, and they can do less with them because they do not understand the language.

Living with one's dreams is a process of self-understanding which prepares one to receive ever-deeper insights which can also become integrations. The more experienced one becomes in living with dreams, the more it is possible to see themes of major importance in almost every little dream. They may not appear on the surface but one can sense their presence not far below. Like waves that beat upon the shore they come ceaselessly and every so

70

often comes a wave of extraordinary size and force which makes exceptional impact.

When I listen to people telling me their dreams I listen out more for the signs of how deeply they felt the impact than I do for the dream content itself; when people describe something that has affected them deeply, the whole atmosphere becomes charged. If the charge is very low, then no matter how potentially powerful the dream content may have been, there is little that can be done with it; it is one of the countless waves preparing the ground.

The occurrence of 'big' dreams *is* a universal human experience and as such deserves a special name; but it should be borne in mind that their bigness is a function as much of the dreamer as of the dream itself. If someone is to experience a really big dream, the right dream has to come at exactly the right moment of readiness for the dreamer; when this happens, it has an extraordinary power to fascinate consciousness and an extraordinary quality of revealing meaningful purpose in one's life.

FURTHER READING

Foulkes, D., 'Dream reports from different stages of sleep', in *Journal of Abnormal and Social Psychology*, vol. 65.

Jung, C.G., *Memories, Dreams, Reflections*, London: Collins.

Mattoon, Mary Anne, *Understanding Dreams*, Dallas, Texas: Spring Publications Inc.

Six

A SEQUENCE OF DREAMS

PART 1

CERTAIN THEMES APPEAR and reappear in our dreams over long periods of time. The same is true of waking consciousness; any moderately reflective person comes to recognize the presence of a number of familiar companions in the shape of certain patterns of thought, wishes, ambitions, desires and fears. These welcome or unwelcome companions may persist for no more than a week or so, or last for decades. Sometimes we experience them as irritatingly repetitive, like a stuck record; other times we notice a change, and realize they are evolving.

Most people who have paid little attention to dreams are sceptical of their being genuinely meaningful. Apart from the experience of a 'big' dream, which cannot be summoned at will, the most effective way to *know* that dreams do indeed carry meaning for us is to study a series of dreams. This requires very considerable *imaginative work* but it can at least be done at will, rather than waiting for something which may not come. By entering into each dream and understanding it as far as possible, and then moving onto the next, one gains an appreciation of the themes which keep recurring, in one form or another.

THE ONE-NIGHT STAND

Even the dreams from a single night constitute a tiny series. Often one can see the same theme appearing first in one way, and at one symbolic depth, and then restated in another way, at a different symbolic depth, and so on. This does not *always* hold true − in fact there is absolutely nothing one can say about dreams (beyond the fact that we do dream and need to) that always holds true − but it is true enough often enough to be useful.

People vary considerably in how they consciously organize their night's dreaming into dream units. Some regularly describe a single long dream within which different dramas unfold with many a shift of scene; others speak of three or four (or whatever) dreams, which they give in order, each with a beginning and an end. Sometimes one can only say one has had lots of dreams, and can't tell whether it was all one dream, or several, nor feel sure of what order they came in.

This dreamer, for instance, described three distinct dreams; but looking through them, alert for similarities of theme, one can immediately see that they could easily have been regarded as one continuous dream:

4.3.77

(a) I am in an hotel room together with Rick and a few others; we are attacked; there is a shoot-out. Desperately trying to kill the attackers, I break the trigger of my special pistol.

(b) With W at a football match; I have taken a rifle with me but W is upset by this; then we are in a church and soldiers come searching for my gun; I dismantle it and hide it.

(c) I am in a car which is too small for me, driving along a terrible road; we see soldiers looking for terrorists; I hide my gun; the girl with me becomes an old man, my father, who is taking me home. I think my special pistol is hidden at home and I want it. A man holds out a pail full of snakes; one crawls out onto his hand; he looks fondly at it and says, 'This one is old; she has learned much.' It has a tuft of hair on it.

The most immediately obvious theme is the dreamer's preoccupation with his weapon. In the first dream it is his 'special pistol' and the trigger gets broken; in the third dream he wants to get this 'special pistol' from his childhood home where he believes it to be. In between he has a rifle which he has to keep hiding.

If one had only the first dream to go on, there would be no way of knowing much about the two sides of the conflict. The subsequent dreams, however, show the dreamer to be in conflict with 'soldiers', i.e. the dreamer's status seems to be one of rebel against the established military authority. With this additional material one can begin to speculate in terms of the son's conflict with paternal authority.

Now it suddenly makes sense that Rick, the dreamer's initial companion, was a friend from his teenage years who had a particularly violent and difficult rebellion against his father.

Many components enter into paternal authority, but sexuality and phallic power is always a central, or at least a major, component; one may guess that the weapons with which the dreamer is so concerned are symbols representing power and strength and phallic sexuality.

The first scene is set in an hotel which, since hotels provide for all bodily comforts, has a maternal quality. But he is attacked in there, his weapon breaks, and he has to leave. In the next scene he is at a football match; this is a setting for conflict ritualized into 'game', made safe by rules and

73

boundaries. Evidently it is not safe enough, seemingly because he has this rifle with him. So the next scene shows him looking for safety in a church, a sanctuary; but he still has the rifle and still the soldiers come looking for it.

At this point (in his waking reflections) it occurred to him that the only rifle he had ever used in fact was one belonging to his father. It is as if the dreams were showing him that since his own weapon got broken he has been trying to use his father's weapon. Psychologically this would suggest he has 'borrowed' aspects, qualities, attitudes, of his father, which he is using as if they were his own.

In the last dream he is still having to hide the rifle from the authorities, but there seems a chance he may be able to recover his own 'special pistol' from the home of his childhood.

Now that he is trying to recover his own weapon, rather than illegitimately using the father's, a more personal father-image separates out from the collective and repressively hostile image of military authority. This dream-father is an older man than the father was in reality; he seems to represent 'the father' in his aspect of benign age and wisdom, more likely to help his son than crush him.

Each dream is further illuminated by the others around it. The same is true for the dreams of a single night within the context of a week's dreams, and the same again for the week within the month and so on.

*   *   *

So far each chapter has surveyed dreams, sleep, and so on, from a generalized vantage-point. For the remainder of this chapter and the following one, though, the viewpoint comes down out of the sky and plunges into the thick of dreams themselves as they follow one upon another. It is not always easy to follow. The dreamer has known his dreams for years, but the reader comes to them cold; it takes most of the first half of the series to discern the main themes. It makes great demands upon imagination, and requires a willingness on the part of the reader to be open to the situation of another; it involves referring back and forwards as necessary, and it may need to be read through more than once.

A long-enough series of dreams can convey what it is really like to *live with dreams*, in a way that the generalized intellectual approach can never do. Furthermore, the acquaintance gained of the dreamer through this series provides the opportunity for a deeper appreciation of his other dreams which appear in later chapters.

THE DREAMER – Dr M

The dreamer, Dr M, I shall call him, was an Englishman born during the Second World War into an artistic and professional family. He had been educated at one of the better-known English public schools.

In the mid-1970s (the dreams are taken from then) he was married and had two children, a daughter and a son. They lived abroad, and he worked as a doctor in a remotely situated hospital funded by a large international company. He had not been in analysis, nor had any knowledge of it, nor was he familiar with any particular psychological approach to dreams. One might describe him as the 'archetypal dreamer', because he exemplifies a type of person who dreams copiously and find themselves obliged to take account of their dreams, many of which involve archetypal themes.

The concerns relevant to this period of his life will gradually emerge through the dreams themselves and the comments which accompany them. It is helpful, however, to know from the beginning that he had for some time been concerned about his relationship with his wife. He experienced a powerful sexual attraction to her but felt painfully the lack of a spiritual or soul bond; the arrival of his daughter had made him all the more aware of this because he began to feel that longed-for spiritual affinity with his daughter.

It would be misleading, and unfair to Dr M, to see him through the glass of his dreams alone. Dream-life needs to be seen against its accompanying context of waking life. Dr M's waking life, as a husband, father, doctor, and company employee, was very different from the events and dramas in his dreams. It would be impossibly cumbersome to provide a full day-by-day waking context; in general his life was conventional and much like that of any other hard-working doctor and family man.

Considerations of space have made it necessary to condense both his dreams and the comments he made upon them at the time. However, the words that remain are his words and Dr M, who has kindly given permission for me to publish his material, has agreed that the essence is undistorted.

The dreams run from 6.10.76 until 12.12.76. But we begin with an overture: a single dream from June 1974 which describes a situation succinctly, and sets the scene for the later dreams.

OVERTURE: THE DEFORMED 'UNDERDOG' WOMAN

11.6.74

(a) In a plane; a beast-man has tethered two dogs one on top of the other in a cramped place for a long time; as a consequence the lower dog, the bitch, is deformed mentally and physically; she has developed a crooked

hump back, and when we release her she shows a passion for filth, e.g. always following us to lavatories.
(b) A woman persistently tries to persuade me to buy a nice dress for W. I see a woman in a museum case dressed like Joan of Arc, together with the words 'Liberté, Fraternité, Egalité'.
(c) I enter an underground warren-like museum; Avril walks past sadly; a man with golden hair, rather like the beast-man, tells me she has lost 6 babies now – all aborted; somehow it seems to be my responsibility.

Dr M: Disquieting dreams ... female hurt, damaged, deformed ... somehow my fault ... does not seem fair, but still feel huge heaviness like guilt or doom. Brought up thoughts and memories of my mother dying. Feel I'm suppressing W; must try to change. Why Avril?

RP: These three dreams confront the dreamer with a deformation that has taken place in the 'feminine', and make him feel guilty.

There is, in the first of the three, a curious combination of aeroplane, modern, man-made and civilized, with beast-man and dogs, primitive and animal. One might speculate that the dream images portray the conscious discovery of an underlying instinctual disturbance. The metaphor says that 'at the animal level the feminine has been so crushed that its expression has become distorted and perverted'. There is more than discovery, though; the dogs are released, so changes may be expected to follow.

Painful memories of his mother followed the dream. Dr M's mother died when he was in his teens; he felt he had to become manly before he was ready, and this involved suppressing feminine aspects of himself. The bitch's inclination towards 'filth' hints at some immature perversion. In a subsequent dream (19.10.76) we shall see that the dreamer's anus, particularly, is linked with his femininity and his fear of being seen as feminine.

The second dream develops the 'underdog woman' specifically in terms of W (*his wife; she appears in many dreams, remember W = Wife; D = Daughter; S = Son*). He is urged to value her more than he is doing, and shown that she is herself struggling for equality, liberty and sisterhood. Most likely the dream-W points not only to his actual wife, but also to his own femininity.

The third dream completes a movement which began above ground in a plane, then moved to ground level in the second dream, and finally goes below ground in the third; each perhaps representing the same situation at less conscious levels.

The word 'warren' suggests rabbits and hence fertility and reproduction, which is relevant because Avril, a married but childless woman-friend of Dr M, desperately wants children and has recently rather thrown herself at him, which he has found awkward. She has not in fact had any abortions. If the dream-Avril is taken simply as the 'real Avril' there is no foundation to the suggestion of the dreamer's guilt. If, however, she is taken as a personified image of the *unhappy feminine* within the dreamer, then the dreamer's sense of guilt and doom becomes dimly understandable. We shall soon see how this also connects with feelings about his mother.

THE THREE-MONTH SEQUENCE

The Gentleman and his shadow

6.10.76

(a) Night-time in a café; I'm cheated by a fair-haired Englishman with an untrustworthy face, but when I confront him he's too frightening. Then daytime, and I see him cycling; can't catch him but think of killing him with a blowpipe; track him to a building but still have problem of how to get hold of him and what to do then; he comes out with an insolent smile and walks away.

(b) At L.House; Justin calculates how much I owe him; Oliver speaks of Mardi Gras; I offer to take everyone out to eat and pay with credit card; D plays with my cash; I reprimand her.

(c) With W in basement flat; golden-haired man arrives, weary and not pleased to see me; he has 2 dogs, huge light-coloured male Alsatian and black Labrador bitch; Betsy there too.

Dr M: Fair-haired Englishman is side of me I don't like ... nasty mixture of public school arrogance and insolence, combined with slippery dishonesty ... the 'cad'. Hate him but fear him too ... don't think I am that foul, but seem somehow to know I am.

Thinking of Betsy ... vivid memories ... painful sadness and guilt at abandoning her ... memories of drowning six of her puppies in basement sink. Ugh. Remember mother standing at same sink before she died.

RP: In the first dream Dr M encounters his 'shadow'; hence his feeling he both is and is not like the odious man. In his outward behaviour he is not like that, he is closer to the admirable qualities of the English public school product, qualities of honesty, integrity, good manners, industry and responsibility. But the shadow of these qualities exists within him too, and they peep through from time to time.

Quite apart from what others may see, he himself is increasingly aware of his shadow. Meeting the shadow in one's dreams involves recognizing, and dealing with the fact of, one's less than admirable and desirable qualities. In this dream Dr M evidently wants to kill them off. This won't work; one cannot get rid of a part of oneself and anyway there are always some positive values in the shadow. Craftiness, for instance, may not be an ideal part of the gentleman but it is still a valuable resource for living life.*

The second dream continues with the same theme, developing it in terms of his credit-worthiness. Many personal associations and memories come into this dream, most of them too lengthy to pursue; some, however, must be introduced because they reappear in later dreams.

L. House is Dr M's home of origin, where he grew up and where his father still resides; the dream, therefore, places him within that home, specifically within the room known as the family room with all its many and emotionally charged associations.

Justin is an old schoolfriend of Dr M; being proud of his ancient and aristocratic lineage, he holds especially precious the ideals of the English gentleman.

Oliver, too, is an old friend from University days and also proud of his country squire background. However he is a more complex and unstable character than Justin – uprightness alternating with unscrupulousness, brilliance with near-madness, and spirituality with brutality. In waking life, both Oliver and Justin are living far away and Dr M has not seen them for a year or so; their appearance in the dream is not, therefore, because they play any part in his present outer life; they appear as reflections and illuminations of aspects of himself. He is shown himself, personified into the ideal presence of the one and the half-shadowy presence of the other.

In the last dream a man, the same as in the dream of 11.6.74, reappears, again with two dogs, one light and male, the other dark and female. Once more he appears in an underground location, and again the meeting between them leaves the dreamer disturbed and guilty. This dream-figure is not anyone actually known by Dr M; he is characterized as golden-haired, sometimes as 'beast-man'; he seems to have a dog connection; and, like a messenger from the depths of his soul, he seems to put Dr M in touch with his guilt. He may be regarded as a personified image of Dr M's self (not his ego).

Betsy was an Alsatian bitch belonging to Dr M; she had come to him in his late teens, shortly after his mother's death. She became, in effect, a mother substitute. Although Dr M seems to have forgotten it, his present comments (on drowning her six puppies) throw light on the six lost babies in the dream of 11.6.74. When he chose to work abroad, Dr M had to leave Betsy with a friend in England. He experienced this as an unforgivable betrayal on his part.

---

*The craftiness of Odysseus was much admired.

It is scarcely visible as yet, and will be clearer when we look back from subsequent dreams, but an understanding begins to dawn that the guilty doom-laden sense around the damaged feminine is connected with his dead mother, his transferral of trust, love and dependence onto his beloved dog, his destruction of her puppies and his feeling of having betrayed her when he left her. The link with his shadow struggle is perhaps because the gentlemanly ideal holds the feminine sacred and demands the most honourable treatment from the man; deep within himself he feels he has behaved extremely shabbily, with ruthless selfishness, and feels guilty because he cannot forgive himself.

7.10.76
(a) Visiting dubious man; I have to find my own shoes.
(b) A shifty man is attached to me; wherever I go he goes.
(c) With Ralph and prostitute; she fancies Ralph but I will have her anyway.

Dr M: Stuck with this shifty chap whether I like it or not ... true enough I suppose! Ralph has spiritual/sexual split; I couldn't enjoy the prostitute ... felt less a man.

RP: Figures of speech like 'stepping into one's father's shoes' or 'putting oneself in someone else's shoes' show how we use the image of shoes to represent attitudes or roles. It is in this sense that Dr M, who is discovering he has to coexist with his shadow, is trying to find the right shoes. The second dream speaks for itself.

Ralph, in the third dream, is a colleague; he is a devout Catholic with intense and lofty spiritual longings, but is also an intermittent alcoholic and a client of prostitutes. Dr M's comments refer to an occasion when he and Ralph engaged prostitutes for the night; Dr M, however, was unable to get an erection, to his chagrin.

The experience made him realize that he needed a sense of relationship for his sexuality to flow. This was a blow to that component of his masculine self-image which was macho and would have liked to be able to perform indiscriminately; it made him reflect how much was feminine in his nature. The dream deepens his growing awareness of the problem with the shadow and the feminine by focusing upon the division in him between spirituality and sexuality.

Sex orgy below, soul worship above
8.10.76 (dream-text Ch.13, p.192)

Dr M: Sad, nostalgic, soulful memories of Beatrice; shocking contrast between feelings for her and lust at Chinese orgy. Still worried about D, fever higher today ... love her so much it frightens me.

RP: The division between spirit and sex, as it involves his feelings about woman, is now made sharper still. The orgy, which so aroused him that orgasm resulted, takes place among 'the Chinese' — i.e. seemingly foreign to the English gentleman; a disowning further emphasized by the dividing screen.

Immediately contrasted is his relationship with *Beatrice*: When he was 20 he became engaged to Beatrice, a budding musician and writer; the engagement could not, however, stand the strain of separation when she left the UK to study abroad. The separation was too close, in time and quality, to the loss of his mother.

In actual fact his relationship with Beatrice had been tempestuously sexual as well as spiritual, but this dream (and many subsequent dreams) represents her with the emphasis entirely on soul-love. The specific denial of sexual feelings seems a bit bogus, given their position in bed.

His father puts a stop to this; a hint, perhaps, that an incestuous theme with the mother lies at the root of it. Some additional evidence for this comes in the last dream, when his paralysed mother appears to be made better by his nakedness.

The anxiety in the intervening dream, concerning separation from his daughter, seems connected with her actual illness at that time. In the light of his love for her (see his comments), however, it is worth bearing in mind that he is, like every father, responsible for protecting her from incestuous desires; perhaps this responsibility is reflected in the anxiety over her possible abduction by a 'bad man'.

Too much violence

10.10.76

(a) Near L.House, walking with D; one Chinese kills another, slashing with razor-like knives; much blood and D gets very upset. Company man asks me to keep noise down; I get stick and subdue them.

Dr M: Feel dizzy, confused, anxious.

RP: The 'Chinese', this 'foreign part of him' which was sexually orgiastic two nights ago, is now blood-lusty; the 'company man', which clearly represents Dr M's professional persona, demands that this instinctual conflict be quietened down, and we now see it does indeed threaten his daughter.

He is becoming increasingly conscious of instinctual urges 'close to home', which appear uncontrolled and orgiastic. They threaten his ego, which experiences waves of anxiety; so he tries to deal with it by beating it into submission.

Abraxas invoked

14.10.76 (dream-text Ch.15, p.224)

Dr M: Spiritual yearnings and sexual longings ... have both, and they get in each other's way ... reminds me of prostitute dream. Again the damaged woman. Strange feeling about invoking Abraxas — excited and nervous; reminds me of *Demian*; must read again. Black man terrifying in his rage. St Tropez - sex, money, sensual 'good life'.

RP: These dreams reveal the depth of his inner conflict. So fundamental is it, and so much a part of everyman, that he is drawn down to mythic images which concern good and evil and the nature of God.

Hermann Hesse's novel *Demian* made a great impression upon Dr M when he read it some 15 years previously. He showed me certain passages he had underlined years before this dream:

'My gradual awareness of sex loomed up before me, as it does before everyone, as an enemy and destroyer, as something forbidden, corrupt and sinful ...'

'I lived in dreams, actions, desires of a subterranean kind over which my conscious life nervously constructed a series of bridges ...'

'... each one of us must discover for himself what is permitted and what forbidden as far as he *himself* is concerned ...'

'Only that part of you which composes your life can know. It is good to know that we have within us one who knows everything about us, wills everything, does everything better than we can ourselves ....'

'Abraxas ... (is the name) of a godhead who symbolizes the reconciliation of the godly and the satanic.'

And lastly:

'The bird is struggling out of the egg. The egg is the world. Whoever wants to be born must first destroy a world. The bird is flying to God. The name of the God is called Abraxas.'

In the struggle going on within his psyche, the attempt to beat his instinctual urges into submission has apparently failed.

In this dream, once again experiencing the tearing pull between spirit and sex, and the damage/loss of the mother, the dreamer resorts to invoking that name of the godhead which 'can reconcile the godly and the satanic', a name which he discovers on *the mother's belt* and which coincides with the discovery of a second heavenly body in the sky. At first he takes this to be a second sun, but the old woman's daughter tells him it is the moon or another star − in other words a heavenly body more associated with night and darkness rather than day and light.

No sooner has he invoked Abraxas than a huge and terrifying black man appears; one might think this figure is Abraxas, but neither within the dream nor in his comments does Dr M appear to have felt so, but rather that this figure is outraged by the invocation of the god. Later dreams (22.11.76 and 5.12.76) link the terrifying black man with the father in his dark threatening aspect (a figure analogous to Darth Vader in *Star Wars*). The dream ends with him experiencing equal desire and disgust for the vast sensuality of the world.

Original sin and The Fall

15.10.76 (dream-text Ch.4, p.56)

Dr M: Monks cheating, should not have dances; cherry = virginity, and apple = breast ... Adam and Eve and apple; animals for sacrifice. Holiness, guilty hidden sinfulness, and sacrificial expiation. Beginning to realize I'm religious ... never occurred to me before.

RP: He now finds himself grappling with original sin, offences against God, fear of punishment. He is surprised; but only the night before he had invoked an ancient God in whom were combined both holy and satanic. Clearly he had not taken this seriously yet.

This very scepticism comes into the dream in the shape of *Dick*. Dick is a colleague, a down-to-earth no-nonsense surgeon, not the least bit religious; his personality (and his work) is penetrating in quality; he places his confidence in scientific intellect and consciousness, dismissing everything else, including dreams.

Being 'with Dick' in the dream means 'having Dick's attitude'. Confronted with the cheating monks Dick would probably say, 'Why not? Don't be superstitious.' The dreamer is trying to convince himself he need not fear the wrath of God; that it's all superstitious nonsense.

This attitude, however, breaks down in the second dream; having no 'fear of God', Dick doesn't think twice about talking of the stolen fruit in earshot of the Chief of Police (God); but the dreamer, who is just beginning to realize he *does* know the fear of God (which is the beginning of wisdom), is scared stiff.

In the last dream game birds innocently approach man without fear of his destructive potential. This is a further allusion to the paradise myth, a pretence that the paradise state is still intact, that no Fall has taken place.

Just to be sure, sacrifice is to be made as well. Finally, the whole inner drama must be kept hidden from the hospital – i.e. his conventional and public life as a doctor.

16.10.76 (vision-text Ch.14 p.211)

RP: Dr M had not yet re-read *Demian*. Had he done so he would surely have thought of the egg that is the world, the egg from which the bird is struggling to emerge and striving to reach God. The snake is an addition to this consciously forgotten but once-known image; the snake around the egg does appear in some myths, and the snake in the garden of Eden was implied in the dreams of the previous night.

Dry heat and animal panic

17.10.76 *In desert; natural disaster, fire or hot typhoon; thousands of big animals galloping madly; then walking seashore with some animals; I have basket of underwater food – hollow, hairy, sausage shapes; I feed the animals and they are grateful.*

Dr M: Dream of fiery desert ... see images of fire ... feel dreadfully hot and dry. Panic at animal level because of fiery heat coming. Hairy food from undersea ... what can this signify? Hairy seems animal, primitive.

RP: He knows something serious is going on now; even awake he feels it. Perhaps he is beginning to grasp how huge a thing it is to have invoked Abraxas. By doing so he has invited parts of himself, previously deeply buried and scarcely known yet feared as evil, to appear and participate. He may not have known he had any sort of God-image within him, but the raging black man *is* his dream image of the 'wrath of God'.

The continuing consequences of his invocation are now fiery heat in the desert and animal panic, as if Satan is drawing near.

A touch of homosexuality

19.10.76 *At a feast a middle-aged fat man rests finger on my anus; angrily I struggle free, then hit him in the face.*

Dr M: Don't mind younger and feminine men being attracted to me, but hate men being attracted to me as if I were feminine.

RP: This dream is more personal in content; it does not involve magic or supernatural events. Conflicts find expression within dreams at both personal and collective levels, the former tending to come in shallower sleep and the latter in the deeper sleep from earlier in the night. Each can illuminate the other.

We saw that he had begun trying to reconcile *gentleman* and *shadow*; but allowing more recognition of shadow became alarming and shocking in its uncontrolled sexuality and violence. Although he was only marginally conscious of it, within himself he became frightened when he found he couldn't control it. The dreams he then remembered brought mythic images and stories to bear on his situation; at that level the desired reconciliation is expressed as being between 'godly' and 'satanic'. And he does begin to understand himself at a dual level, personal and archetypal. Perhaps things begin to feel slightly more in control.

The dream he now remembers is once again from a more personal level, a seemingly straightforward homosexual image. Evidently he does not fear homosexuality *per se*; he is flattered by those attracted to his masculinity. His fear and anger arise only when a more masculine man wants to penetrate his femininity.

Mythological names or ideas such as Satan or the devil only really make sense in one's ordinary daily life when they can be seen to have a personal connection. In distinct, personally recognizable terms, this is a 'satanic' touch for Dr M. The man touching his anus is, as it were, touching his femininity which, having been repressed (as we have seen) is split in two: a 'heavenly soul-mate' and a 'deformed bitch with a passion for filth'; and the latter is so unconscious in him that it is indistinguishable from archetypal evil. But we must bear in mind that he has no hope of redeeming the feminine within himself if he has to keep it suppressed.

In fact, in Dr M as in so many men who are quite evidently heterosexual in predominant inclination, the extraordinary anxiety surrounding homosexuality is less to do with the sexual expression in itself, and more to do with a still-precarious masculine self-identification which feels threatened by feminine tenderness, sensitivity, emotionality and feeling because they are seen, from the viewpoint of a still undeveloped masculine, to constitute weakness. Only once the masculine qualities have been sufficiently proved through experience will there be enough confidence in strength to allow weakness, and only then is the discovery made that there exists a new and different strength in the feminine.

Enter the devil

20.10.76
(a) Walking rough ground with old Indian man who gives me food.
(b) In room with two women, a mother and adult daughter; daughter says she and I can only make love after seeing Devil 'cover' her mother. Devil

84

locked in room nearby; they seem depraved to me; Devil escapes, black monkey sort of creature with demonic energy and pointed tail; he overwhelms many people.

Dr M: Indian man like wise teacher; I liked him ... reminds me of Don Juan; there's a devil on the loose and Don Juan knew how to protect Carlos.

RP: Don Juan was a sorcerer and knew how to keep his balance while living in 'both worlds' at once. He is a wise-old-man figure, an inner teacher. The previous night an older man had frightened and angered him by touching his feminine place. Now this masculine energy is divided in two: one is a wise, nourishing and protective teacher; the other is the sexually overwhelming devil. There has again been a descent to the collective, mythic level, perhaps because of the violent repudiation at the personal level.

The daughter, who we may take to be a personification of his feminine aspects, knows she and he cannot unite unless the devil first 'covers' her mother, a term emphasizing the animal nature of the union. Although the dreamer has effectively summoned the devil by invoking Abraxas, he cannot accept all this, finding it depraved. Perhaps because of his disapproval the devil, which is distinctly subhuman (and appears as a black monkey in subsequent dreams), goes on the rampage.

21.10.76 *Reversing my car, it half falls in swamp; with a huge effort I lift it out. I am sent as ambassador to say that the wealthy oilman has attractive things to offer.*

Dr M: Devil is now wealthy oilman ... have to reverse my position and speak *for* him.

RP: Oil is 'black gold', a residue from the primeval forest trapped below ground which can be released by drilling to provide valuable energy. If these outer realities are interpreted as inner realities in terms of resources within the psyche, and the wealthy oilman is understood as the owner of the oil, then Dr M is surely right to associate him with the Devil. The image is a contemporary version of Pluto, rich god of the underworld.

Reversing his car and the huge effort in pulling it out of the swamp portray what an effort he has to make to change his attitude towards the 'satanic' and all that this term means for him. In psychological language he is overcoming his resistances and accepting the value of ancient residues in the unconscious, both personal and collective; in mythological language he is daring to begin to deal with the god of the underworld, whose dark realm is full of treasure as well as danger.

22.10.76 *Medical dinner; Karate man says I must have mushrooms and gives me a pretend kiss.*

Dr M: Homosexual again; Karate man very strong and masculine; reminds me of S (more powerful boy at school), that time he overpowered me and masturbated me and I felt incredible melting release.

RP: Back to the more personal level again. But now the approach to his femininity is not repudiated so violently and his associations are of a rare and extremely enjoyable experience of his feminine sexuality.

25.10.76 (vision-text Ch.14 p.211)

RP: The fiery theme of the last waking, visual impression, which was linked with the devil, reappears but now it is situated within a church and matched, as it were, by a shaft of light from above. It has taken on the formal shape of a triangle.

Defensive flight? Or inflation?

26.10.76 (dream-text Ch.5 p.69) (vision-text Ch.14 p.211)

Dr M: Anxious tense feeling all night ... sense of illegitimate doings, fear of being caught out. Man in E-type, Japanese man, the engineer Emperor, and Dick all the same figure ... technology, science, head, intellect. Thinking too much and cut off from feelings; cut foot in sea this evening without even noticing.

RP: The last dream before this one brought vivid memories of a homosexual episode in which he experienced his femininity. It seems this was too much for him. Tonight's dream is all about flight and pretences of extraordinary powers.

He finds himself 'with' a strange, shifty, many-faced companion: this companion represents aspects of his present attitude. To begin with the companion has a rather Mephistophelian quality: impious, inventive, magical, deceptive. This may indicate that Dr M is experiencing an 'inflation', meaning that he is puffed up with a superhuman feeling of devilish cleverness and potency.

But everything has a manic and fragile feeling about it, and no sooner do the police catch up with this 'emperor-ingenieur' than he falls and dies, his bottle broken. His spirit (alcohol), however, immediately reconstitutes into Dick. We have already seen the 'Dick' attitude: rational, materialistic, intellectual, sceptical.

From his comments it is clear that Dr M has understood his dream in terms of defensive flight into this 'Dick' attitude, presumably because he knows he feels anxious about things getting out of hand. Certainly, when, following Dick, he tries to fly away from the 'world' in the metal globe, this does represent emergency flight into intellectualization, the globe at the top being like the head which tries to separate itself from the material body. But there is a distinct impression that they have to fly *because* the Mephisto character has been exposed. The inflation that seems to be present is not being admitted.

The attempted escape from the world fails. He cannot escape the sexual pull; his gaze is drawn back down and into the world by sexuality in a monastic setting. His orgasm is immensely powerful; it brings the flight to an end.

His return to earth places him in, yet again, a Garden of Eden scene, with woman, tree and serpent – Satan's first form on earth according to the myth. He wants to kill the serpents (the archetypal shadow), but cannot.

His waking fantasies involve the Moon and Venus, Artemis and Aphrodite, virgin goddess and sex goddess. Perhaps these differing aspects of the feminine which are causing such difficulties for him (as they have done for most of the Christian West) are beginning to be put together.

27.10.76 (dream-text Ch.9, p.132)

Dr M: Stolen and make-believe powers . . . nasty taste in my mouth . . . like a fraud. Feel dominated by sexual desire; wish I had more mastery over it, but surprised how much I deny it in dreams . . . as if something in me is more moralistic than I know.

RP: Now, in dreams and in comments, he recognizes the inflation, the false magical power. He claims, in a nightclub, that he is immune to the charms of sex, and, in the second dream, delights in his control over inanimate matter. The reference to opium virtually tells him that these are illusions.

It is the third dream in which he becomes aware of stealing; his conscience has reappeared. It does so when the curiosity shop owner offers him something legitimately. What the two stones may have been and why he stole them is not clear at present (but see 29.11.76, p.222) where his father has his 'stones' around him).

28.10.76 (vision-text Ch.14 p.211)

Dr M: Fantasies beginning to alarm me as much as intrigue; slight fear of madness. Pure and good and spiritual feelings I sometimes have in a church being brought together with burning desire for sex, power, recognition, and worldly things.

RP: His anxieties about the waking fantasies are understandable. Dreams, even when very disturbing or terrifying, at least feel as if they are in their proper place from which one can escape by waking. Suddenly to see, in the midst of the waking day, a different world in which one is experiencing events and performing actions, really confronts one with the realization that 'there are many mansions in my Father's house'. The certainty that one will be conscious and tolerably well-adapted to conventional reality so long as one is awake is immediately threatened.

Vivid fantasies like these confront one with an autonomous and purposeful power within the psyche, which might be welcomed if only one could be certain that its creativity were going to serve consciousness and the development of the personality. But one can't be sure; rightly or wrongly there is always the fear of madness.

Incest

30.10.76 *In Harrods; find package with same name as mine on it and bluster assistant into giving it to me; contains glacé cherries and a rudder arm. Later challenged by real owner; offer him remaining cherries but hide rudder; feel ashamed and wonder why I'm behaving like this.*

Dr M: Mother had all provisions delivered by Harrods. Passion for glacé cherries when I was little . . . used to steal them from larder. Called Rachel's nipples her 'cherries'. Without rudder cannot steer own course. Felt in foul mood all day.

RP: The inflation has further subsided; he is no longer an emperor or magician. But he is again stealing from a shop. Harrods is readily understandable as the 'rich mother' and his associations to Rachel's (his sister's) nipples, together with the name on the package being his own family name, leave little doubt that incest fantasies are involved. The real owner of the rudder and glacé cherries from Harrods may be assumed to be the 'father'. Having to steal the rudder shows how rudderless he feels at present.

Like the stealing of the two stones, this effort ends in shame and confusion. The father's ownership of the mother now begins to come into view as a problem for the dreamer. This mainly concealed state of conflict with the father parallels at a more personal level his stealing the fruit of the Garden of Eden and his fear of punishment from God the Father. The interweaving of archetypally mythic and historically personal is beginning to become clearer.

Seven

A SEQUENCE OF DREAMS

PART 2

Father and son

2.11.76 (vision-text Ch. 14, p.211)
(a) A breakfast feast; I hear son tell father that the Church is the drilling department; notice my clothes are filthy. A vast storm begins; I hold D because she's frightened by flashes and bangs; our house slides toward edge of cliff; I take D to Church which is strong; a nun takes her while I go to rescue W; then in another church which is half-full of water; danger.
(b) Problem with oxygen supply. I realize I'm naked; patient vomits into big water container.

Dr M: Finding Christianity within me . . . never felt it had anything to do with me. Son and father . . . me and my father . . . Christ the Son and God the Father.

Drilling reminds me of wealthy oilman dream, so . . . son tells father that Church is way to release devil's wealth. I'm the son, my clothes dirty from drilling. Father reacts like Zeus in a rage, thunder and lightning, destruction of my house.

My eyes being opened . . . thunderstruck . . . religion and my family life, my personal history are somehow one and the same thing.

[Referring to vision] . . . becoming aware of Jesus within me is very comforting.

RP: These dreams and waking image/thoughts were an important stage in his journey, one might even say a turning-point.

His comments show that he has really got hold of something which is also symbolically expressed in the second little dream: the patient vomits into a big water container, which is the Church half-full of water; in other words, the patient empties his uncomfy personal contents into the collective container, the Church. This is indeed the true role of the Church in psychological terms: to receive the personal into its collectivity. He is grasping how this happens as an inward experience, and it impresses him.

The specific nature of the personal contents at present are the *entry into and possession of the mother, and the inevitable clash with the father.* This is being tied in with our Christian myth.

We see, in this tapestry of personal and collective language, the son challenging the father, claiming that his drilling (evidence of which is visible in his dirty clothes) is OK because it 'is within the Church' (i.e. sanctified). The father clearly doesn't think so and flies into a rage. Faced with this exhibition of godlike wrath and power the dreamer abandons his drilling into Mother Earth, and concentrates on keeping his daughter and wife safe.

4.11.76 *At sex party; I orgasm twice while watching man ramming penis into woman; hostess wants sex with me but I have no more desire; later she is still after me.*

Dr M: New angle on the drilling! Hostess like mother. Can only be voyeur.

RP: Back again to the personal level. While 'drilling' the previous night referred to an image of screwing into Mother Earth, tonight's dream shows a man drilling into a woman. But Dr M is no longer the driller! Having been daunted by the father's rage, he cannot get in there himself; he can only, as he remarks, be the voyeur. There is a broad hint that his mother is (or was) seductive.

Drawn down into childhood

5.11.76 *I have been loaned a strange vehicle, a car with an outrigger; in the twilight W and I have to clamber over a roof to get to it; there I find my scalpel (the one Daddy gave me), but it's broken because someone tried to throw it; the car has one flat tyre so I take off outrigger; then on roof again I see python and cobra; think they will fight and not sure which will win, also fearful for myself; but get back to car which I have to reverse blindly. W worried, but it works OK.*

Dr M: Nausea, dizziness, feel loss of control of my mind; uncomfortable memories of incest games with Rachel ... Mummy close ... brother/sister love, and physical love, are very powerful ... waves of hot/cold rising from base spine to top of head.

RP: The dream involves a complex web of personal associations. The overall sense of struggle and personal history is reflected in his comments, and it is important to notice that 'Mummy' and 'Daddy' are used rather than the terms 'mother' and 'father' he has used hitherto. The change, probably unconscious, shows how much he has been drawn back into the atmosphere of his childhood.

6.11.76 *In loaned motor-boat; when I start it it shoots backward very fast; the rudder-arm breaks off.*

Dr M: Memories of teenage girlfriends, love and sex. Again a loaned vehicle, and again trouble controlling it. Shooting backward is what my mind is doing . . . effort to be in present.

RP: He is being confronted with the fact he is using things which do not belong to him, and hence cannot control. The broken rudder echoes the broken scalpel from his father, and also links back to the dream of 30.10.76 when he stole a rudder from a man (associated with the father). He has to see the difference between what is his and what belongs to his father; ultimately this means differences between his own individuality and the attitudes and beliefs of his father, many of which he will almost certainly have taken on unquestioningly. He needs his own rudder to steer his own course.

A wounded gazelle

7.11.76 (dream-text Ch.15, p.233) (vision-text Ch.14, p.211)

Dr M: Sadness all day. Back in childhood; atmosphere around Mummy's death thick in dream . . . but gazelle part of me as much as her . . . tender, feminine, lovely, gentle. Soho . . . prostitutes . . . after Mummy died I used to go there.

[Referring to vision] Grey stone column in cathedral like Jesus inside; tie myself on for safety.

RP: Now, instead of trying to steal his father's objects (such as rudder, stones, and scalpel), he is recognizing his father's authority and asking his permission. He wants very much to show the gazelle to his little boy. It is as if he is now asking the father's permission for the little boy in him to have some of the mother's beautiful tenderness. This is really kowtowing to the powerful father.

Mrs P was the housekeeper who became woman of the home following mother's death; she is blamed for the gazelle's death, which occurs beside the black cupboard (a real, and sombre, article of furniture, here symbolizing death and the darkness of the sarcophagus).

The gazelle 'dies' in the dream; but it is also shown as being underwater except for its head. This is typical dream imagery for a part of the self 'dying', or being lost, in the sense of being *submerged below the surface of consciousness*; in other words, the death is not absolute. In this instance the head part remains conscious but the body has become unconscious.

Psychologically, this would mean that the gazelle, which appears to be an image both of mother and of his own feminine nature, has persisted as an intellectual (head) knowledge, while the feelings and emotions (the body) are unconscious. The specific wounds, to right foreleg and right shoulder, have some distinct symbolism because they reappear in two later dreams, eventually being healed by the 'queen'. (See Ch.15, p.233.)

The wounded gazelle is a development of the deformed bitch which came into the 'overture' dream (11.6.74, p.75).

Getting his 'little car' serviced in Soho speaks rather poignantly of his need for a mother-substitute (distinctly sexual) after his mother's death; Mrs P (an elderly lady) was evidently useless in this respect.

8.11.76 (dream-text Ch.13, p.192)

Dr M: Sexual feelings all day ... had to hide erections from patients.

RP: After the gazelle 'died' the dreamer went to Soho. Apparently continuing this theme, there is uninhibited sexuality in tonight's dream, but little sense of the whole person being loved. He experiences, very intensely, 'part-object' desire, and then jealousy. One has a sense of being close to the roots of that separation between soulful love and sexual love which is of such concern to him.

Infantile experience and fantasies of his mother's body are very close, and the 'other man' (rich and powerful) is the father.

10.11.76 (dream-text Ch.4, p.47)

Dr M: Fallen in love with Anna over last week; no sex though ... walking the beach in the evening. Dream heart-stoppingly beautiful and magical.

RP: As his dreams bring back painful memories of his rivalry with his father over his mother, together with the later wound of losing his mother in death, he becomes infatuated with another woman. This is not meaningless coincidence!

The dream is laden with a sense of legendary romance and, with the emphasis on photographing, a desire to capture it for ever. Coming so quickly after a very sexual dream, it seems that his divided opposites of sexual female and soul-love female are lurching from one side to the other. But they are also brought together in a way: the symbols of the dog and bitch, with which this series began, are rather neatly shown to the dreamer to be one and the same as the beautiful black mare and golden unicorn.

12.11.76 (dream-text Ch.5, p.68)

Dr M: Little different from notions I've had about Anna as second wife; girl in dream like her.

RP: This appears to be an unrealistic solution to the problem of how to bring together the separated components of his feminine. The Oedipal conflict in the background finds an allusion in Regina, a wealthy woman friend who is a mother, and is experienced by him as motherly.

16.11.76

(a) Driving my MGB at night; I fail to stop at pedestrian crossing because I'm sleepy; trouble with police.
(b) Night-time in dark street; Sophie, tall girl with unshaven legs, comes up from behind and greets me.

Dr M: Got MGB after Mummy died; Sophie was Mummy's name. Hair grows after death. Need all my will to do decent day's work.

RP: Dr M has been quite deeply depressed these past days. Having attempted to short-circuit his inner conflict by having an affair with Anna, but then realized its unsuitability, the real psychic task goes on and he finds himself drawn back again to images of his mother and the past. The darkness, night, and sleepiness all suggest low consciousness and depression. His association that hair growth continues after death, in connection with a woman who bears his mother's name and joins him out of the darkness, perhaps helps him to realize that although his mother is dead in outer reality, she is still alive *within him*. The loss of Anna has revivified his buried anguish about his mother's death.

18.11.76   Fever and rigors

RP: Not surprisingly perhaps, he has fallen ill. One can often see it coming when the inner world is known through dreams and self-reflection. When psychic torment is too much to bear it finds physical expression.

The anguished monk

21.11.76 (dream-text Ch.12, p.177)

Dr M: Feeling better today, thank God. Monks dream exactly how I've been feeling ... has been inside me for years, but didn't know it.

RP: His interrogation of the family shows how anxious he is not to break the incest taboo and incur the father's wrath again. But it seems his sister has indeed been sleeping with him, i.e. in the febrile blurring of alert consciousness, his femininity *has*, so the dream says, been 'in bed' with him. The guiltiness of this is evident.

His comments show how important the second dream is; he both sees himself, and is himself, making contact with an anguished part of himself represented by the God-forsaken monks. These are feelings that have been long-buried; they are not only the feelings he has been affected by, but unconscious of, during the depression of the past few days, they go back at least to the unreleased feelings around the death of his mother, and almost certainly from before that too.

The father is attacked

22.11.76

(a) Close to University; an amazing river/snake of conglomerate humanity comes into view; it moves forward but has no beginning and no end; from it comes a powerfully seductive call for others to join it. I wonder if it is caused by a Don Juan drug; I'm told I can ask by touching it; I do so and feel the answer 'yes'.

(b) Army of Chinese youth comes into view near University; I am with Negro who takes instant decisions; a fight between Negro with 16-bladed cross as weapon and Chinese with 2 daggers curved like moons; Chinese stabs Negro in the eye; then I'm walking away with W down African road; a vast black man comes towards us.

(c) At L.House; talk with Rachel; Daddy comes in, his face bruised, right eye empty, nose missing. He tells me it is injury not disease, a junior doctor maliciously gave him an explosive bleep; my heart groans for him.

Dr M: Such sadness for Daddy ... came from pit of my heart. Terrible sense I did it. Negro = father. Weapons had sacred or ritual appearance.

RP: The first dream contains an image of the collective unconscious itself and its immense seductive power. The second seems to deal with a racial clash, i.e. a conflict still expressed at a collective level, but at least distinguished into races, each with its different symbolic weapons which hint at the cross and the moon. The clash between these two picks up the same theme as in the Abraxas dream, when the dreamer saw the moon as he invoked Abraxas, and then the raging black man appeared. Later dreams confirmed the negro as the image of the terrifying and tyrannical father. Seen in this way, the dreamer, as the son, would seem to be 'the Chinese' which, from previous instances of the 'Chinese' symbol, has pointed to the instinctual urges of the son.

Recent dreams have shown Dr M is still dominated by the power of the father and feeling he cannot gain possession of the mother. We know too that his inner fight with the personal father is simultaneously being experienced as a fight with the paternal tradition of Christianity in which he grew up. So far, that Father-God image within him has not tolerated any attempt to acknowledge another God-image. That, nevertheless, is what he somehow has to do because the imago of his personal father within him has a very archetypal quality, and hence he can scarcely distinguish it from the Father-God imago.

The first two dreams are so collective that personal connections are minimal. The third dream, however, plays the same theme through a more personal level. His actual father has been terribly injured (showing the father = Negro link) by what one may take to be the son's rivalry and malice.

Until now the father has had the upper hand and the son has retreated before his wrath. Now, having integrated his buried anguish (represented by the God-forsaken monks), it seems the son has more strength and has truly managed to make a dent in the father. However, he loved and admired his father dearly (hence his difficulty in separating from him) and this damage to the father-imago has hurt him deeply; a fact which also shows how truly it has been done.

The magician enters

23.11.76 (vision-text Ch.14 p.212)
Music recital; audience of blue-rinsed women, spiritually dead, talk of strange entertainer to come. Magician enters through door with 'Daleth' written above it.

RP: In some earlier dreams his dream-ego itself has played about with illusions of magic, but these puffings-up with spirit quickly subsided. Now the magician, as a collective archetypal figure, makes a real appearance. The word Daleth, which he must have come across but forgotten, is the name of the fourth letter in the Hebrew alphabet. All the letters have ancient symbolic meanings in the *Cabbala*: Daleth signifies 'the door', and in the Tree of Life it connects Binah (Understanding) with Chokmah (Wisdom). For some reason he made no comments on this dream, but the appearance of the magician through this door is an important development for him, as we shall see.

The image of the black sun (see vision), which burst in while he was reflecting upon Christ and the crucifixion, is one that has appeared among various mystic traditions, notably alchemy. It signifies the paradoxical idea, or experience, that there is a source of power and even illumination which comes from the dark depths rather than the heavenly heights. Once again this is reminiscent of the Abraxas dream with its reference to the reconciliation between the satanic and holy godheads.

Having made some headway in his massive inner fight with the father archetype, it seems a mystical and dark power is making itself known to him.

Destroying a world

25.11.76
(a) Walking in Kilburn; a research scientist gives me a bomb to end the world.
(b) A world disaster has happened; I'm in USA with girl and sheriff; we are all running in a river.
(c) I'm in a strange and very powerful house; there are 10 people, all on drugs. A chart on a round table can tell one about one's sexuality by using one's date of birth and Zodiacal qualities. I discover I am 'voyeur'; Dick is 'lusty'. It is Timothy Leary's house; many strange books on mind and religion; I look through them, secretly searching for sexy ones. The owner arrives, he has a face like the moon; he gives me fruits which are also strange drugs. A girl gives me money; the King is there.

Dr M: Can't remember feelings from first dream – only idea. Second dream not quite real either. Third felt exciting, forbidden, strange, like entering realm of drugs, sex, secret knowledge. I woke right out of it at 3.33 a.m., walked beach; sat until dawn watching moon and sea.

RP: Kilburn is a district in North London with a large Irish population. But, to guess from the context, the name is probably used by the dream to mean 'kill and burn'. Again in very global and collective symbols the hugeness of the paternal cultural identification he has to destroy is portrayed: he has to *end a 'world'*. This echoes back to the Abraxas dream and one of the Hermann Hesse associations:

'The bird is struggling out of the egg. The egg is the world. Whoever wants to be born must first destroy a world. The bird is flying to God.'

Now the deed is done although, being rather remote from his emotional reality, one may guess that this is no more than the first deep sign that it is going to happen for him consciously. Nevertheless, the orthodox and solar-light world having been destroyed, we see him, in the third dream, entering the occult lunar world and discovering many strange things – including a king. The themes of the magician, the arcane knowledge, and the black sun are all developed.

Apollo and Dionysus

27.11.76 *With Rick and Justin; Rick driving us fast in his big car; I find I live close to Rick whose home is a tower; see broken recorder, then long* *axe; I'm happy because Rick and Justin are getting on well; see man trying to catch his girl who is floating from high window of vast cathedral.*

Dr M: Rick had explosive rows with his father ... Justin quite the opposite, never had a row with his father, looked like him, moved like him, talked like him, believed exactly the same things. Both friends of mine, but they never got on with each other. Rick is Dionysian, Justin Apollonian. Still trying to bring them together in myself. I stand between them but not balanced; sometimes wholly one and sometimes wholly the other, or so it feels.

RP: Rick is an old school-friend who became a rock star in the early sixties; his world, as seen through Dr M's eyes from the times they spent together, was an orgiastic night world of drugs, sex, and wild abandon; hence his description of Rick as Dionysian. Justin, who has appeared in these dreams before, is quite the opposite: fastidious, formal, controlled, philosophically minded, intensely loyal to his personal father and to the cultural traditions.

Dr M has not seen either for a year or more; their appearance in this dream undoubtedly represents an attempt to harmonize within himself these very different relationships between son and father. Despite his joyful feeling in the dream that they were 'getting on well', the broken recorder and long axe hint that relations are not as good as they seem, and the girl floating from the cathedral window is not yet even held, let alone grounded. Note also that he 'lives close to Rick' — the side that challenges the father.

Decay in the power of the Father

29.11.76 (dream-text Ch.15, p.222)

Dr M: What's in my dream house is what's in me. Lot inside that's on its last legs; the 'father's' in state of decay. It's true ... I don't have much sympathy with their old values, scientific, military, moral. Realize I've felt that for ages; difference is — now I *know* I feel it.

RP: It is clear from his comments, that the major shift we have seen boiling up in his identification with certain traditional paternal masculine values, has now become conscious. This is far from meaning it is complete, but it is a big step forward.

The dreamer's father is portrayed sitting in a chair made out of the bones and hide of a cow. This striking symbol makes it plainer why Dr M had to mount this challenge to the father. The cow, for obvious reasons, is a mother symbol; hence the father is shown in possession of the mother and surrounded by his power symbols (including his 'stones' which the dreamer tried to steal from the curiosity shop).

In the course of his dreams we have seen numerous attempts on the part of the dreamer to possess the mother (or equivalent woman), ranging from overt challenges to covert stealings; the former failed and the latter were unsatisfactory. Those earlier efforts to possess the mother, when they failed, were followed by the fling with Anna, but he was sensible enough to realize this was no good. Giving her up was very painful and was followed by depression and illness, which resonated not only with his anguish from the time of his mother's death, but also with an earlier loss which happened when his father returned from the war; until then, the three-year-old boy had had mother all to himself.

Since recovering from the illness, and digesting the pain expressed in the image of the monks whose God had forgotten them,* the strength to challenge and distinguish himself from the father has grown. His identification with the traditionally correct father archetype, that is to say the Father as presented by Christian orthodoxy, has been loosened with a simultaneous movement toward the mystical, magical, dark and Dionysian. This feels dangerous and slippery but it is essential because so long as he is still subject to the power of his father he cannot truly become a father himself, nor can he truly possess the mother.

At this point it is necessary to make it clear that the 'mother' does not of course refer simply to his actual and long-dead mother. In terms of an actual other person the 'mother' would now be an incarnated person mainly in the figure of his wife, who is mother to his children. But the 'mother' means more than this, the 'mother symbol' points also to the feminine creative fundament of his own being, his unconscious potential, the substrate of his conscious personality; possessing her does not so much

---

*It becomes increasingly possible to see that the 'God' loved by the monks was an early God-image for Dr M, one whose roots lay in the experience of the mother: i.e. the God who had forsaken (her) faithful lovers (monks) was his mother who had transferred so much of her love to her returning husband, and later the mother who had died and abandoned the son who still needed her.

To see that the roots of this God-image lie in the *feminine* makes it much easier to understand why the new lunar God, for which Dr M appears to be forsaking the Father-God, is characterized with all the feminine attributions of moon, darkness, mystery, magic, drugs, etc., and also why it first appeared in this dream sequence as Satan or the devil. Profound themes to do with gender, sexuality and the God-image are involved here. Dr M is a man of his time and the aeon of the Father God is indeed coming to an end in the collective, with a resurgence of the older feminine mysteries. Nor must it be forgotten that in his 'big dream' of 25.3.75 the two heavenly bodies, sun and moon, are revealed side by side in marriage. This longing too was sought in the invocation of Abraxas — that the holy and the satanic godheads be reconciled. These, however, are tasks which stretch into the years ahead for Dr M.

mean owning her as earning the right to enter her and fertilize her – the inner mystery of the creative individual.

'Le roi est mort; vive le roi!' goes the old saying for succession to the throne. We have seen a new king appear in the house of the 'moon-man', and we have seen the old king decaying in his cow-throne. The dreams of this night have taken Dr M a significant step closer to the royal succession.

Synchronicity

30.11.76
(a) Karate club looking for new champion.
(b) Driving my MGB, but it has no power; I'm close to the Rolls-Royce garage.

Dr M: Suddenly decided today that I want to return to England. By extraordinary coincidence heard this afternoon that Company want me in UK where they have big future planned for me. Don't think I want it with them, but ... a good way to go back.

RP: Jung used the term 'synchronicity' to connote moments when outer and inner events coincide in a way which defies causal explanation, the coincidence being experienced as striking and meaningful. Experiences of synchronicity tend to come at moments of important change in the psyche.

In the light of the discussion of the previous night's dreams, the search for the new champion is obvious enough. The second dream suggests the dreamer has grave doubts about his power; in some subsequent dreams Rolls-Royces with royal number plates belong to his father, and beside them his little MGB is puny. Even in his decaying state the father still has great power. However, the synchronism of inner decision and outer event must underline the sense that Dr M's personal development has taken a major step forward.

The inadequate son

1.12.76 (dream-text Ch.9, p.127)

Dr M: Suggests I do not feel up to the big future they see for me, which is odd; I do feel up to it, though I don't really want it.

RP: Outward events, now that return to the UK is a definite future, are no doubt preoccupying him and probably that is why he has taken this dream in an outward way as referring only to his future with the Company. Certainly it does portray a Company setting and, despite his conscious protestations, reveals some feeling of childlike inadequacy in relation to the

Company executives and the rich future proposed for him. But the contrast is so like the previous night's dream in which he felt puny and powerless in his MGB beside the rich Rolls-Royce garage that there can be no doubt that the inner complement of the outer situation continues to be the son feeling small and inadequate beside the father at the food-rich table of the mother.

2.12.76 *I'm trying to release men locked in a building but fail; then begin making love with Regina but realize after a while we are being seen by everyone in the big hotel. Then re-enter building to try to release men; confront inadequate young man and spit at him. Now it seems one man has died and another is sick and somehow because of this the others will be free. Again I begin to make love with Regina.*

Dr M: Regina means Queen. Couldn't make love with her until I had freed the locked-up men. Inadequate man like dream previous night when I felt small. Need to become more masculine.

RP: The paternal values he has been wearing like a borrowed cloak no longer have the strength they once did for him; what strengths does he himself have with which to replace them? He is discovering he does not have enough. Some of his masculinity is 'locked up' and he has to release it. After a feeble attempt he gives up and tries to possess the Queen right away but this, of course, does not work.

He then makes a somewhat more determined effort to release the masculine, which involves an actual confrontation with the immature and inadequate youth within himself.

The man and his shadow

3.12.76 *(a) Fight with fair-haired Englishman.*

RP: This sounds like a more earnest struggle with his inadequacy. The fair-haired Englishman echoes back to the dreams near the beginning of the sequence, at which point he was too scared to tackle him. I have called it 'the man and his shadow' now, rather than the 'gentleman and his shadow' as I did before, because he has relinquished certain identifications with the 'gentleman'. By now we can see more clearly what 'shadow' qualities he is struggling with: inadequacy, immaturity, weakness, an excessive thraldom to the feminine.

5.12.76 *There is civil war; I have W and kids with me; we're told to stay in a room; rebels come and a hand grenade is thrown in but goes off with* *only a small bang. With my rifle I try to shoot Idi Amin but nothing works properly. He gives the order, 'Kill'.*

Dr M: Woke in a sweat. Anxious about the future, worried about financial security if I leave Company; heavy sense of responsibility for family. Idi Amin is mad but powerful tyrant, ogre dictator.

RP: The huge and terrifying black man has appeared several times before, and each time there has been some link between him and the father's shadow; in other words, within the spectrum of Dr M's archetypal images of the father there is the 'white' father with his spiritual symbols of power, his microscope, books and stones; but there is also the 'black' father who is huge, muscular, raging, and terrifying.

In this dream-situation of civil (internal) war, it is not quite clear whether the dreamer is bravely guarding his family . . . or being herded into a room with the women and children. He seems to be threatened not only by Idi Amin but also by rebels; he is impotent in his attempt to kill Idi Amin. In his comments, his anxieties are realistic and properly paternal. His intention to make a more individual life for himself and his family outside the protective shelter of the Company is brave and is the objective evidence that all this work within his psyche is bearing fruit in waking reality. Somewhere inside him he is terrified by the prospect. Facing and overcoming that terror will bring him the stronger masculinity he now knows he needs.

Beatrice

6.12.76 *Evening light and Beatrice with me in the jungle; wolves howl; we see shrunken-head trophies on poles. Beatrice and I have to find the chalice near the river and take it to the King.*

Dr M: Dreams of Beatrice come with sad nostalgia as if she is my true soul-mate and I have lost her. Been thinking today about trying to find her again. When Beatrice haunts me I see W as coarse and materialistic, which is horrible for both of us. Know it's unfair to W, but the feeling envelops me. Beatrice seems to fit with King Arthur.

RP: For the past fortnight his dreams have concerned themselves mostly with the son's more effective challenge to, and separation from, the father. Now he has found that although he may have separated himself from an excessive identification with the good father he cannot yet stand up against the 'Darth Vader' dark aspect of the father. His masculinity is not yet strong enough and his possession of the Queen is incomplete. In this dream we find him once again with Beatrice, the dream figure for whom he feels spiritual, but not sexual, love.

The setting is wild and primitive and the shrunken-head trophies remind one of tribal wars where the victor eats the brains of the vanquished (which probably links with the Idi Amin dream). Beatrice is to be his ally in the task of finding the Grail-like chalice for the King. The dream reference to Arthurian legend points to the true king being wounded in spirit, a wound which can only be healed by the Holy Grail.

12.12.76 *I'm sitting with W and kids, but looking towards Beatrice and her family; Beatrice is sad. Then I'm caressing her but not wanting sex; I want to put things right. Then in boat with D; fear of collision; Beatrice is so sad she's rocking with pain; she has to have operation; I try to catch her eye but she rejects my wish to help.*

Dr M: Decided to find out where Beatrice lives now and meet her again. Operation reminds me of surgery Mummy had to have and how sad I felt for her, and how bad to be going out with girlfriends while she was dying.

RP: So powerful are his feelings for the Beatrice of his dreams that he is confusing the actual Beatrice, whom he has not seen for many years, with the meaning for himself of his dream-Beatrice. He did, in fact, pursue his intention to find her, and they met some six months after this dream. Only when he actually met her and saw how different she and her real life were from his dream experience was he able finally to let go the notion that she (the actual person) was his true soul-mate.

A crucial component of the emotions making her so important a figure is clearly revealed in this dream and his comments: his caresses come from a profound desire *'to put things right'*. He needs to make better, to repair. This theme of guilt and reparation has been around from the very beginning of the series. The guilt of betrayal that he felt over the figure of Avril in the first dream, and over his dog Betsy in later dreams, has now reached Beatrice, and through her, his mother.

Now he can feel his guilt that he abandoned Beatrice because she left him for too long a time, and this guilt is intermingled with the guilt he felt in transferring his affections to girlfriends while his mother was dying. As we know, he feels he has lost his soul-love, which has appeared variously as Beatrice, mother, and God; the reason it is lost, and disconnected from his instinctual sexual love, is *because his guilt is lying heavily on top of it.*

We see his need to *make reparation* in order to free him from his guilt and unblock the springs of his heart-love so it can reach out into the real world again.

* * *

We must leave Dr M and his dreams. His dreams, like everyone's dreams, will continue to the last day of his life, an unceasing evolution of his soul. A few dreams from subsequent weeks and months appear in other chapters, and although they are used primarily to illustrate the particular theme relevant to that chapter, many of the figures and dramas we have come to know through this series continue to appear, including more of his process of reparation.

The inner world of the psyche that appears before us in our dreams is not meaningless. Certainly, dreams do not have to be remembered, any more than we have to be conscious of our hearts beating or our lungs breathing; they do their work whether we notice it or not. Nor is anything we have seen in Dr M's dreams in the least unusual; the Oedipal conflict is, as Freud revealed to us, universal; so too, as Klein has shown us, is guilt and reparation; so too, as Jung discovered, is the interweaving of collective myth and personal history as the self unfolds. The only thing that *is* unusual about Dr M and his dreams is the number of dreams he remembers, and the commitment he gives to his inner life.

But there is a good deal to be said for allowing our dreams some conscious space and time; they provide the opportunity to become consciously aware of a great deal that underlies and interweaves with our conscious lives. Engaging the brilliant illumination and sharp focus of waking mind with the emotionally laden twilight realm of dreams, and doing so through time, may bring much doubt and sometimes fear but will also deepen and enrich the understanding of oneself and one's engagement with life.

FURTHER READING

Hesse, Hermann, *Demian*, London: Peter Owen.

Jung, C.G., 'A Study in the Process of Individuation', in *The Collected Works*, part 1, vol. 9, London: Routledge & Kegan Paul.

Dreams, London: Routledge & Kegan Paul.

'Synchronicity: an acausal connecting principle', in *The Collected Works*, vol. 8, London: Routledge & Kegan Paul.

Maguire, W. (ed.), Notes of Jung's *The Seminars*, vol. 1, London: Routledge & Kegan Paul.

Dr M's dreams in other chapters:

25.3.75: Ch.5, p.62
3.6.76: Ch.13, p.191
8.10.76: Ch.13, p.192
14.10.76: Ch.15, p.224

2.1.77: Ch.4, p.52
7.1.77: Ch.9, p.137
11.1.77: Ch.9, p.138
12.1.77: Ch.4, p.48

Eight

AN APPROACH TO DREAMWORK

HAVING DREAMED A DREAM, remembered it, written it out, how then can you set about getting the best from it?

Simply living with your dreams and learning what you will from them is the most important thing of all; but it has to be admitted that dreams are so confusing and imprecise that most of us need somewhere or some way of beginning, some orientation in approach. The sex of the dreamer suggests itself as a preliminary question. One might anticipate some characteristic differences between the dreams of males and females.

DREAMS AND THE SEX OF THE DREAMER

There *are* differences, it's true: but it must be said that they are dwarfed by the samenesses of dreams, most of which reflect the *human* condition rather than the *gender* condition. Although we find the differences between the bodies of men and women very exciting, and therefore very noticeable, the fact remains that our anatomies have a great deal more in common than differences. And this is no less true for our minds and our dreams.

Many dreams — be they dreamed by men or women — show us our hidden sides. Whatever there may be about ourselves that, knowingly or unknowingly, we conceal from the world at large, we will be reminded of it in our dreams. The man or woman who wears a brave face will find in their dreams their secret fears and timidity; the ones who broadcast their honesty will see their lies, little or big; the shames, guilts, hidden rages, hollow pretences, envies, jealousies, unacceptable sexual desires — all are laid bare in the privacy of dream. This is the nearest and awkwardly painful face of dreams, and although it may look back at a woman with a woman's face, and at a man with a man's face, in its essential meaning and purpose it is the same for each.

In the same way, many dreams to do with mislaid or developing parts of ourselves — whatever they may be: sad, terrible, joyous — are not different in their essence whichever sex one is. Naturally the dreamer 'knows', or rather takes for granted, his or her sex and experiences the dream 'I' as being their own sex. But many dreams, if written out and then read by another, do not reveal whether 'I' is male or female:

> There is terrible war: destruction, invasion, confusion, fighter planes, etc. It goes on around me as if I'm in it but somehow remote and detached. I feel like a very young child. Then, after a long time, it is over. A man approaches; he was a fighter pilot, a 'flying ace', but he is older now, sad and somehow wise. I see him go to one of those war cemeteries where ranks of white crosses stretch to the horizon. He cries, and says, 'I never knew that so many people had died.'

One really could not tell whether this was dreamed by a child, a man, or a woman. In fact the dreamer was a young woman, but although the personal and terrible experiences in her life are, for her, bound up with her female identity, the feelings and knowings in the dream are essentially *human* and might be experienced by either sex.

But there are of course some characteristic differences. Naturally enough, they appear particularly when dreams focus upon the dream-ego's anatomy, or when sexuality is involved, or in all the many aspects of gender-role activity.

Mostly these differences are no more than what one would expect: men *may* dream they have breasts, women *may* dream they have a penis, but it is much more likely that the dream-ego will have the same anatomy and be the same sex as the dreamer. Similarly, men can and do sometimes dream that they are pregnant, in labour and so on, and women can and do dream they are charging into battle with a machine-gun; but usually it is the other way round.

In very broad terms, men dream rather more of physical conflict, while women dream of verbal or emotional conflict; women, at least when describing their dreams, pay more attention to clothes, fabrics, etc., while men notice technology and tend to be more aware of orientating principles such as points of the compass and time.

Both sexes are likely to experience rivalry with dream-figures of the same sex, while romantic feelings and sexual acts most often take place (as one would expect) with figures of the opposite sex. When it comes to authority figures the variability is greater according to personal circumstances and experience, but each sex tends to see authoritative and parental figures, whether critical cold judges or wise kind teachers, as the same sex as the dreamer.

EXPERIENCE AND THEORY

The gender of the dreamer is a beginning; but some kind of map is needed for the far greater common humanity of dreams. Experience is the sine qua non. Continuity of experience brings gradual understanding, and understanding naturally begins to formulate itself into theory. Over the centuries many individuals have approached dreams with as little prejudice as they can muster, and gradually formed their own theories. Other people's theories can be immensely valuable, especially to begin with; but unlike purely scientific theories which may be learned dogmatically and applied (more or less) as technical tools, theories of dreams and dreaming are closer to artistic theory and need imaginative adaptation to one's own personal material.

One cannot begin to form one's own theoretical model until one has had extensive experience, and prior to that it is useful to have a ready-made approach. It will serve, at first, as a structure to hold onto, and gradually become a 'standard' against which one can compare one's own experience, see differences, and make modifications.

This approach to dreamwork may be divided into three parts: first, an attitude or belief about the whole nature of dreaming and dreams, which is simple in itself but not simple to describe; second, the more or less regular structure of a dream, which is straightforward; and third, a model of the psyche, which is both complex and complicated to describe.

1   THE NATURE OF DREAMS AND DREAMING

In the prologue to his novel *Demian* Hermann Hesse wrote:

> The life of every man is a way to himself, an attempt at a way, the suggestion of a path. No man has ever been utterly himself, yet every man strives to be so, the dull, the intelligent, each one as best he can. Each man to the end of his days carries round with him vestiges of his birth — the slime and eggshells of the primeval world. There are many who never become human; they remain frogs, lizards, ants. Many men are human beings above and fish below. Yet each one represents an attempt on the part of nature to create a human being.

Granted enough life-experience it is not hard to recognize the truth of these metaphors in the world we see around us. But this quotation says much about the nature of dreams. So often they bring the strongest feeling that one is somehow being shown the 'way', the 'suggestion of a path'. And dreams are themselves natural metaphor. Within them the slime and the eggshells, the lizards, ants and fish within our nature can appear exactly as such. The dreaming 'I', male or female, looks down into the water and perceives the fish in her own deeps; or, at the mouth of the cave he encounters his own benign or malevolent lizard:

> 26.1.77 Carefully looking out for snakes, I approach a lake, eventually finding myself close to the mouth of a cave; there I see a strange creature, squat and malevolent, browny-grey in colour, like a lizard. We stare at each other; I am disconcerted that it does not run away. Then I'm in an underground maze through which wind convoluted and ancient-seeming tree roots; the monster has now become half-human and is chasing me; I know it could turn me to stone; I escape but wake in a drenching sweat.

NATURAL PHENOMENA

Dreams should be seen as all natural phenomena are seen: they are as simple and as mysterious as a tree or a stone.

Think of a particular tree or stone you know well: it is, in itself and all by itself, the best possible expression of what it is. We may know more *about* it by drawing upon botanical or geological classifications, but only at the cost of submerging its uniqueness into the generality of a species or type. In the same way every dream is the best possible expression of the psychic situation at that moment; hiding nothing, disguising nothing; it just is; no less apt than the momentary pattern of branches dancing to the tune of the wind.

Dreams belong however to a peculiar category of natural phenomena; unlike trees or stones, and unlike other bodily productions such as urine or sweat, dreams are neither outside us nor are they objectively material. They are natural phenomena of the mind.

MIND AND PSYCHE

(a) Mind is something which exists. No one knows exactly what it is; no one knows its origins for sure; no one knows its limits. We can divide our idea of it (using our minds) into conscious and unconscious, personal and collective, etc., but it remains one of the great mysteries of existence. The problem is, of course, that we cannot get out of it to see it from the outside, we are always within it. Our situation is one of mind gazing at mind within mind. Whatever it is, it is not static; it is dynamic, restless, rarely leaving 'us' in peace. The terminology is difficult and confusing: mind is often called psyche – which is the term

I usually use — but it may also be called 'soul' or 'spirit', both of which also have more specific meanings (see Ch.10, p.151).

(b) What happens in dreams is that *psyche appears before itself.*

(c) Psyche is immaterial, not in the sense of irrelevant, but in the sense of 'not material', 'not matter'.

(d) Being immaterial it is, in itself, invisible. To become visible to itself, which also means becoming understandable to itself, it has to 'clothe' itself in something.

(e) The 'clothes' it puts on, in order to become visible to itself, are made from sensory images which derive from the natural world; it has infinite variety in its wardrobe.

(f) The sensory images of the natural world, as they exist in an objective or 'real' way, cannot express all that psyche is. By combining images in a way which is outwardly unrealistic, however, psyche can transcend the limitations of sensory world images and in that way fulfil its urge to appear before itself as it is. The image of one's own body, for instance, can be combined with the images of flying and of looking down from a height to result in a composite image of oneself flying, which is outwardly 'unrealistic' but gives visible shape to some invisible reality of psyche.

Tabulated like this the psyche sounds ponderously mechanical, as if it were carefully selecting clothes for the late-night show. This is not how it is, of course, any more than invisible wind laboriously chooses to set ears of corn a-swaying and leaves a-dancing to reveal its presence.

So ... dreams are psyche which, being invisible in itself, appears before itself in our dreams clothed in all the sensate images of nature.

This is simple enough as an idea; it is like imagining an invisible ghost putting on clothes in order to become visible. But when the abstract idea begins to be known as inward experience, there is something awesome and eerie in the awareness of invisible psyche moving beneath, beyond, on the other side of, your dream images. One begins to feel the communicative urge of this psyche, which is so much oneself and yet so strange, unknown, and 'other'. What mysterious and petrifying part of invisible psyche, for instance, finds visible expression through the image of the squat lizard monster?

INTERPRETING

Dreams are psyche appearing before itself. The 'itself' before which it appears is, of course, psyche as conscious 'I'. Within the dream, and still more so when awake, the 'I' struggles to understand, and this struggle involves words.

The conscious impression from a remembered dream is, first of all, a seamless and kaleidoscopic wealth of ever-shifting imagery. It would need the simplicity of a child's eye and the heart's understanding of a poet to know directly, to understand effortlessly. Very few are so gifted, and even they must still wrestle with the task of translating (i.e. interpreting) seamless imagery into words. We need some conceptualization in language in order to articulate the higher developments of consciousness with the world-clothed soul of dreaming. And so dreams are 'interpreted' — nature is translated into concept.

Each of us has to build our bridges, has to find the way from the dream as it is to rational conceptual consciousness as it is.

Both the dream and the operations of waking consciousness are psyche. There is, I repeat, no 'outside of psyche'; not even the most scrupulously objective scientist can for one moment stand outside of psyche. Psyche-in-dream is ancient, universal, arising from a deep where our personal soul and the 'soul of the world' are indistinguishable, perhaps even one and the same. Psyche-in-consciousness is evolutionarily more recent, focused in time, centred around ego, enchanted by whatever contemporary fashions and notions are currently prevalent within collective consciousness. All too easily it can lose touch with the depths of the psyche whence it came, as one who lives in a skyscraper can forget about the simple earth upon which we all depend.

Each night, remembered or forgotten, the skyscraper 'I' is immersed in a succession of dreams. Even if they are unremembered this natural process ensures that psyche-as-conscious-ego cannot wholly lose touch with that world-psyche from which it has budded forth.

Although the vast majority of dreams are never consciously remembered, and some people hardly remember any, still one cannot escape the strongest impression that psyche actively intends to communicate with itself, and that one of the ways in which it does so is through dreams.

One might, therefore, speak of the language of dreams, much as we speak of body-language; but this metaphor would blur over the most essential point of all. Dreams do not use language; language refers to communication through words ('la langue' being the tongue). Words are the symbols employed for the communication between conscious and differentiated minds.

Dreams are deeper than written or spoken language; although they occasionally employ speech and distinct words or ideas verbalized in a particular language, they are essentially pre-verbal and universal. All the world over they are no less and no more understandable than the mountains

110

and seas, the houses and hedgehogs in whose images they appear. An Eskimo's dreams differ from a Tahitian's only to the extent that each has a somewhat different stock of sensory images of the world.

The psyche's urge to communicate through dream uses as a vehicle its own deep identity with the material world in which we live; '*as above, so below*', as the alchemists used to say, meaning that the macrocosm without is one with the microcosm within.

When, waking and conscious, we gaze upon the stars or the ocean or a snake, these external objects of perception are not experienced as detached camera-like perceptions; the sensory perception is all of a piece with the most subtle reverberations throughout our soul. When the dream-maker shapes an image in our dream, these inner echoes are being played upon like the harpstrings of life-experience. Dreams play upon the web of our being, and that is how they communicate.

So it must be understood that the translation into ideas, concepts, words, is *not* a translation into the real thing, or the better thing, or the real meaning, or what the dream is really trying to say. Quite the reverse: the dream itself is the real thing in its completeness of experience, in its subtle shades of emotional and spiritual meaning and allusive echo.

The conceptualizations we draw from its living depths are always more limited and, paradoxically, more generalized. If I dream of an unknown older woman, for example, kindly in face and comfortable in figure, I may translate her into such words as a 'good-mother figure', and that abstraction is both an impoverishment of the actual dream experience as well as a generalization.

The advantage of the abstraction is that it can far more easily be manipulated, correlated with theories, categorized, and so on. The dream series from the previous chapter threw up some fifty differing images, ranging from a chair made out of cow, through a variety of dogs, to a number of human female figures, all of which were conceptualized in one way or another as 'the feminine' or 'the mother'. It is useful for rational consciousness to do so, but it is essential not to lose touch with the wealth of associations around the particular by seizing upon the utility of the general.

2   THE STRUCTURE OF DREAMS

The idea that dreams have a structure needs to be taken with a pinch of salt. Many remembered dreams feel to their owners like a fragment from a longer dream, and often these fragments are too short to reveal much structure. And there is an unmistakable tendency for the waking 'I' to organize the dream, arranging sequentially dream experiences which somehow, impossibly, seemed simultaneous within the dream; or deciding that such and such an event *must* have come before such and such ... because it makes more sense that way.

Nevertheless, I hear many dreams each day and among them there are always a few so clear and vivid that the dreamer is quite certain that it really did unfold just as he or she has narrated it. Within these dreams, at least, and by extension perhaps within all dreams, a generalized structure can be discerned. A woman of young middle-age, beginning to struggle with the enormous repressions of sexuality that had taken place in her early childhood, dreamed:

I'm with my mother, looking out of an upstairs window onto a garden [association to a particular one of her childhood homes]. I'm visiting, not living there. I would like to go into the garden but it's misty and cold. The house changes, becomes L-shaped, and we are higher up now [association to the home which they lived in after the previous one]. Snow on the ground and cold clouds billowing over lawn. Can't see because of the cloud, but sense that the garden to the left merges into vast plain. A strong wind blows from behind and to the left.

Then see animals appearing out of the cloud, running with the wind; wildebeest and other African animals. Between garden and house there are five gates, each only wide enough for one or two animals to pass through at a time, so most crowd at the gates trying to get through. Dusk falls and I see a fire begin near the furthest gate. Animals are being burned. I'm afraid. House made of wood. I see three young men close to the fire. They seem to have lit it but now they're beating it out. One seems angry; he takes the last burning brand and, resentful and envious because we are in the house while he's outside, he shouts and throws it into the kitchen, setting the house on fire.

We panic. My mother, now seeming not my mother but an older child, runs downstairs into the burning kitchen. Q [dreamer's 7-year-old son] is now with me; grab his hand, snatch two coats — any size will do — and run into main wing and down central staircase [association to many-flighted stairs at boarding school]. At the bottom I see a man standing in a doorway, not family but I seem to recognize him. Q and I are barefoot and it's cold outside; thrust Q into man's arms, shouting that he must take care of him. I mean to go back up and get shoes, but no lights and fire spreading. Too dangerous. I give up.

All the family seems to escape. I hear mother screaming she's forgotten to move the car. House seems to be in very remote place and we are stranded without help.

I have divided the dream narrative into paragraphs, each paragraph being an example of the structural components common to many dreams.

In the beginning of a dream the dreaming 'I' becomes aware of a certain *initial state*. It perceives its surroundings, often discovers it has some accompanying persons,* and more or less immediately begins to take in the situation in which it finds itself. This situation is virtually never completely static; it has some dramatic tension inherently within it.

In this instance the dreamer is with her mother (who was also instinctually repressed), they are above ground level, inside a house which takes her back to a particular age in her childhood. She knows she wants to go down and outside, into the 'nature' part of the home, the garden. But it's cold and misty, i.e. a chilly atmosphere, which is experienced as impersonal, prevents her from going. Then the house is from a year or two later in childhood, but things seem to have got worse. Now the 'nature garden' is covered in snow and cold clouds; the freezing of feelings has increased. But she senses a vast collective wild nature into which the domestic garden-nature stretches, and a wind blows, a movement of spirit from the unconscious (from behind, and from the left), and wind brings change.

Having set the initial scene the dream proceeds (now in the second paragraph) with some actions or events which change the status quo and lead to developments in dramatic action.

In this instance the wind seems to bring *wild African beasts*. One imagines there must be heat and sun and wilderness somewhere in that direction. All this animal energy tries to get into the house with her, but can only trickle in because the five gates (five senses?) are so narrow. Already the feeling of threat is gathering. A fire begins, as if the frustrated animal energy is becoming inflamed. Now the danger is acute; the animal instincts are suffering and the whole personality could be brought down. Now the animals seem to personify into three men, as if her repressed sexuality is being shown to have a special connection with the masculine she has shut out. They want to get in, and reducing now from three to one, he and his fire (because they are, in a sense, one and the same thing) *do* break into the kitchen, that particular chamber of the 'personality house' suggesting that the instinctual repression is more than sexual; feeding and the oral instinct of hunger are involved too.

In the third part the dreaming 'I' tries to do something about the

---

*'Presences' might be a better word: they may be human, animal, vegetable or mineral. Any of these, including mineral, may be 'animated'.

situation, often not being very clear about what it is doing; sometimes being effective, sometimes not. In general the second and third parts of a dream together constitute the great majority of the whole.

In this particular example there is panic to begin with. The natural realm of instinct, frozen out at home, had begun by being sensed as a vast invisible plain; then it had taken animated shape as wild African animals trying to stampede their way into her; then it had developed itself further into three men with fire; then into a single man who has got in and set her house on fire. She has become inflamed by a man (and this corresponded with her waking life). The next thing is that she and her mother go separate ways (a separation long overdue). Her chief concern now is for her youngest son. This may reflect her anxiety for him because her falling in love has made her worried about her marriage; or, being much the age she herself was in these homes of her childhood, he may represent the 'masculine child-her'. This house, this old personality structure she shared with her mother, has to be abandoned. She grabs essential protection and flees. One can only wonder if the man she now finds in the house is the one who was outside. Probably he is, but now it seems she can entrust her child to him.

In the fourth and final part of a dream there is some sort of resolution or statement of the concluding situation.

In the dream of this woman, it is that nothing catastrophic has happened, but she feels very unprotected and helpless. When she considered the dream she could recognize these feelings within her.

3   A MODEL OF THE PSYCHE

Each of us has to build our bridges, has to find the way from the dream to rational conceptual consciousness. Sooner or later it will be found that this task involves more than seeing dreams in a certain way; some kind of model of the psyche is needed. It would be idealistic to expect everyone to develop their own theory of the psyche. Only a very few individuals have done so, and it is the work of a lifetime. Most people employ one or other of these ready-made models more or less en bloc according to how completely they seem to satisfy the situation, usually modifying them in the light both of their own experience and of the persuasive attractions of other models.

This approach to dreamwork is based upon Carl Jung's model of the psyche.* The psyche is not simple, certainly not from the only perspective

---

*But the outline of psyche which follows is not purely Jung's. I am describing my own approach, which owes an enormous debt to Jung, but has been modified by the work of many other psychologists, both earlier and later, in addition to insights gained through various artistic and scientific authors and, last but not least, my own experience.

114

available to us − the human perspective − so any theory which strives to formulate understanding of it cannot be simple either.* Naturally, then, the following description is no more than a thumbnail sketch with particular reference to dreamwork; it is included only to provide some idea of the conceptual tools with which one can build the bridges between dream and waking consciousness.

CONSCIOUS AND UNCONSCIOUS

To begin with, psyche is conceived to be divided into conscious and unconscious. The division is not sharp and 'all or nothing'; I often imagine the transition in images of sunlight and sea. With one's head above the water's surface there is the brilliant clarity of full consciousness; with one's head immediately below the surface the brilliance is dimmed, things look bigger and vision is accompanied by awareness of vague and formless limits. The deeper one goes the darker it gets until eventually there is utter darkness, save for those weird creatures who make their own tiny lamps by the light of which they cruise the slow cold currents of the abyss.†

EGO

Neither the light above the surface nor the darkness below would count for anything were there no eye to see. In terms of the psyche this brings us to the 'I'. This 'I' simply *is* consciousness, at least in an everyday sense. In theories it is usually called the 'ego' (which, of course, is no more than the Latin word for 'I').

It is vital to understand the central importance of the human ego. If we are awake, and in sound mental health, then the ego is strong and alert and we are fully conscious; in light sleep, and in REM sleep, the ego is weaker, has diminished powers, but it is still functioning so we still have some consciousness, which is experienced as dream-consciousness and sometimes remembered. If we have a big bang on the head, or are deeply anaesthetized, or in certain deep and dreamless stages of sleep, then the ego has, to all intents and purposes, ceased to function and we are wholly unconscious.

In some mental illnesses, the ego is seriously damaged; in depression, for instance, large quantities of energy are withdrawn from ego, which can be

The Collected Works of C.G. Jung extend to twenty large volumes; Freud's are longer still.
†Using the image of ocean to convey something of the unconscious comes very naturally because dreams so often employ that very same image (see 'Water' in Ch.15, p.214).

left almost devoid of thoughts, feelings, will and courage; and in schizophrenia, archetypal components of the psyche (of which more later) which normally play a contributory but secondary role within ego occasionally seem to possess the ego altogether. There are times when it might appear that a mentally ill person is conscious of what they are doing, but because of ego-damage it is quite possible that some behaviours are going on completely unconsciously.

EGO NUCLEUS

One can conceive the ego as having a centre or nucleus which consists of that most central experience of consciousness – that consciousness of being which can say 'I am'. In some ways it seems this ego nucleus has an organizing capacity which it can exercise over other contents of the psyche. For instance the ego has a certain availability to the memory banks so that 'I' can sort through memories, choosing some, discarding others. Similarly 'I' have a variable amount of disposable energy which can be used as 'will'; if I try to be strong-willed I might be able to deny the hunger instinct for a few days. If this relatively small quantity of will is fuelled by ideals (and the ego is very susceptible to ideals, which have archetypal sources) then it may become strong with a strength borrowed from the 'self'; hunger-strike protestors, fired by their ideal, can sacrifice ego and starve themselves to death.

EGO FUNCTIONS

There are four basic pathways by which 'I' can know something: thinking, feeling, intuition, sensation. To some extent 'I' can choose to use one or another, although people tend to be types in the sense of favouring one or other of these four functions.

These primary functions of conscious ego often appear in dreams as companions to the dream-ego. If, let us say, you are predominantly a thinking type and your feelings are not so differentiated, then your dream might begin with your most distinct companion being someone you know who is very intellectual, while another companion, far less distinct, might be a friend who is a feeling type; together, the group of you go through the dream drama.

To anyone who has made a serious effort to understand him or herself and other people, it will come as no surprise to hear that the psychology of the ego is immensely complicated; indeed, so huge and all-embracing can it seem that some psychologists do not accept that there is *anything but* ego and consciousness.

The ego-complex (by which I mean the ego-nucleus together with all the contents of consciousness which must be related to the nucleus) is at its largest and has most energy when it is 'above the water's surface' (referring to the ocean image above). But it is not a phenomenon of the psyche which is either 'there or not there'; for quite some distance below the surface it continues to function but with ever-diminishing attributes and potencies. As befits its enormous importance in the overall economy of the psyche, the ego appears in almost every dream; it is the 'I' of the dream.

Before turning to the dark depths of the unconscious, it is worth saying something about one particular and specialized function of the ego. All functions of the ego are important (just like all functions of the liver are important; they would not be there if they were not), but this particular one is relevant because it plays a prominent part in so many dreams of ordinary people. Jung called it the 'persona', borrowing the term from the name given to the masks worn by actors in classical drama.

PERSONA

The persona is the public mask; it is that part of the ego concerned with outward and especially social adaptation. It plays a large part in the clothes we choose; it often influences our mannerisms, style of relating, even accents. Some people allow their persona to dictate choices of car, house, holiday, even marriage.

To have a persona is entirely natural and healthy; all people in all cultures do; in fact to have an inadequate persona is often represented in dreams as being inadequately dressed. We all know what it's like to feel depressed or unhappy about something going on in our private lives and, often quite rightly, to keep it hidden behind the mask while at work or out and about. Society could not function, at least in the way it does, if everyone wore their heart on their sleeve all the time.

But the persona can get out of hand, actually suffocating other vital needs of the ego; when this happens the situation will generally be reflected in dreams. Jung observed that dreams tend to complement or compensate the conscious attitudes, confronting the dreamer with the alternative or opposite attitudes which exist in his or her unconscious. In the specific conscious situation of over-identification with the persona, for instance, the dreams will tend to reduce the attachment to the persona in some way, mocking it as stuffy and foolish perhaps, or depicting it as constricting or strangling.

Every occupation has a more or less characteristic persona: the judge, the soldier, the surgeon, and the society hostess each have their characteristic working clothes and working manner. So long as they *are at work* this is fine; but they are not just professionals, they are also human individuals and should be able to lay aside the persona in private situations. As everyone knows, some people cannot; they have identified with their persona or, in other words, have ceased to distinguish between their 'I' as a whole and that function of it which is persona.

UNCONSCIOUS PSYCHE

Most people are humble enough to admit there is more to man's psyche than his consciousness. In fact consciousness is by far the smaller part of our psyche, just as the wave that spumes and sparkles in the sunlight is very much the smaller part of the ocean.

If we are not conscious of something then, by definition, we know nothing of it. This being so, how can we say anything about the unconscious? Indeed we may only know the unconscious by inference. The situation, however, is not as bad as all that as one person may at least observe what another person does unconsciously.

Everyone's life is full of little unconscious actions; mostly they are quite unimportant, but they do at least show plainly enough that there exists some shaper or guider of actions beyond ego-consciousness. Recently, for instance, I stayed for some time in the home of some friends; after a day or two I happened to notice (i.e. I became conscious of the fact) that my hostess never walked the straightest way across the living room to the kitchen door; she seemed to deviate as if to avoid an area in front of the fire.

I asked her why she did this but she was completely unaware she had been doing anything of the sort. The following day she said she had been *watching herself,* and had to admit I was right; but she still had no idea why and what's more, found it quite an effort to change her ways. This shows what we all know perfectly well, although we tend to know it rather in the way of an instinctive knowledge: that ego may be the centre and organizer of consciousness, but there is also some centre and organizer of the *whole being,* conscious and unconscious. As my hostess said she '*watched her self*' to see what *it* did.

SELF

Indispensable as the ego may be for anything that can reasonably be called normal humanity, it is limited, transitory, and weak, compared to the self. Jung's life-work was devoted especially to the psychology of the self, which he showed to have a very special relationship with the ego:

The term 'self' seemed to me a suitable one for the unconscious substrate, whose actual exponent in consciousness is the ego. The ego stands to the self as the moved to the mover, or as object to subject, because the determining factors which radiate out from the self surround the ego on all sides and are therefore superordinate to it. The self, like the unconscious, is an a priori existent out of which the ego evolves. It is an unconscious prefiguration of the ego. It is not I who create myself, rather I happen to myself.

As Hermann Hesse said, 'No man has ever been utterly himself, yet every man strives to be so'. In the psychological terms we have been using, we may say that our ego has evolved out of our self; always in and through our ego we both seek and are impelled to become the most complete exponent of our self that we may be. As we know by immediate experience, our ego is self-conscious (that is, conscious of self) but always feels limitations in its self-understanding. Not constantly, perhaps, but certainly again and again, life seems to demand that 'I try to understand my self'.

But so all-embracing is the self, so containing of all opposites (saint and sinner, coward and courage, masculine and feminine, etc.), that ego cannot ever be wholly self-conscious; it would burst with the inner tensions. Always there is more, always something beyond the ego's understanding. It is a way with no final end unless perhaps it may be in death; it is a way in which the journey matters, not the goal.

The self may be imagined to unfold during the course of life like, let us say, a sunflower. There is active debate among psychologists concerning the ego-consciousness of the very young baby, but it is fair to say that what ego-consciousness there is is very much less then than later in life, and first appears only for very limited periods of time. Mostly, therefore, the whole being of the baby is being 'run', as it were, by the self, just as we see with the animal kingdom.

The self can run things very well; like the Tao, one might say it *is* the way. But it is not conscious; it does not know itself. The human psyche, presumably related in some fashion with the evolutionary development of the brain, has developed the capacity for self-reflection. The expression of this development, as we see it in each individual, is, precisely, the evolution of the ego out of the self. One may imagine the sunflower-self unfurling one petal after another throughout life, from beginning to end. As each unfolds, an inner predisposition, similar or identical to the 'innate release mechanisms' described in biology, will begin to operate.

The inner predisposition is at first hard to describe; it is like an almost inchoate image; it is like a hunger for something which will be recognized when it is found; it is like a searching for something which is going to be findable somewhere.

In very early unfoldings of the self such a development could be the inner predisposition to 'find' something which we would call the nipple; a later unfolding would involve discovery of 'more' of the mother and a better grasp of her wholeness and separate being; later still there will be an unfolding discovery of the father.

If these unfoldings* are matched more or less well by the appropriate realities in the environment around the developing individual, then recognition takes place in multiple little explosions of consciousness and the self's unfolding petal then becomes a part of the forming ego. No longer is something *just happening*, now there is *ego knowing it is happening*.

By way of this unfolding self the ego, in normal development, gradually knows and becomes firmly anchored in its own body experience, in the mother, then the parents, the family, the wider world and so on. We may understand now that no matter how brilliant an ego may be in any particular decade of life, it cannot possibly know all the self because there are always petals yet to unfurl.

It should not be thought that the self's unfolding and evolving of ego is concerned only with relating to other objects, people and the world around us. Every aspect of all human consciousness comes from this source. Intangible human concerns such as religion, philosophy, ethics, art and science, have their roots in self. The idealism typical of late adolescence is an unfolding of self; the deeper interest in and responsiveness to religion characteristic of the second half of life, is again an unfolding of self. Wherever we see *typical* stages and developments, they are typical, or archetypal, because things are so arranged that just those petals of the self unfurl at just those times of life.

How does the self appear in dreams? Compared to the self the ego is weak; at least for some time every day it needs to slip back into the measureless eternity of the self, relaxing its tiring and energy-sapping consciousness in the dark womb of creation.

One might say that *all of the dream* is self; that the weakened remnant of the ego that is known as the dream 'I' is truly immersed in the self. All the characters in the dream, all the images of cars and rooms and rivers and mountains, etc., all the dramas ... all is self. Within the state of dream, 'I' perceives self, experiences 'I' happening within its context of self.

*Which Michael Fordham, in an important development of Jung's psychology, has called 'deintegrations'.

ARCHETYPES

This statement sets the overall scene, but is so broad that it provides little specific help. This can come, however, from beginning an acquaintance with the *'archetypes'*.

The archetypes may be regarded as noumenal existences within the self in its entirety. They may be imagined as riverbeds scored into the geography of the self through countless aeons of human life-experience. They may be understood to be potentialities for conscious experience. As actual images of the real world flood into the self through the living sensory apparatus, they bring life-giving water to the riverbeds and what was archetypal potentiality becomes archetypal image.

Take the 'witch', for example. No matter what country, no matter when, children have dreams of witches, know about witches. All their images of the witch are not identical; they vary greatly of course, but they are typical enough to be known as the witch (in whatever language). The witch is an archetypal image, one which is particularly associated with childhood, of course, because the witch image itself is no more than one of a spectrum of archetypal images arising in connection with the mother.

Differing archetypal images tend to hold sway at different stages of life, not only because one archetype may, at a given time, become more constellated than another, but also because the archetypal images themselves, in any given individual, undergo change with advances in knowledge and growth of the ego. Nevertheless, there are a number of well-recognized and invariably present archetypal images in the adult and the task of understanding oneself through dreamwork is much helped by having some understanding of them.

(a) Shadow

When someone first begins to engage with their dreams, one of the first dream figures they will encounter is the 'shadow'.

The way to imagine the shadow is to see that while the self contains all human potentialities, the ego does not. Often the ego does not yet recognize much that is in the self, let alone acknowledge it or exhibit it. There exists, therefore, a discrepancy between what the self is and what the ego thinks it is.

Many influences, both from within and without, act to make the ego wish and strive to be good: 'I' like to believe I am honest, faithful, caring, strong, gentle, conscientious, not-jealous, not-envious, non-violent, etc. The reality, however, may not be quite like that and usually is not.

So long as there exists a significant discrepancy then the shadow will

121

appear in dreams. When a person too much believing himself honest, faithful (etc.), goes to sleep, he will find himself tangling with a figure who embodies and manifests the very opposite. In the dream series of the two previous chapters we saw Dr M's dream-ego confronted by his shadow again and again. His shadow was characterized as weak, effeminate, dishonest, insolent, immature. Understanding the nature of the shadow we may tell from this that Dr M's ego wished to be, and believed itself to be, stronger, more masculine, more honest, more correctly polite, more mature, than was actually the reality.

Confronting one's shadow is not pleasant at best; at worst it can be harrowing. Usually the personification of the shadow is the same sex as the dreamer. Its appearance and behaviour is made up from images of other people, known or unknown, who tend to be disliked or even hated because the individual can see in them the very things he does not wish to see in himself.

You might ask why one has to face the shadow. The real answer is that nature, or God, seems to demand it of us and it is unwise to ignore the demands of this all-powerful mystery. One can also find virtue in necessity by understanding that success, contentment, and other commonly desired goals are more likely to come in a lasting way to those who know what they are rather more than believing themselves to be what they would like to be.

It should not be thought that 'integrating the shadow' means handing over the reins to the shadow; far from it; so long as the shadow is not recognized and acknowledged its actions remain unchecked and frequently lead to no end of trouble. Once one does know one's shadow one then has to take responsibility for it, and govern it as best one can.

(b) Collective shadow

So far we have been dealing with the 'personal shadow'; that is to say, aspects of the personality which could become conscious and owned but tend, not to be because they come into conflict with the ideals that influence the ego.

As with all the archetypes, however, there exists a collective level as well as a personal, although the two weave in and out of each other, rather than being discrete and separate. To give some idea of what I mean by the 'collective shadow', it would, for Christians, be known as Satan, the principle of evil.

In Dr M's dream series both the personal and collective shadow appear in a number of dreams. By and large the collective shadow will, for any culture, be represented by images and ideas associated with the dark side of the godhead, or the enemy of god. Images such as witches, wizards, demons, magicians, etc., belong more or less midway along the spectrum from personal to collective; how much they are one or the other can best be felt by the dreamer, and will be known by the intensity of weirdness or magic quality.

(c) Anima and animus

Another archetype almost constantly present is the '*anima/animus*'. These are the names chosen by Jung to connote the image of one's own opposite sex within one; '*anima*' (which means soul) appears as images of woman within men, while '*animus*' appears as images of man within women.

The figure of Beatrice in Dr M's dreams represented the 'holy' or higher aspect of his anima. But, inasmuch as the majority of his dreams were concerned with his relationship with the feminine, one could say that many of the female figures represent various aspects of his anima.

When a man and woman 'fall in love', the man has found an actual woman who fits or corresponds sufficiently closely with his own unconscious feminine, his anima, so that he experiences that person as if she were a part of himself and passionately wishes to unite what feels (almost consciously at times) like the divided halves of a whole; the converse being true for the woman.

Let us say this couple marry. After some time that state known as 'in love' will wear off, although it may well be that they discover they can grow to love each other as two separate individuals. The point in mentioning this is that the relationship between two individuals is not all that is involved here. That is a vital biological part of it, but there is also the urge of each of their psyches to become more consciously whole in itself. In other words the man has innately within him the urge to integrate into his masculinity the feminine in his nature, while his wife equally has the urge to integrate her masculine into her femininity.

We saw how Dr M struggled to maintain his realistic love for his wife, and recognition of her separateness-in-herself, while nightly being tossed in his dreams between divided and opposing poles of his anima: sexual-anima (often the image of his wife) and soulful-anima (usually the image of Beatrice).

Such situations are not unusual. In fact they are bound to exist and they lead to no end of problems in life. They are better and more easily negotiated when one has some idea what is going on and can follow the images within one's dreams.

Like the shadow archetype, the anima/animus archetype manifests both at the personal and collective levels. (Once again, this is true for all the archetypes.) Whereas the shadow, by its very nature, always appears in a negative light, the other archetypes not only have a spectrum from personal to collective; they also have a spectrum from 'good' to 'bad'. A simple example of good and bad images of the collective anima might be, respectively, the Virgin Mary and the Whore of Babylon; similarly, examples of collective animus might be Apollo and Bluebeard.

OTHER ARCHETYPES

Other archetypes manifesting in personified images and frequently playing a part in one's dreams are the Mother and Father, the Hero, the Child, the Wise Old Man or Woman, and the Self itself. The reading list at the end of the chapter provides sources for following up all these, and more.

An excellent way of getting a feel for these personified images of the archetypes is to read myths, legends and fairy-tales: they all have much in common with the self-world of dreams and provide illustrations of these figures time and again.

FURTHER READING

Hall, James A., *Jungian Dream Interpretation*, Toronto: Inner City Books.

Jung, C.G., *Dreams*, London: Routledge & Kegan Paul.

Jung, C.G., 'On the Nature of the Psyche', in *The Collected Works*, vol. 8, London: Routledge & Kegan Paul.

Ryecroft, Charles, *The Innocence of Dreams*, London: Allen Lane.

Samuels, A., Shorter, B. and Plaut, F., A *Critical Dictionary of Jungian Analysis*, London: Routledge & Kegan Paul.

Nine

THE DREAM 'I'

FROM THE POINT of view of inner experience a dream, just like waking experience, has the simple structure of subject and object: 'I' and 'it', where 'it' is everything 'not I'.* That is to say, the dream 'I' finds itself in a particular setting, a room, or boat, or hospital or whatever, and encounters other living creatures in the dream, be they human or other. More or less dramatic action then involves the dream 'I' and the dream 'it'. There are four aspects to consider:

1. The dream 'I' (or dream-ego), which is a thing in itself.
2. The setting(s) in which the dream-ego is placed.
3. The connections between the dream-ego and the other figures in the dream.
4. The aims and achievements (or lack of them) of the dream-ego within the dramatic action, and the effects of the experiences upon the dream-ego.

1   THE DREAM-EGO

The way our 'I' is and feels and behaves in dreams has much in common with our waking 'I', but it is rarely identical and occasionally it is entirely strange.

Unless the differences are startling, such as finding oneself to be a mouse or a robot or paralyzed or magical, we do have a tendency to take the dream-ego for granted, scarcely remarking on considerable discrepancies between it and the waking ego.

One possible reason for this hypocritical attitude may be that the dream-ego often appears and behaves in ways which are privately not so strange to the waking ego, although they may seem strange from the perspective of another person from whom certain things have been concealed. A woman

---

*The psychoanalytic 'Id' (from the Latin '*id*' meaning 'that'), connotes the instinctive impulses of the individual, and expresses the same 'I' experience of the 'not-I' that is nevertheless oneself.

who prides herself on not being seductive or flirtatious, for instance, may not be startled to find she is making a sexual exhibition of herself in a dream because she knows that urge to exist within her; others, however, may know nothing of this tendency of hers, and might be surprised by the dream-ego's behaviour. It is always worth bearing in mind that many ego possibilities lie hidden not too far behind the persona.

Because our 'I' is what we consciously know of ourselves, and because 'I' is our most immediate experience and the part of ourself we actually live with, the way 'I' appears in our dreams, no matter how strange or bizarre, is both of immediate importance to us, and also likely to be the element of the dream most accessible to our understanding.

As always, the infinite variety of dreams defies any rigid schematic approach but the headings which follow, which overlap each other, can help as starting-points for reflections upon the dream-ego.

Differences in age

Usually the dream-ego is familiar but unspecified; one's natural assumption is that one is the age, sex, and in general terms the person one knows oneself to be. Sometimes, though, despite feeling this, the dream surroundings suggest otherwise:

> A married lawyer in his mid-thirties dreamed he was in Iceland. He came to a cottage, went inside, and there found a very big woman who suggested he look upstairs; the stairs began normally but as he climbed they became so tiny he had to squeeze himself up; at the top, he found a little bedroom which could only be a child's room because room, bed, and furniture were all very small. At the same time as thinking everything was tiny like a doll's house, he realized how very comfortable and happy he felt, as if it fitted him.

For this man, Iceland (he had never been there nor had anything to do with that country) was the 'land of ice', i.e. frozen water; it stood for the 'land of his childhood' because much of his childhood had been so painful that its feeling-memories had frozen over, and were no longer available to him as the living-water that flows through all parts of the soul. Although in the dream he felt himself to be his adult age and size, it is clear that he is being helped towards connecting with himself 'as child'. Over subsequent months he went on to unfreeze his own beginnings.

In this instance, littleness in surroundings have directed an initially adult dream-ego to feel little and childlike. Somewhat more commonly the dream-ego finds itself unwillingly little beside other figures or objects in the dream which appear extraordinarily large:

1.12.76 I'm sitting at a refectory table laden with rich food among many senior Company executives; I do not really feel part of them; increasingly, the table and my colleagues seem to get bigger and I feel small compared to them.

This dream reveals a part of his ego which feels little, childlike and daunted.

So far, these have been indirect expressions of different age or size; but it is not at all unusual for dreams to be direct:

● A woman, recovering from a breakdown, dreamed that she was a baby lying in a cot and sucking on a bottle.
● Another woman, a therapist, dreamed she was walking to school carrying her satchel; it was the morning of her eighth birthday.
● A girl of five dreamed she was an old woman, wrinkled, carrying a stick, walking through a forest.
● A boy of seven dreamed he was a strong hero like James Bond, rescuing his sister from a sea-monster.

Anyone can be any age in their dreams. Often these dreams feel very realistic, which may not be hard to understand in the case of someone dreaming of themselves as they were at a younger age, but it is a little more surprising, perhaps, when a child dreams, and really feels itself to be, an adult.

Naturally enough, all stages and ages of life are programmed into our being; but it seems as if prefigurations of them already exist in the psyche, lying present as parts of the ego-complex which can occasionally be experienced in the dream state.

Differences in appearance

Alterations in appearance are very common. Peculiar clothes, or the uncomfortable discovery that various articles of dress are missing, are the commonest changes, and usually have something to say about the state of the persona.

Every conceivable change in appearance can come up in a dream, some fairly obvious in their meaning — e.g. a man in a state of high excitement over a business deal dreamed that he had no feet and knew immediately he was not 'grounded' — while some are quite bewildering at first sight. The following example illustrates a generally useful approach to baffling dream components:

> 27.2.77   I am making my way to L.House through difficulty and danger because there is war; soldiers and police are everywhere. Then I'm with Daddy in L.House; I discover I have a warty green growth like a malignant melanoma on my left arm, then see that Daddy has same beside his left eye. Daddy prepares a peculiar cone-shaped instrument with which he is to treat me.

Already knowing other dreams of this man helps considerably. We know about the dreamer's conflict with the 'father', which finds expression here in the war surrounding the father's house. But his dream-ego is portrayed with a cancerous growth on the left arm, and a peculiar bond is made between him and his father inasmuch as the father has the same growth beside his left eye.

The meaning of all this is certainly not immediately obvious. In such a situation the dreamer should ask him/herself 'what things are' in fully conscious language, and then return the answer back into the dream context and see where that leads.

In this dream we have, first of all, a cancer. What is a cancer? It means a number of body cells, of some particular type, which have broken away from the relatively harmonious integration within the self as a whole and become autonomous; their autonomous behaviour is destructive to the self as a whole. This cancer is specified: it is a malignant melanoma. What is that? It is a cancer of the pigment cells in the skin; such growths are usually black but may be greenish or brownish (it must be understood that the dreamer, being a doctor, was familiar with these facts; dreams naturally use the sensate imagery with which the dreamer is familiar).

So ... using this information to try to make some sense of the symbol of the melanoma (neither he nor his father actually had any cancer; the dream employs the image of the cancer to communicate some invisible reality of psyche itself), certain things come to mind. Firstly, the 'war' theme is picked up in the war between cancer and self; secondly, the 'terrifying father' has appeared in other dreams as a black man (a possible link with the skin pigment cells), and thirdly, the autonomous character of the cancer introduces the idea that both father and son are trying to deal with a destructive part of psyche that has not been integrated.

In other words, this dream image suggests that the war may not be the simple opposition between father and son. Rather, both father and son have something in common in that they *both* suffer from the existence of some destructive and warring energy which has to do with the terrible aspect of

128

the father imago; this is not experienced as an integral part of themselves but as 'outside' like a war, or alien like a cancer, and which needs to be treated. The fact of the green colour remains; possibly it may indicate that the nature of the autonomous and destructive psychic energy is jealous or envious.

Translating the immediate imagery from the dream into the conceptual structure of conscious knowledge, then returning this into the context of the dream, often helps to unravel meaning. However, it is a practice which must be used with caution; the conclusions should be held tentatively until developments in subsequent dreams show whether or not one is on the right track.

Differences in sex

To find that one is the opposite sex in a dream is certainly less common than alterations in age or appearance, but it is not uncommon, particularly when gender identification is rather weak. Since gender identity tends to strengthen with age, dreams in which one appears as the opposite sex are commoner in childhood and youth:

A young student of 20 or so dreamed: I am walking along the King's Road. I see a policeman and feel a strong desire to hug him and kiss him; I feel a strange sensation around my belly; looking down I discover, with surprise at first, that I have breasts and am wearing a skirt. After a moment of utter confusion I remember that I am in fact a woman but have been lost in a long dream (which seems to have lasted for years) that I was a man. Then I am in bed with a man, perhaps the policeman, who hits me angrily; at first I don't know why, but then I find that I seem to have become a man again. I feel confused and ashamed.

This young man had grown up without a father; his mother was domineering and hostile to men. He was, as is clear enough from the dream, in a state of confusion about his gender and sexuality. The 'King's Road' and the 'policeman' hinted that he was searching for the strong father, and his subsequent development proved this to be true.

Not all sex-differences in the dream-ego arise out of gender confusion however. Often in middle-age, or later, men and women who are husbands and wives, fathers and mothers, become increasingly aware of their inner contrasexual personality. That is to say, a man, having established his masculinity and confirmed it through life-experience, begins to find awareness growing of the femininity within him, and this often takes on a personified form, especially, of course, in dreams. The opposite is equally true for a woman:

> A woman in her late forties dreamed she was in the bathroom washing her face in the basin. When she stood up the face looking out of the mirror was a man's face; his face was unknown as a specific person and yet she knew it as if she had known it all her life. She was particularly fascinated by the firm lines of the jaw and the boldness of the eyes.

Differences in life-form

Occasionally the dreaming ego finds itself to be some other form of life altogether – a mouse, tiger, horse, etc. They tend to be dreams remembered with pleasure and felt to be important:

> A woman art dealer of about thirty, extremely dependent and insecure, dreamed: I am a bird in a nest, a chick. I fall out and think this is the end. But I find I can fly; intense relief.

> A woman in her mid-forties, having been in analysis for three years, dreamed: I am in the river of life; I have no specific shape or form, perhaps a blob of jelly. All around me there is a mass of creatures like enlarged protozoa, both in the water and the banks, some being amphibious. I remember one especially, a crab with one central human-like eye; also something with tentacles. I feel content; I know [my analyst] is close by.

Differences in active presence

The dream 'I' can be entirely absent from the dream, save for a 'seeing eye' which observes but seems otherwise uninvolved and inactive. A young student, at a time of fairly severe confusion and distress, dreamed:

> A monk dressed all in white stands on a cliff holding an iron cross and crying out, 'Where are you God? Where are you?'
> Each time he does so, Satan, who is standing behind him dressed in black, leans forward and says, 'Here I am.' After the third time Satan whacks the monk on the head; the iron cross becomes a cross of light, the monk dies and is buried with the cross, and Satan makes his throne above the place where the monk is buried.
> The dreamer awoke with the thought that his task was to discover where the monk was buried and uncover him.

It is not hard to guess that the monk (and Satan too) is, as it were, a personality not too far away from the dream-ego, but the fact remains that the monk was not experienced as 'I'; he was seen as object not as subject. Dreams in which the dream 'I' is absent apart from a recording eye tend to occur when the ego is paralysed by a powerful pull of opposites, in the above instance the opposites of good and evil.

A broadcaster and entrepreneur of thirty or so, whose mother had been ill when he was a baby, was liable to experience his hunger and his need for security in an extraordinarily impetuous way; it was like a ferocious ravenous energy that scarcely seemed to belong to him but, rather, took him over so he might be unable to stop himself ripping open tins and gulping the food down like a beast. Naturally enough, this ferocious energy was bound to create problems in his intimate relationships. At a time when he was profoundly distressed by his girlfriend's infidelity and doing everything in his power to recover the feeling that she belonged 100% to him, he dreamed:

Six or seven big hungry hunting dogs are sitting below a tree and gazing hungrily up into it; their gaze is so intense that they make lines of light which all intersect upon a lump of raw meat which is hung on the tree.

His dream ego does not appear; there is nothing but his instinctual hunger and the object of that hunger. Casting it within the lifespan of a human, it might make one think of the raw instinctuality, the unconsciousness, the ruthlessness, of a baby's extreme hunger. Dreams such as this one, by bringing him conscious understanding of his inner experience, helped him a great deal in his valiant efforts to maintain some ego control over his ravening need; this he had to do if he were not to risk destroying the much-needed relationship altogether.

At the opposite end of the spectrum, and rarely in normal mental health, the dream-ego may appear as the sole activator and mover of events — a veritable god. Far and away most often it lies between these two extremes.

Differences in potency, will, and resource

Between the extremes of complete absence and total god-like presence, confusion is probably one of the commonest experiences of the dreaming 'I'. It finds itself with less clarity than the waking ego, its memory tends to be hazy and uncertain, its orientation is regularly being confounded, and its aims and decisions tend to go awry. Very common too are experiences of impotence, of trying to punch someone but being unable to summon any power, trying to get control over events and situations which seem ungraspable as water, trying to walk as in soft sand, trying to pass exams for which one seems hopelessly unprepared.

Experience shows that when the dream-ego feels weak and confused etc., the very same feelings are afflicting the waking ego, although they may have been unnoticed or unacknowledged. In other words, such dream states come when we are rather depressed or anxious or confused, and especially if we have covered it over (with brittle jollity or compulsive activity, for instance).

Far less common, but still common enough for almost everyone to know, are dreams in which the 'I' has powers beyond the normal or possible, magical powers. Flying dreams seem to be the best known, and usually bring delight, but walking on water, exerting power over others through the power of one's eyes or personality, changing shape, or being irresistibly fascinating or desirable, are also common enough:

27.10.76
(a) W angrily takes the children and leaves me in the hotel because I have smoked opium; I feel happy; then I'm being driven in luxury to a nightclub; there I cause amusement among the hostesses by telling them I'm no longer interested in sex.
(b) At a formal dinner I bewilder the guests by making a number of toys move magically. I bask in their astonishment at my powers.
(c) I'm inside a dimly lit and remotely situated curiosity shop; I find two strange stones and pocket them; the owner returns, he offers me a thurible and a horse and cart golden charm. I accept them but feel guilty and crafty.

Wielding magic power in dreams brings a marvellous feeling of delight in the power of the will and no one likes to have it diminished by interpretation. But, far more often than not, interpretation is actually very important because the ego is in a rather perilous condition of illusion which is bound to spill over into waking life to some degree, and usually brings regrets in its train. The greater the delight, in fact, the greater the illusion. There are some dreams in which the dream-ego sees from a great height, as if flying, but the feeling in the dream is more of being *shown something,* rather than the delight of escaping the laws of gravity, and these are different because the exercise of magical power is not being 'claimed' by the dream-ego.

These three dreams (above) show an ego in a state of inflation and illusion, claiming what is not real. The dream says as much with the opium. The dreamer had never really smoked opium; he believed, as most people probably would, that it brings vivid fantasies, so powerful that imagination and sensory hallucination can create the illusion that the body can actually do, or is doing, all that the psyche imagines.

While it is not an illusion that mind can float free of matter, it *is* an illusion that the body can escape the laws of matter. This is, in effect, what the dream-ego claims in the first two dreams: he begins by claiming to be above that mighty power of matter — sexuality — and goes on to claim that his mental will can make physical objects move. His purpose seems to be the winning of admiration and wonder.

The third dream sees him feeling differently; no longer a saint or a magician, he is now a thief, confused, unhappy, and somewhat guilty.

The susceptibility to *ideals* seems to be peculiarly human; they tug at us like the calls of sirens. Ideals such as purity, nobility, and goodness can seem so very fine that we long to attain them but, again and again, the hungers of the body are our downfall. The vast majority of us eventually come to terms with the fact that glands, if not actually stronger than ideals, are certainly no weaker.

But we struggle, and in our struggle an intense wish can arise to get rid of, or overcome, the earthbound limitations of our material nature. This is the psychic situation reflected in dreams where the dream-ego delights in the magical powers of its will. They portray the desire (and attempt) for mind to dominate matter.

Differences in emotions and feelings

It is perfectly possible, even common, for people to have emotions and feelings and yet not know them. Quite often the waking ego can be 'woken up' to the presence of unconscious emotions and feelings by the dream-ego's experience of them. Any emotional state can be brought to consciousness in this way. This example is of envy:

A middle-aged advertising consultant, in analysis, had persistently and vehemently denied the existence of envy within her, although it was plain to her analyst that she was suffering pangs of envy to do with what she fantasized to be the analyst's rich life. After some time she dreamed: I am in a cheap café eating fast food with (my analyst) at a small plastic table; he is telling me about all the wonderful restaurants he eats in. Then I'm outside, alone, on a road with cobbles just below the top of a hill. I press my face up against the window of a beautiful warm cosy restaurant where couples are enjoying candlelight intimacy while they eat. I feel lonely, empty, shut-out and miserable.

Her own recognition of her envy began with this dream.

A divided dream-ego

Sometimes the dream-ego is split; that is to say, the dream 'I' sees another figure in the dream and knows it is also 'I'. This can range from quite comfortable and congruent feelings where the 'I' location moves between observer and actor:

> I am on the bridge of a ship; there is a big storm but the ship feels sturdy and safe; I watch the captain at the wheel; somehow I am both him turning the wheel, and also me watching him from behind.

to severely shocking confrontations with oneself which leave the dreamer in no doubt that there exists a serious division within themselves:

> I'm looking down on a hospital room, as if I'm seeing from the ceiling; I feel completely calm and detached, unaffected by any worldly concerns. Directly below me I see I am lying on the bed, grotesquely swollen and discoloured, riddled with cancer everywhere. Fluid begins to leak out through the skin all over, including the eyes. Several others stand around the bed; I can see they are horrified but I feel nothing.

This was dreamed by a woman in young middle-age, who did not have cancer. Among her images of herself (for we all have many) there is evidently this really ghastly one. She cannot yet let in the feelings which would belong to or accompany this part of her, they are too awful; so her 'seeing' observer ego begins awareness of it in a way that is cut off from the feelings, separate and detached like a little bubble up above.

2 THE DREAM-EGO IN RELATION TO ITS SETTING

I am in a desert ... I am in a house close to the sea ... I am entering a tunnel ... I am in my car, driving ... I am in space, holding onto a piece of metal ... I am in a baptismal font ...

The variety of initial settings is infinite. Much like the tendency to take the dream-ego for granted, there is also a tendency to ignore the setting and jump straight to the main action. 'I had a dream I was bitten by a cat', as someone told me, became 'I was at Jane's house, in the back yard; there were several cats chained up; Jane wanted me to take them to the garage; when I released them one of them ... it was like my own cat ... bit me; but I managed to get them all to the garage' when I pressed for details.

The settings around the dream-ego, changing throughout the dream, *can* tell one a great deal; but, being so much more *it* than *I*, it takes more effort to find one's way into their meaning. This may be easier if they are known and familiar, so that the associations are personal, but less easy if they are wholly unfamiliar, in which case the meaning will be carried at a collective level.

Although it might be possible to classify the infinite variety of settings — e.g. water settings, land settings, air settings, fire settings; buildings, which may be collective like hotels and offices, or more individual like apartments or houses; vehicles which may be powered or self-propelled, collective like buses, individual like bikes, etc. — it would be a very lengthy business and nor could it hope to deal with all the personally familiar scenes. The collective meanings of some settings come into the last chapter 'Common to all'.

What is most valuable to grasp is the principle that the dream setting itself has meaning in relation to the dream-ego. The many examples throughout the book can be used to see how one may *feel* oneself into an understanding of each individual situation.

3 THE DREAM-EGO IN RELATION TO OTHER DREAM-FIGURES

In the vast majority of dreams other living figures, usually human, play some part. Very often the dream opens with the dream-ego's awareness of certain companions. They may be quite distinct, recognizable as this or that friend or acquaintance, or reminiscent of two or more known people blended together; or they may be very indistinct, vague presences, undistinguished in age, sex, or number. One should note when they appear, whether they accompany the dream-ego throughout the dream, and if not, when they disappear. If one appears just when another disappears they often carry much the same meaning, which is being developed.

These dream figures are *with* the dream-ego; in other words, although they are not experienced as 'I', they are nevertheless close to 'I'. They are personifications of various components of the total personality which are close to the ego and exercise influence upon it; usually they are helpful to the dream-ego, but they may be obstructive or simply inactive. Evidently they are either not consciously recognized enough to be experienced as 'I'; or they appear in this separated existence so that the dream-ego can 'see' aspects of itself.

For instance, a woman with a highly developed (and therefore very conscious) feeling function, but whose thinking is relatively undifferentiated (and therefore not very conscious) may dream she is accompanied by some friend who can think well. That person's image in her dream is the personification of her own thinking function, present and contributing, but not quite felt to be herself. In general, when the dream provides the dream-ego with companions right from the beginning, it is showing that one is, in some way, like them.

A girl of sixteen, whose parents were embroiled in an ugly divorce, dreamed:

> I am with Megan and a little boy who seems to be my son; he's about three or four and close to tears but trying to be brave. We're running and hiding through the streets; terrorists or something have invaded London, they can make people unreal if they catch them, so you can't tell if they're enemy or not. We have to get to North London to save someone because he is important and if he's made unreal everything will be lost. But the bridge is blocked with barbed wire, and guarded. I begin to cry and feel it's hopeless but Megan leads us up-river and finds a boat hidden in some bushes. Then we're rowing over; I can't work the oar properly and the boy falls overboard and nearly gets drowned, but Megan catches him and we pull him back inside. We reach an island. She says we've done the worst of it.

At the time of the dream she was living with her mother in South London and had not yet seen her father since he left home and moved into a flat in North London. She had been feeling unhappy, confused, angry and, at times, frightened that her sanity was crumbling.

This fear of madness comes into the dream with the power of 'the terrorists' to make people 'unreal'. It would seem that her grip on reality was not a very strong one. Indeed, she described herself (and so did others) as a rather dreamy and introverted person, highly intuitive but ungrounded.

The most obvious understanding of the dream overall is that she needs to see and confirm the reality of her father so that he doesn't become an 'unreal' figure for her. The dream shows her with two companions in this task, the little boy who seems to be her son, and Megan, who is a fourteen-year-old friend from school. The little boy personifies her own masculine courage, still very immature but nevertheless present and her very own. Megan has a personality opposite in type to the dreamer; she is practical, decisive, earthy, full of common sense. Her helpful presence in the dream indicates that the dreamer has more of these qualities within her than she has realized. As is so often the way with dreams, the 'Megan' part of her became more conscious after this dream and she began to explore and develop her sensation function.

Other figures in dreams – that is to say, other than the initial companions – may be peripheral and fleeting or vivid and in some distinct relationship with the dream-ego. There will be enemies (supernatural, human, animal), desired ones, loathed ones, chasing ones, ones to follow, ones to teach, ones to be taught by, ones to mistrust, ones to trust, hated ones, loved ones, relatives, colleagues, strangers ... Once again the variety is as rich as life itself. One has to ask oneself exactly *what* relation or connection is going on between dream-ego and the 'other':

> A clever, epileptic, man of about thirty, in analysis, had buried emotions of anger and grief (among others) to do with his deprived childhood. He kept them buried by determinedly living in and with his intellect. His fear of consciously experiencing these emotions was mixed up with his fear of his convulsions over which, of course, he felt he had no control; they came from the 'it' without warning, hurled him about, hurt him, and humiliated him. After about two years in analysis, he dreamed: I am standing in a sandy place; all around me the sand is being heaved about from below; I realize there are reptiles buried beneath the surface. I know I have to touch them, but I loathe the very thought of it. Making a supreme effort I overcome my revulsion, put my hands in and touch one. Astonishingly, I find a wave of love and value courses through me and I embrace it fully.

He recognized that these buried reptiles were dream portraits of his emotions, portrayed in this way partly because the image was apt for the way he felt about them, and partly because they *were* very primitive; having been buried, or repressed, when he was very young, they had not undergone the normal evolution of development.

Here the 'other' figures are reptiles; we see that they portray parts of his self, parts which could, at least in some measure, be embraced by the ego and eventually be felt to belong to it. Before this dream they were, most definitely, felt to be 'not I'.

> 7.1.77 I am in the far north, standing on a cliff. Far below the cold green foaming sea rages through a gorge. I see a moody discontented man wandering below me, kicking stones; then he's got above me somehow and he dislodges a rock which might have killed me had I not caught it. He sets off down a dangerous track and I follow him.

What is the relation between the dream-ego and the 'other' here? First, one of seeing from above; then seeing from below; then being threatened by destruction; then a following down to the sea. There can be little doubt that this 'other' is the personification of a sullen, angry, dangerous mood. At first he feels 'above it', on top of it; but then it gets on top of him and

137

becomes a danger in its self-destructiveness. Does he follow it down towards the sea (also dangerous and angry) because he can't escape its power? Or because, dangerous though it is, it can take him somewhere of value? Certainly one can gain benefits from consciously following moods on down to their very source.

4 THE DREAM-EGO IN RELATION TO THE DRAMA

What one must try to do is to define and understand the dream-ego's relation to the dream drama.

> I arrive at a house where there is a party. Inside I find a big room full of my father's relatives, immigrants from East Europe; all are old, wearing frock coats. Seeing them all a gust of hatred arises and I scream out, 'Cunts. You're all cunts!' Then I begin to tremble; I'm afraid I will be left all alone. But they take it OK and tell me I don't have to lose everything.

The dream-ego's relation to the dream drama is firstly angry, active, initiating, then fearful and insecure, then reassured and relieved. The dreamer – a student of about thirty – had never had a chance to battle with his father, who had been quite old when the boy was born, then died before his son was ready. He was full of anger with a father who wasn't there, and he did not know where to put it, constantly afraid that any exhibition of his anger, which often seemed irrational and excessive, would be met with rejection. The dream encouraged him to have some faith in familial tolerance.

> 11.1.77
> (a) I'm in a bookshop browsing through mystical books; a little old man with a violent abrupt manner shows me a particular book and tells me it's a fraudulent cheat. 'Prove it,' I say. He walks me along a lane and I find cherry cake and chipolatas on the ground. 'Taste,' he says. They taste horrible. 'That's how you tell,' he says. Later he plucks a white flower ... 'This tastes good ...' I smell a wonderful honeyed fragrance.
> (b) I'm on dry land but swampy floods surround me; Hoi-Chu and Regina are wading and I can see their dark pubic hairs through the wet uniforms. Then I'm playing squash with Rachel; her pants split; I want to watch her changing but another woman comes in to play.
> (c) Night-time and I'm in an expensive call-girl's flat; many dancing girls and erotic films. While I sit on top of a cupboard eating walnut chocolate whirls, a powerful old politician sadly tells me of Macmillan's death.

When morning comes I realize the girls have given him sex. There's a parking-meter woman prying about; I don't care, I'm leaving.

The overall theme describes a mystical or spiritual inclination finding itself in conflict with an equally powerful and relentless desire for matter in the shape of woman.

There is ambiguity in the first scene: the dream-ego is pursuing its mystical bent when the eccentric old man denounces a fraudulent cheat, presumably referring to one of the mystical books, and then proceeds to demonstrate something by way of sexually symbolic food and a virginally pure flower. It would appear that the dreamer is being taught a way of purity and spirituality by the old man: how to satisfy desire through perfume alone, rather than the coarse chewing and swallowing of food. But is fragrant honey the honeyed fragrance of woman, the white flower the irresistible virgin?

Certainly the drama continues with sexual woman appearing before him. Perched upon his little island of dry land, allurements beckon him from the surrounding swamp. The scene changes: he is playing squash with his sister (squash being a theme woven in from the film *Emmanuel*, where women made love in the court) and her pants split. The sexual desire now centres on brother – sister incest, the union of like with like. This was once the prerogative of gods and goddesses and their royal representatives in the ancient dynasties. Why does this theme appear? The answer is that he is trying to bring sex and spirit together. In the archetypal images of the collective unconscious, brother – sister marriage is a spiritual and mystical union as much as a sensual and sexual union.

This is no longer ambiguous; but it is unacceptable as an external reality. The dreamer would like to go further, but cannot without being seen. This is a desire he must keep secret.

The scene changes, developing the theme of desires that have to be pursued in secret: expensive call-girls, respectable public figures of weight and worth who visit under the cloak of darkness. There is disillusionment in this last part of the dream; a recognition that the universal longing for some mystical union where opposites conjoin in holy orgasm, finds itself driven to seediness, concealment and self-deception. One can sense the dreamer's struggle to keep hold of that archaic gnosis, that innermost truth which tells him there can be a honeyed and fragrant purity in sexual transports. But, like so much commercial sex, the reality falls pitifully short of our innermost desire for total experience. Wearied again, in a petty world of prying officials, de-spirited and exhausted, he leaves.

139

THE DREAM-EGO IN RELATION TO THE SELF

The dream-ego is always immersed in the self, but usually without knowing it; only occasionally does the dream-ego remind itself that 'this is a dream'. There are dreams, few and far between, in which the dream-ego is shown and understands something of its relation to the self *as a numinous whole*. In such dreams the self may appear as a divine figure, or perhaps as an actual person who is immensely rich and powerful and to whom the dream-ego feels strongly attracted; or it may appear as a source or centre of tremendous energy within which the dreamer feels caught.

Such dreams fuel the slow developmental growth in which egocentricity diminishes while a humbler and more religious attitude grows. To be egocentric is to experience 'I' as the centre. To begin to let go of the egocentric state is to begin to know, not only intellectually but to know with the heart's knowing, that the figures appearing from the soul's dark and inscrutable centre are truly other and yet truly self. It is to know that self is the centre, and that 'I' is *the moved not the mover*.

A woman, the last of whose children had just left home and whose husband had recently died, felt afraid that she had nothing left to live for. While in this state she dreamed she was standing on a cliff above the sea; she could hear it but see nothing because everything seemed dim and dark. In despair she threw herself over. As she fell she felt afraid and regretted what she had done. Then she landed — but not on the rocks and cold water she had expected: instead she found herself cradled by the sea which held her with a knowingness, a love for her being. She felt she was in the arms of the goddess. She woke up with an immense feeling of love and gratitude, and a conviction was born in her that she was sustained from within.

FURTHER READING

Jung, C.G., 'The Relations between the Ego and Unconscious', in *The Collected Works*, vol. 7, London: Routledge & Kegan Paul.
Neumann, Erich, *The Origins and History of Consciousness*, New Jersey: Princeton University Press.

Ten

SYMBOL

THE ASTROLOGICAL SYMBOLS ♂ and ♀ represent Mars and Venus; @ is known as the 'at' symbol; Marilyn Monroe is called a sex symbol; Rolls-Royce and Porsche are status symbols; hammer and sickle, rising sun, cross, crescent moon, Christmas tree and Easter egg are all symbols we know well and associate with nations, cultures and religions, but understand less well than we might.

What is a symbol? Attitudes vary so much, some seeing almost everything as a symbol, some almost nothing. Is something a symbol only if we think of it as a symbol? Or can it be a symbol without our realizing it? Why can some merely know a symbol while others are deeply affected by its power? Do symbols draw us into an understanding of our past, or lead us into our future development, or both? Can we look up the meanings of symbols in symbol dictionaries, or does every symbol hold unique shades of meaning for each experiencing individual? Are dreams symbolic from beginning to end, or do they have a few symbols embedded within them?

There are no answers everyone would agree upon. But at least the dictionary provides a definition which can serve as a starting-point.

DEFINITION

The Oxford English Dictionary offers three definitions, one of which is apt and relevant for dreams: A symbol is *'something that stands for, represents, or denotes something else (not by exact resemblance, but by vague suggestion, or by some accidental or conventional relation); especially a material object representing or taken to represent something immaterial or abstract.'*

One does not have to search far to find corresponding dream-material. We often dream, for instance, of finding ourselves in some house which reminds us of a specific house, perhaps our own, but which is at the same time different:

21.12.76

(a) I am in a big house which seems in some ways like L.House, but is different; I find a staircase I never knew was there; after the second floor it becomes a spiral staircase with stone steps. I explore and am amazed to find that Beatrice lives up here in one of the attic rooms; it seems she has always been here, or at least for a long time. I try to interest her but she seems neutral about me. Looking around I realize it's the same room Mummy used to write in.

Dreams are perfectly capable of using images which correspond exactly with the waking reality. 'L.House', which was the dreamer's childhood home, has appeared in many of his dreams and often its dream-appearance seemed just the way it was in fact.

But here the dream-house is both L.House, and yet quite different. At the most obvious level it fits the definition in that it would seem to stand for the dreamer's childhood home, but does not resemble it exactly.

But this is hardly satisfactory. The childhood home can be, and often has been, presented as it is. There must be something deeper than this.

REPRESENTING THE IMMATERIAL

The last part of the definition observes that a symbol may be '*especially a material object representing or taken to represent something immaterial or abstract.*' This is the key to the understanding of dream symbolism.

The images in dreams are not material objects from an objective view-point. But they are *experienced* as material objects, and this is what counts.

Not only the altered house, but even the unaltered house, can be a symbol because both are material object images, and both may be taken to represent something immaterial or abstract.

What I mean by this is that a dream image of the childhood home, experienced within the dream as a material object, re-presents to the dreamer not only the visible physical appearances but, through them and woven into them, the invisible psychological and emotional experience attaching to that place. One might say that the childhood home in a dream can symbolize the shape and quality of the containing structure within which the dreamer grew up.

But this means more than the physical structure. The images of the environment absorbed by the child all have their matching complements of inner experience, much of which was and is invisible, but terribly important. The dream can call up this invisible inner experience by surrounding the dream-ego with the physical appearances that went with it.

The dream-house, in general, is a symbol standing for the dreamer's own

142

inner structure, almost a sort of emotionally coloured diagram of his personality, in which there is a front door out to the public interface, a back door into his personal patch of nature, a kitchen for transforming raw materials for digestion, a drawing room for formal intercourse, bedrooms for privacy, and so on. The home and all its denizens, family members and animals, make visible representations of invisible parts of oneself.

Dreams very rarely communicate directly in immaterial and abstract terms; that is just the way they are. They employ symbols through which immaterial and abstract understanding may be grasped.

PAST, PRESENT AND FUTURE

Returning to the dream: why does his old home appear other than it was in reality? Clearly it is to show him that things *inside his personality* have changed; they are not the way they used to be.

A part of his personality characterized as feminine and spiritual, which can write creatively (as both Beatrice and his mother did), can be found in the loftier part (the attic) of his mind. The dream shows that he is only just discovering this, and that the relationship between his 'I' and this potentially creative part of himself is 'neutral', which suggests that it could be better.

This understanding of the dream actually corresponded very well with his waking situation at the time; he was, as we already know, beginning to see himself in various new ways and a part of this new self-understanding took the form of daring to imagine that he might have a talent for writing.

Symbols draw upon past experience, appear in the present, and point to the future. They are pregnant with meaning. Swelled with fertile and procreative seeds from the past, they tug at our understanding, seeking to transform it so that they can continue to grow into what is to come.

TAPESTRIES OF SYMBOL

Seeing dream imagery as − in the words of the definition − material objects which stand for or may be taken to stand for something immaterial or abstract, effectively means that one can see *all dream imagery* as symbolic. So dreams are symbolic from beginning to end.

Dream images have, usually, associations with experience from somewhere in one's life. By stringing the associations together, meaning begins to appear. This meaning can be interpreted into concepts which deal with the essentially immaterial, such as statements about the personality.

Of course one does not have to do this; with some dreams, at least, one

143

can choose to view them as no more than portrayals of external objective events. But most dreams will make no sense seen this way, while they certainly do make sense if one views them as symbolic representations of the state of affairs within the self, or between the self and others.

From this broad perspective of the nature of symbol, we see that symbolism in dream is not confined to the occasional appearances of collectively known symbols such as unicorns, green lions, mermaids and phallic weapons; dreams are wholly composed of symbols because they spring from some depth of our psyche which 'thinks' in symbols.

So dreams are tapestries of symbols from which conceptual understanding can be derived. This does not mean, however, that dreams use symbols to hide their true meaning. Only if one could know the intentions of the unknown dream-maker could one know for sure why dreams are the way they are, but experience teaches that dream symbols, far from attempting to conceal, have an urge towards revealing. This deep realm of our psyche where dreams are formed naturally communicates through symbol and it is up to our often over-cerebral selves to try to meet it halfway.

CONVENTIONAL RELATION

The definition speaks of a symbol denoting something else by '*vague suggestion, or by some accidental or conventional relation*'.

If one accepts that the entire dream is a composition of symbols, then most of it must surely be personally symbolic in the sense that no one but the dreamer could understand it fully. It follows, then, that dream interpretations based upon conventions can never be fully satisfactory (not least because there usually exists more than one competing convention).

A sword, for instance, may be conventionally understood as a phallic symbol, referring to phallic instinctual drives and suggesting a desire for power and penetration with specifically sexual connotations. But another convention understands the sword as a symbol of the intellect which penetrates and divides and thus has the power to know one thing from another. Both conventional interpretations might be useless, however, if someone had stolen a sword for gain, and the dream-sword's associations were actually to do with guilt.

Inevitably, when considering dream material, whatever conventional interpretations one has heard of will be bound to suggest themselves as possibilities. And it is always easier to employ ready-made interpretations than to have to struggle through to one's own. The real benefit, however, lies in doing precisely this; even if one ends up in the same place as one or other of the conventional interpretations, one has now made it one's own.

COLLECTIVE SYMBOLS

Nevertheless, one cannot deny the existence of a vast array of symbols which belong, or have belonged, to the public domain in the sense that everyone recognizes them as symbols and shares an understanding of their meaning:

I see a girl of about 15, in a rustic cream-coloured dress; she is waiting for someone. Two men appear – one old and tall, the other short and gnome-like, with an ugly face and huge bulbous nose; his right arm is a bandaged stump. He's wearing a skull cap; he is a Catholic priest and impotent, maybe castrated. The tall man leaves them together; the gnome tells the girl 'some people would say what I'm going to do to you is wrong. But it's not. It's beautiful.' She nearly faints with fear but knows she has no choice but to submit. He holds up his stump and waggles a huge, bulbous thumb at her. I understand he's going to use this thumb to deflower her.

This was dreamed by a married woman. Within the dream she felt the girl's feelings as vividly as if they were her own. Her waking attitude towards sex was very positive and she would not have said that it was dirty or sinful. But she had been brought up as a strict Catholic and the dream reveals how much the age-old conflict between sexuality and purity or innocence continues to exist within her. The collective symbol which should surely be taken in its conventional meaning is the 15-year-old girl in the rustic cream-white dress: although the creaminess perhaps hints of sensuality to come, she is nevertheless a symbol of purity and innocence.

This, and countless other symbols (e.g. the lion denoting courage and royalty, or the goat denoting unbridled sexuality), are already part of the very fabric of collective consciousness and more or less familiar figures of speech cluster about them.

Such conventional understandings can be an immense help; the broader the traditional base upon which they stand, the more they can be trusted. Knowledge of them, combined with sensitive application, frequently provides a short-cut to the heart of the meaning. At the same time it is wise to be cautious; however collective the symbol there are almost always some personal associations which must not be brushed aside or underestimated because they will be the very things that bring the symbol to life *for that individual*.

ENGAGING WITH SYMBOL

If a symbol doesn't come to life for the individual, it is useless. Simply recognizing the presence of a symbol counts for very little; what matters is the extent to which it engages one's whole consciousness – memories, imagination, thoughts, feelings, intuitions, sensations, emotions, and, eventually, morality and will.

Having recognized a well-known collective symbol, it is always worth asking what one understands about it. Often this is surprisingly little. One may dream of the Cross, and be engaged by the symbol, and only then realize that there is more one does not understand about it than one does.

KNOWN AND UNKNOWN

Symbols would no longer be symbols were they wholly understood. Symbols fascinate; they contain paradoxes; they puzzle; they combine within themselves the known and the unknown; they seem to promise a knowledge of the as yet unknown; we sense more in them than we can understand, and this hinted, half-known yet unknown moves us whether we notice it or not; it pulls at our interest, we worry away at it, trying to find our way into its mysteries.

The Cross is one of the great symbols inexhaustibly overarching our Christian culture; how many thousands of individuals have spent decades thinking about the Cross, meditating upon it, visualizing it, studying examples of it, dreaming of it, arguing about it, unable to get away from that irreconcilable opposition between the vertical and horizontal. And it was a worldwide symbol long before Christianity.

SYMBOL AND PROPAGANDA

The advertising industry, seeking to manipulate wishes and desires, knows well how to take advantage of symbols; not only is their communicative power more international than language, they have the added advantage of exerting an influence at a mainly unconscious level.

Quite recently, for instance, there was an advertising billboard which consisted, quite simply, of a very large, very beautiful, very dramatic photograph of a golden eagle near its highland eyrie, and it bore the caption – 'There are Kings and there are Superkings'. It was advertising a brand of cigarette.

Obviously this is a symbol, but why did they use it? What meanings does it carry for us in fact?

It is eye-catching, of course, and its natural beauty has particular appeal at a time of collective concern about our poisoned environment. And at a simple symbolic level we all know the eagle to be the King of the Birds. So beauty, nature, and royalty are being associated with smoking this cigarette.

But there is more to it than this; the eagle is a long-established symbol and has a cluster of associations which are similar the world over. Although most busy passers-by will have hardly given it a thought, these vast images of the eagle will have automatically evoked some echoes from that level of the psyche where symbolism is the primary mode of communication.

The eagle was the symbolic bird of Zeus (Roman Jupiter) for instance, and Christ has sometimes been represented symbolically as an eagle; in the Brompton Oratory, as in many churches, the lectern is supported by a carved eagle, which symbolizes the holy 'Word'. There was the Roman eagle, and there is the German eagle, and the American eagle.

These are only a few examples of the eagle symbol; if one looks through a lot of them, learns about them, tries to understand the significance they had (and have) for people, and compares one with another, one begins to sense some bundle of qualities which they all have in common. In other words one begins to draw out certain conceptual abstract qualities for which the symbolic eagle has stood. These are qualities such as high-aboveness, all-seeingness, divinity, royalty, power, gloriousness, unconquerableness.

The symbolic image is an expression of certain understandings more primitive than abstract concept. *Most importantly, though, this is not to say that the symbols are no more than archaic vestiges of the psyche, now superseded by abstract mentation.* Symbols can be unpacked or translated into abstract qualities, true, but their real power to move, to fascinate, to compel, to excite worship . . . remains with the symbol. The crusaders did not write abstractions across their chests; they emblazoned themselves with the Cross that went before them.

Quite often one symbol comes linked with another, which tends to be opposite in its cluster of meanings, thereby throwing the qualities of each into greater relief. The eagle, for instance, has traditionally appeared in conflict with another long-established symbol, the snake. A mythic theme, which can be found at the very dawn of history and yet still lives among people to this day,* tells of the Tree of Life and how an eagle lives on its topmost boughs while a serpent lies coiled about its roots; everlasting conflict both joins and separates the two.†

One finds, time and again, that religious eagle symbols are interpreted into abstractions such as 'good, holy, celestial and true', while religious serpent symbols are interpreted as 'evil, unholy, material and false' (e.g. eagle symbols for God the Father and Christ, serpent symbols for Satan).

---

*Essentially the same story found in the Mesopotamian cylinder seals, was also told to me by a Punan tribesman in Borneo.
†The same symbol appears in the caduceus, the medical wand, which has wings at the top of the staff and either one or two serpents crawling up it.

Coming back to the advertising billboard: on the face of it, it may seem absurd to suggest that all this − and more − is evoked when we glance at a cigarette advertisement. And yet it is true. Whether we know it or not (a matter of learned consciousness), the symbol reverberates within us because symbols are not and never have been artificial constructions. They are natural productions of the psyche.

Beneath our individual differences there is a vast majority of each of us that is the same as everyone else, and this applies to the structure of the psyche no less than to the structure of the body. In the regions where our psyche is collective there exist collective symbols. One may think of them as common denominators of universal man's experience through aeons; experiences of eagles have evoked a certain regular, recurring pattern of sensations, feelings, thoughts and intuitions. Naturally, then, if psyche seeks to evoke that particular pattern it does so by presenting the eagle image.

The advertising industry understands this well enough to know that money is well spent in stirring symbolic associations, all the more so when they exert their potency in a region of the mind so dimly lit that questions concerning the validity of associating cigarette smoking with feeling like an eagle are never raised.

FIGURES OF SPEECH

In addition to the huge variety of genuinely collective symbols, one finds many symbols in dreams which *approach* a collective meaning, usually because they provoke immediate associations to figures of speech. For example:

> I am with most of the management committee and we are all flying in a hot-air balloon which I am trying to control. The controls are like a ship's wheel, but it's made out of rope so it's ridiculously floppy and I can't control the thing.

A hot-air balloon is hardly a universally known symbol, but the business-woman who dreamed this readily understood it as meaning 'full of hot air'. She had been in a mangement committee the day before the dream, and she always got very exhilarated and excited when discussing big business with powerful men. 'It's true, I very easily get carried away,' she said, 'and talk too much and too fast'. Obviously the hot-air balloon symbolizes this state of herself, and its floppy controls symbolize a lack of firmness in her self-control. The dream-experience brought this home to her very vividly and it is not hard to imagine that it helped her towards gaining more self-control.

When figures of speech come readily and fittingly to mind in connection with dream images — and this happens very commonly — there is obviously a collective aspect to the symbol inasmuch as it is using a metaphor understood in common by some large cultural group. Such visual portraits of figures of speech are enormously helpful in the work of interpreting dreams but, as always, one must be on one's guard not to impose meaning where it does not belong; like Cinderella's slipper, it must not be forced, it must fit.

So long as these relatively collective understandings of symbols are based upon a truly popular and long-established understanding, and so long as they fit both the dream and the individual's circumstances closely, then things are fine. But interpreting symbols by any sort of convention always runs the risk of sterility. The danger, of course, is that we all have a tendency to confirm what we already believe and to resist change.

TWO HALVES

The word 'symbol' comes to us from the Greek language. 'Syn' means (roughly) 'together'; and 'bol' is from 'ballo', 'to throw'. So a symbol involves the notion of *'thrown together'*.

In classical Greek times a 'symbolon' was an actual thing; it was a mark or token such as a notched stick which was split down the middle in such a way that only the same two pieces would fit together perfectly. If two individuals made a pact of some kind, each could be sure of knowing the other because only their two half-sticks would fit. The symbolon is a popular theme in novels and films (more often appearing as the two halves of a broken coin or medallion).

Knowing the roots of a word almost always helps to understand its meaning better. Symbols do indeed throw things together, or bring halves together; a phenomenon which can be viewed from both a psychological and a metaphysical perspective.

Whether one calls it instinct or archetype we are born with inner programming (presumably genetically based) for certain expectations; unconsciously, the infant 'expects' the nipple, the breast, the mother, the father — not all at once, but each in due time. These inborn and inner expectations are matched, more or less well, by the environment; in other words a nipple, or bottle-teat, appears, and so does a mother, a father, and so on.

INSIDE AND OUTSIDE AND ARCHETYPAL IMAGE

In this natural arrangement of things, we may understand there to be a 'half' inside and a 'half' outside; so long as the two fit together more or less well (the infant's need for an initially near-perfect fit finds an instinctual, or archetypal, response in the upwelling of the mother's early devotion) there springs into being a satisfying sense of relationship between inner world-half and outer world-half.

Experiences of the fitting together are accompanied by the dawning consciousness of images, images which one may think of as having been latent in the unconscious before the experience; images which may be accompanied by a blissful quality at moments when the fit is experienced as perfect; but may have a hellish, tortured quality if the fit is experienced as very bad or non-existent, and in-between images for the mainly in-between states. The specific content of the images will in some way involve the outer object, and will be emotionally coloured by the way the experience of it has matched or failed to match expectation.*

The expectation is archetypal, and the images which come into being are known as archetypal images† and they are symbols. Rather like a magnetic field, which is present all the time but only becomes visible when iron filings reveal its hidden presence, so the power of the archetype is always present but only becomes visible when its matching environment reality is experienced and so provides the sensory input which enables the visible formation of archetypal images.

Thus a component comes from within and a component comes from without. The image which forms is not a photographic rendition of the environmental reality, but nor is it unconnected with the environmental reality.

If a young child (like the little boy at the beginning of the first chapter) has experienced a painful discrepancy between what he needs and what he actually gets from his mother, the experience may portray itself in his dreams as 'the witch'. This image is the portrait of *his experience* of the archetypal 'bad mother'; his inner experience is made visible to him within the psyche; this both provokes consciousness and enables consciousness to begin to grapple with it. In other words, it plays a vital part in the development of the ego.

---

*Inner images, dreaming or waking, within the very young baby can only be guessed at. The guesses take into account what one can observe of behaviour and expression, and also what is known of inner images from a bit later in life when the child can draw pictures or make some verbal communication; guesses also take into account analytic and psychiatric experience of regressed adults. These ways of guessing what was there in the infant by knowing what is there in older humans may well attribute more definition to the images, which might well be very inchoate visually in the very young; but as earliest experiences of good and evil the guesses seem likely to be accurate.

†Jung described archetypal images as self-portraits in the psyche of the instincts.

SYMBOLS, ARCHETYPES AND FATE

Symbols, as they join inner world and outer, mediate Self to ego. All through life they confront, provoke and expand consciousness, leading the ego into ever greater self-understanding and world-understanding.

As the years pass, slowly changing constellations of archetypes govern the unconscious disposition of our expectations and, through their psychic expression in symbols, exert a profound effect upon our conscious interests and passions.

SOUL, SPIRIT AND SYMBOL

In the older language of body, spirit, and soul – a language now regarded as more metaphysical than psychological – symbols can be seen as the manifestation within the body of the meeting between soul and spirit.

When some work of art, such as the ballet *Swan Lake,* moves us deeply, we experience something quite ineffable in our soul. We see Siegfried and Odette die for their love and so break the enchantment of the evil spirit; moments later, knowing them to be dead, we see them together in their eternal life, floating past in some beautiful world beyond our world.

Certainly these must be symbolic images, for we see nothing of all this in waking reality; but equally certainly our soul already knows about it, recognizes it, rejoices in tears rather than words. The soul seems to know of an existence beyond form, which is all *meaning and feeling.* No doubt a number of factors go into making certain works of art popular, but chief among them must be their ability to put us in touch, momentarily, with our soul. This is indescribably precious to us because our soul feels with a heart that is in touch with the heart of God.

As soul is deep within the heart of earth, the wordless earth of heart, so spirit is overarching and above, the mind of sky and the sky of mind. As symbol reaches downwards into soul, so too it reaches upwards into spirit. Spirit is *meaning and understanding;* spirit sees, spirit understands with an eye like the eye of God, and spirit creates the 'Word'.

Sky above, earth below; in that potential space where the two both join and separate, we live. Little living creatures of flesh and blood with our heads in the sky, our feet on the ground, our individual bodies at that very plane of meeting.

So it is in the invisibility of our psyche. 'I', our ego, our unique body-based individuality, exists at the interface between spirit above and soul below. Between the great blue above and the great red below we burn with our own little personal clouds of energy, our own bipolar auras, blue above and red below, for our personal intellect is our little spirit and our personal feelings are our little soul.

A symbol is like a phantom brought about by intercourse between the beyond-I soul and the beyond-I spirit. Springing into existence before our eyes it has the power to draw us down through the path of our feelings into the wordless depths of universal soul, and to draw us up through the path of our intellect into the heights of universal spirit. Understood in this way, symbols no longer have to be seen to stand for something else because the something else, both below in soul and above in spirit, is already understood to have condensed or materialized into the symbol. The symbol does not stand for or denote something else, it leads the way.

SYMBOLIC ATTITUDE

Like wave and water, symbols and dream are inseparable. Nor are our dreams alone inseparable from symbol; our lives waking and sleeping are threaded through and through with symbols. But what of the conscious attitude towards them? There is a *symbolic attitude* of the ego, and not everyone has it. How much or how little one has of it can mean the difference between wisdom and madness.

Let us imagine that three people have the same dream, an unreal situation since dreams are supremely unique to the dreamer. But the exercise serves to illustrate differing conscious attitudes in relation to symbol:

> I am in my bedroom, lying on the bed but can't sleep because there are sounds like rats or birds running above the ceiling. I get a stick and hit the ceiling. For a moment there is silence but I feel an indescribable terror gripping me. Suddenly the ceiling is ripped open and my father's head pokes through from above with a contorted leering evil expression. I wake in shock.

The first person, who has been acting more and more peculiarly for some time, wakes in a frenzy of terror and anger. Still lying in bed it comes over him that he has had the truth revealed; his father is actually the devil and he's trying to pretend he's God. He knows what he must do. For the sake of all the world. Surely they will understand. Even if they do not, he must still do it, though it may mean his own sacrifice.

In his dressing gown he gets the axe from the garden shed. His old father lies in his falsely neat bed, pretending as always that he's just a decent ordinary chap. The contorted leering face floods his mind; now he sees it on the pillow. It's easily done. More easily than he'd thought; three blows and the thing is severed. Putting it in a plastic bag from the kitchen he takes it round to the police station. 'I've killed the Devil,' he says, with modest pride.*

The second person wakes in a cold sweat and a full minute passes before the sense of fear and horror ceases to permeate the room around him and withdraws back inside him. Still, though, he feels disturbed by vague sensations which seem to come from far away and long ago. His mind, unwillingly on his part, replays the terrible image; fragments of memory appear before him for split seconds, Dad coming back from the pub drunk, unbuckling the broad black leather belt, shouting and screams and moans from his parents' bedroom. After ten minutes he heaves a great sigh and, glancing at the alarm clock, resolutely puts the dream from his mind.

Four o'clock. Three more hours before he must get up. He begins to think of his boss, the unreasonable smug bastard, so self-important and dictatorial. Perhaps he should look for another job. But why for God's sake! All because of this vile man?

He indulges one of his favourite fantasies in which he sees his boss jostled on the platform and falling in front of the train, and then he himself being asked to take over as account manager. He drifts into an hour's uneasy sleep. Over the following days flashbacks to the dream flare up for an instant but he thrusts them away with a shudder.

The third person goes through the same experiences on first waking as the second person. As she recovers from the shock and gets her mind around it (rather than *it* being around her mind while it permeated the room) she begins to wonder why. Why should she see her father in so horrible a way when she loved him so much, when she had been devastated by his death on her thirteenth birthday? She feels it is cruel of *her* to dream about him in this way, like a wanton besmirching of his memory.

Half-recoiling from the thoughts while half-allowing them, she finds things that her mother has recently told her echoing in her mind; things she had not wanted to hear, things about her father, how he had had the crash while on his way to his mistress, the mistress she had never known about. Unable to get back to sleep, she lies in her bed, suffering a turmoil of conflicting emotions and thoughts as the idealized image of her father she has so long protected begins to face up to another side of him.

In the following days and weeks she has more dreams, she talks further with her mother, now beginning to feel better about her. It dawns upon her that, without ever knowing it consciously, she has kept this bad side of her

---

*A man did just this. Later he told the psychiatrist that a dream the night before had showed him his father was the Devil.

father 'out of mind', hidden in a part of her house she could not see. She begins to understand why she has never felt seriously about any boyfriend; none of them could ever have been good enough to match up with the all-good father she had clasped inside her.

The first person, at the time when he committed this disastrous action, had no *symbolic attitude*. Simply to have survived at large until the age he was, he must have had some capacity to distinguish symbol from reality; but probably that capacity was small, a mere skin covering over a very undeveloped part of himself which could not see that something was *as if* it were something else. One may imagine that the effort of maintaining that skin of sanity became too much. With this dream he could not think, 'This image of my father appears *as if* he were the Devil', he could only think, My father *is* the Devil. Equation instead of equivalence. He has, in effect, become possessed by the symbol; it has swallowed his ego up.

The second person clearly has the capacity to distinguish symbol from reality; it happens more or less automatically, as it does in any healthy person. But he turns away from the symbol, pushes it away. One has the impression that he regards the dream as no more than a horrible incident, best forgotten as soon as possible so that he can get on with the real business of life. And yet one can sense how much he is enmeshed within the power of the symbol; the image of the bad father is simply being replayed with his boss and he is quite unconscious of this and refusing to face the potential for consciousness offered by the dream symbol. His symbolic attitude exists, but it is poorly developed.

The third person has a more highly developed symbolic attitude. Painful though it is she allows the symbol to act upon her, allowing it to draw all its contents of association before her conscious eye. The more she allows it the more she recognizes the value of it.

LEARNING ABOUT SYMBOLS

Development of the symbolic attitude is not necessarily the same thing as learning a lot *about* symbols. No doubt symbologists must have a highly developed appreciation of symbol, but it is not essential to know a great deal about the history and interweaving meanings of symbols in order to be receptive to one's own important symbols. This said, however, it is still true that the more one learns of symbology, the richer and deeper will be one's appreciation of one's dreams and life in general.

Walking and talking are natural developments in the child, yet we speak of *learning* to talk and walk. Living with symbols, understanding symbols, using symbols, is much the same: innately present, naturally proceeding through a process of development, and yet also needing some learning.

In this age of the world, in a civilization transformed in almost every way by the efficacy of science, the precision of intellectual knowledge is understandably valued above all else. While the best minds know that the symbolizing faculty exists like an inexhaustible mine providing the raw materials for the intellect to work upon, the climate of opinion makes it easy for minds of lesser insight to look down upon and devalue the symbolic faculty, pointing to its vagueness, its manifest unreality, its predominant subjectivism. This does little to foster the learning of symbolic understanding; just like the growth of language, the natural development of symbolic understanding proceeds anyway, but without conscious learning it remains more unconscious than it might be.

Artists of every kind learn about symbol; religious people of every religion learn about symbol; historians of culture learn about symbol; the advertising industry, including all propagandists, learn about symbol; some psychologists learn about symbol. Most of the remainder of society *experiences* symbol (on every poster, in every TV advertisement, for instance, as well as in every dream), is affected by it more or less unconsciously, but has learned little about it because it does not seem important enough.

How does one learn about symbols? There are dictionaries of symbols in which one can look up the author's view of symbols and their meanings, and very helpful they are. But the best way to learn is to follow one's nose through the arts, mythology, folklore and fairy tales, religions, alchemy, anthropology, and so on.

Symbology is a field where there are no beginnings and no endings. An apt symbol for symbology itself would be the uroboros, the serpent in the form of a ring, eating its own tail, a symbol bringing ideas of eternity, endlessness, self-sufficiency.

Anyone who has ever tried to organize a body of myths — such as the Greek myths — into a logical structure with a beginning a middle and an end, will know the task is impossible; all are connected, overlapping, weaving in and out of each other, and, more impossibly still, one soon comes to realize that there are not even any true lines of division between the myths of the Greeks and the myths of their neighbours in time and space.

Like the mind itself, myths and symbols are one endless tangle from which both ends disappear into infinity. By imposing causal or teleological views upon it all one can, for a while, seem to see lines of regression or development but sooner or later they turn back upon or into themselves, eternally transforming, merging, disappearing, reappearing.

FURTHER READING

Cooper, J.C., *An Illustrated Encyclopaedia of Traditional Symbols*, London: Thames & Hudson.

Jung, C.G. (ed.), *Man and His Symbols*, London: Aldus Books.

Jung, C.G., 'Symbols of Transformation', in *The Collected Works,* vol. 5, London: Routledge & Kegan Paul.

Eleven

NIGHTMARES

FROM ALL THE infinite range of dreams, few have so typical a character that they possess a title of their own; but nightmares *are* in a class of their own. Known by all, even if only from childhood, and dreaded by all, they have certain qualities unique among dreams.

One characteristic of the human mind, a blessing indeed, is the natural way in which we forget extremes of pain and distress. Only the outline remains, like a dry husk. This lingering memory has the power only to remind us that we don't want to experience the same again.

Don't want to, but sometimes have to. Persistent nightmares, like persistent persecutions experienced in the waking world, have driven people to drugs, madness, murder and suicide.

What is the nightmare, that can oppress us so terribly from within? Does it bear the possibility of meaning, which might then serve us well? Or is it a meaningless torment we must endure from time to time because we have no choice?

MARE OF THE NIGHT

The contents which characterize a nightmare are unbearable distress, very often accompanied by the sense of being suffocated and/or paralyzed, and the strenuous but unsuccessful attempt to escape or free oneself from an often *nameless* horror. But perhaps the most important thing of all to note about nightmares is that they wake one up. So abruptly is one awoken that waking consciousness *has no choice but to remember the dream*. In this insistence upon conscious remembering one may begin to see the purposive nature of their occurrence.

The term 'nightmare', until not so long ago, actually referred to a supernatural being, a spirit or monster or witch, typically female, that beset people in their sleep, settling upon them and suffocating them by their

157

weight. There was little difference between this nightmare creature and the evil spirits known as succubi and incubi in medieval belief.*

The female quality traditionally ascribed to the 'mare' does not seem so apparent nowadays as it used to be. In medieval times the feminine was culturally repressed, feared, and even persecuted. Perhaps this may explain why it rose up in people's dreams with such malignant fury.

Since then, women, and feminine values, have clawed back a good deal of the power and respect they lost with the arrival of the Father Gods some two to three thousand years ago. The improvement in the balance of power between masculine and feminine must surely have lessened the resentful vengefulness of the bottled-up feminine in the unconscious, and no doubt this accounts for some of the change in the way we experience nightmares. Another reason for change lies in the prevailing climate of scientific rationalism; this has influenced consciousness enormously and made belief in *spirits* almost impossible.

As a result, all that we mean when we refer to a *nightmare* nowadays is a dream characterized by the subjective experiences described above. Even when the old nightmare-hag appears very much as she might have done a few centuries ago, the contemporary dreamer will be more inclined to search for explanations in terms of his own psychology rather than return to the terrifying realm of belief in evil spirits.

> I'm in a museum deep underground; strange, intriguing ancient objects on display or lying about in the narrow tortuous passages. Entering a room, I find a peculiar gathering; the people look normal in one way but something feels wrong, sinister, as if they are playing normal. Then I'm making love with a very attractive woman; lifting her dress she sits astride me but the very moment I enter her she turns into ghoulish malignant sponge oozing stale urine and grinning fearfully because she has me in her power.

The dreamer, a young doctor, described how he woke gasping for breath, still trying to throw the malignant creature off his chest, and fighting to control his panic at being caught up in her evil magic, powerless to resist. Later, when he was reflecting upon the dream, his thoughts circled around the fears he had known in his childhood when his mother began to slide towards a nervous breakdown.

Down There by J. K. Huysmans gives a disturbing account of vicious cravings for these more specifically sexual dream-monsters among turn-of-the-century Paris, and tells some stories of their medieval lineage.

NIGHTMARE AND CHILDHOOD

No one needs to be told what nightmares are like because everyone knows; none escape childhood untouched by nightmare. These terrifying dreams of supernatural evil seem to occur, or certainly to be remembered, more often in the very young. This is not surprising since magic and the supernatural are altogether more available experiences for the child than the adult.

The child's ego is still in an early stage of its growth; less of the child's self has been integrated into the ego, and what ego there is has less cohesion than in healthy adulthood. Even while they are awake the conscious experience of young children is very permeable to archetypal images which are heavily coloured with collective psyche. This is what makes childhood the time of life so open to charm, freshness and 'magic', but by the same token makes it equally open to horror, terror, and 'black magic'.

There does exist a natural and necessary purpose in the ordeal of childhood nightmares: the ego actually grows by way of its encounters with and survival of these terrors. The ego is, as it were, the hero whether it likes it or not; it *has* to fight against the dragon; refusal leads only to the stagnant waters of neurosis.

Girls dream that they are boys rather more often than boys dream that they are girls, but apart from this the nightmares of boys and girls do not differ significantly by sex. Whether the image of terror embodies itself as witch or ogre seems to be determined more by personal circumstance than the sex of the dreamer. In fact the nameless evil that is 'coming to get you' is somewhat subject to passing fashions. The comics, films, and fiction of the time reflect closely the children's nightmare images, although which comes first is hard to know. Both, it would be true to say, are the changing manifestations of the ultimately invisible and unknown horror that stalks us below the surface, the thing we have most rejected and repressed.

Forty years ago, when Negroes were still a rarity in Britain, youngsters had nightmares of masked, ritually dancing black men and women who ate children and cast magic spells. In the seventies, dinosaurs figured prominently, combining the mirthless walking hunger of the tyrannosaurus with a ghastly human knowingness in the fixing eye. More recently, zombies and blood-thirsty vampires, the 'undead' hungrily lusting for life, have persecuted the young ones in their sleep:

I'm riding my bike; come to a hill and begin to go down faster and faster. Know I'm going out of control and bound to fall off sooner or later. Bad neighbourhood now, and there are zombies shambling towards me, waiting for the crash. Then I've crashed; I'm lying on a stone table in a cold room; the zombies are all around in a ring, shuffling closer. I cannot bear for them to get me so I try to kill myself by stabbing my heart. But I hit a bone and fall to the floor. They begin to clutch at me . . .

NIGHTMARES AND TALION LAW

An *'eye for an eye; a tooth for a tooth'*. This is the talion law: harm is returned with equal harm. The law of getting even. No forgiveness.

In their conscious thoughts, feelings, and actions, most of humanity now tries to rise above the law of talion; makes a very conscious effort to understand, forgive, reconcile. But it is very certain that we do not have to go far below the surface to find both the urge to retaliate and, even more so, the fear of retaliation.

Immediately below the surface of civilized consciousness we are all, child and adult, wary of retaliation; we know the fear more or less consciously, and we know it is more or less realistic. For the child, physically weaker and still dependent upon adults in many ways, the fear that adults may retaliate if annoyed or hurt is a more terrible possibility.

But deep within the ancient darkness of psyche, talion law is a great deal more than the fear of outward and real retaliation. It is one of the dominating forces within the young child, governing relations between figures *within the psyche*.

If you are a baby and you are filled with rage at your mother and in your imagination (conscious or unconscious) you smash her up and tear her into pieces, then the talion law operating deep within you will ensure that you live in fear of her retaliation. Perhaps not all, but very much of this, can go on wholly unconsciously.

In the realm of the psyche where nightmares are born, the very same destructive violent hatred you direct upon another will flow into that other and be returned at you. Nor is there any escape by killing the other off, so that they cannot hurt you back. In the magic realms of psyche you can tear someone to shreds, only to find they have reconstituted themselves and are after you again, more vengeful than ever.

A woman had an abortion in her early twenties. At the conscious level she said it meant nothing to her, she did not feel guilty, depressed, sad, or anything. But she began to sleep poorly, to drink, to wake screaming. Eventually she had a nightmare:

I'm cutting up a baby in a basin and trying to wash it away down the drain. It is more a foetus, really, but even when it's in bits the eyes stare at me with deadly accusation. They are 'knowing' eyes, like those of an adult not a baby. I shove it all down the drain and wash the blood away, but then a movement catches my eye. I look down and see it's still there, on the floor, staring at me.

Many women have abortions, but most don't have nightmares or such deep disturbance as this woman. The reason was that in many ways her psychic functioning was still that of a young child. Her own infancy had been so disturbed that the primitive talion-based terrors of her psyche had remained virtually unmodified in the course of her growing-up.

Another woman, a writer, had had within her from earliest childhood a cold unquenchable fury with her mother. At the time of this dream she was still entirely unconscious of it, although she later came to know it well:

I'm standing on a road like a racetrack; round the bend comes a car with my mother driving. She is hunched forward over the wheel with a maniacal expression. She is completely intent upon her own purpose, oblivious to anything which might stand in her way. I am almost rooted to the spot with horror. At the last moment I throw myself to one side, falling into a sort of waste-land . . .

So long as she knew nothing of her own murderous rage with her mother, it seemed incomprehensible that she should dream of her mother being such a threat to her life. A year or so later, by which time she had become conscious of her rage (which now kept her awake with pounding heart and violent hate-filled fantasies), she could begin to understand not only the reasons for her own fury with her mother (for having been so insensitive to her needs), but also that such hatred as there was festering within her is bound to be accompanied by the fear of retaliation.

RECURRENT NIGHTMARES

Nightmares have a distinct tendency to recur; often they seem to hijack other dreams, so that a dream may begin innocuously enough but then, as if suddenly locked onto inexorable railway lines, it lurches into the nightmare journey and cannot then be wrenched off track. With the sickening dread of foreknowledge the dreamer is caught up in an unfolding sequence already known too well.

A woman in analysis (Ms X) told me of her childhood nightmares; they started, as far as she could recall, when she was about three or four and recurred over many years:

They began in all sorts of ways, but always ended the same. The nightmare part began when she realized she was in a certain street; this

161

terrible street seemed to be somewhere near her home and somewhere near the sea, but she never knew exactly where. As soon as she found herself in that place she also became aware that something was behind her, or rather, a lot of somethings. In some spooky way they seemed to be tied to her so that run and run as she might, she could never escape them and the sense of them always behind her filled her with dread and terror until she could breathe no more and run no more and knew they would catch her. At this point she would wake in a state of panic, often screaming, bathed in sweat, exhausted.

This ghastly and overwhelming sense of dread for a thing unknown, unseen, and supernaturally evil and magical, is central to the very worst of the nightmare. It is the dark heart of the nightmare.

We shall see that the more the dreaded horror begins to take on shape and visibility, the more possible it is to begin to deal with it. Quite extreme experiences of guilt, shock, horror, and grief, may still be there, but that blind archaic panic, that mindlessly running from one knows not what, will have begun to come under control.

The little girl who dreamed these dreams was desperately trying to have no knowledge of and nothing to do with something that was attached to her. Of course she could not escape it because she could not escape herself. This is the grim truth of all nightmares.

The understanding that gradually emerged, years later in her analysis, was that the 'things' she was trying to escape were her feelings of anger and hatred with her mother; I say 'her feelings' because in an objective sense they were of course hers, but it must be understood that at the time they were not consciously hers. Indeed, it was *from the conscious ownership of* them that she was running in panic.

There have to be reasons for a child's psyche to find itself in such a situation, and there were: her mother had had almost no mothering herself and was markedly narcissistic, always needing to be recognized as the most clever, beautiful, talented, and lovable one herself so that her children, even when they were tiny, were invariably compared to their own disadvantage. Little children *need* certain amounts of praise and admiration for the specialness of their selves and their achievements, and they look especially to their mothers for its provision; without it the development of self-confidence is seriously impaired. Such a shortfall in the natural needs of the self provokes a very central and deep rage.

Why could she not express her rage as lots of children do, and so come to know it as her own? She had no model from which she could take in experience of violently angry feelings being safely expressed. Her father was a living example of how terribly dangerous they were; he was an alcoholic and a violent unpredictable danger to himself and others when he was drunk, although, as she came to realize only when she was adult, a lovable and sensitive soul when he was sober. Her mother could not tolerate anger or criticism at all and would retaliate viciously in one way or another.

So what could be done with her rage? It was too dangerous to express it in the normal way, but it can't just vanish. She tried to get rid of it, tried to extrude it from her self-image. As we see in her dreams, 'it' remains attached to her dream-body, but not inside it. It became a part of her that pursued her wherever she went.

NIGHTMARE AND SELF-REFLECTION

In the way that nightmares recur, often exactly the same, time after time, one cannot escape the impression that some content of unconscious psyche is trying to force its way into consciousness. It is as if something *must* be recognized, something which has been shut away and ignored for too long already. The dream-ego, for its part, is so threatened at a primitive level that it loses all its faculties of reason, courage and will, becoming little more than a petrified, jellified or convulsive animal.

That capacity for self-reflection, perhaps the greatest divide between man and other species, is temporarily immobilized and even though it returns soon after waking, the dread of the nightmare experience is so great that reflection upon oneself and the dream is often almost wilfully withheld.

Possibly this explains why nightmares are not very common among people in analysis. People who choose to go into analysis have chosen to face themselves; all have had nightmares before and some have had years of them, but once they make that choice and direct their capacity for self-reflection fair and square upon themselves in their entirety, the nightmares quickly begin to lose their most nightmarish quality and become 'bad dreams'.

It is impossible to be sure of the true frequency of nightmares among the general population, but I have records of some 200,000 dreams and there are no more than about 500 nightmares amongst them, most of which do not come from analytic patients but from psychiatric patients.

When, in the course of Ms X's analysis for instance, the old rage with her mother began to come out, much of it in dreams to begin with, the dreams were frightening and terrible to be sure, but they were no longer nightmares in that spookiest sense which grips the soul with supernatural terror because, in the containing and supporting presence of an analyst, she had begun to face the unknown and reflect upon it.

The transition from panic flight, through self-reflection, to integration of

163

the once-dreaded content, can nowhere be seen so clearly as in dreams themselves. Early in her analysis Ms X dreamed several times that:

> I am driving my car. I smell smoke and then see that the back of the car is on fire. I drive faster and faster, very scared.

The once-unknown terror behind her has taken on a more distinct character because she can now turn around and see what it is. No longer supernatural, it is portrayed as fire. Not only is fire a collectively understood symbol for emotions dangerous if uncontrolled, but fire had specific associations with her violent father who had once set fire to himself in front of her. Still, though, she is running as fast as she can, not far from panic, one senses. Somewhile later she dreamed:

> I am sitting on a cliff overlooking a bay where a galleon is anchored. Beside me a cannon is firing shot after shot into the belly of the ship but I try to shut it out of my mind by concentrating on the book I am reading. But the page begins to smoulder.

Associations led to an understanding of the galleon as a symbol of the mother-imago and the cannon as a symbol of her anger. Altogether there is an atmosphere of greater control and order, the fire disciplined into directed explosions; but still she tries to put it out of mind as if none of it had anything to do with her. The smouldering page of the book shows how it is beginning to confront her fully conscious understanding.

True enough, it was not so long after this that she began *consciously to feel* her rage with her mother; the very beginnings of knowing these feelings as her own were accompanied by a dream:

> She was with someone (who she later associated with her mother); they reached hands towards each other and touched; as the contact was made a swarm of bees flew up from her own hand.

The symbol of the swarm of bees was subtle and many-sided, involving honey and the love-goddess as well as the stinging darts of aggression. In the same way as she was beginning to experience her rage, and know it as a natural thing she had no need to fear so terribly, the dream portrays it as the stinging potential of a swarm of bees. Not only has it been reduced to a level one can deal with; it has been shown to be inextricably linked with a loving potential within her.

THE PURPOSE OF NIGHTMARES

Nightmares *do* have purpose and meaning. They confront the ego, whether it likes it or not, with something that *has to be assimilated* if there is to be full psychic health. They may seem cruel but their cruelty springs from that careless-seeming and inescapable wisdom which characterizes nature, fate, and God. Something, so insists the dream-maker, *has* to be faced by consciousness; it has to be taken in, swallowed, digested, absorbed, made one with one's own substance.

Plainly this is not always possible; many individuals fail; our mortuaries and mental hospitals are full of them; the wisdom of nature neither professes nor realizes those equal rights of individuals so cherished by socialist ideals. Every day, in every land, there are those who turn to the last resort, to the hoped-for peace of death, because they can no longer face the nightmare of their life.

PERSONAL AND COLLECTIVE

Something must be said concerning the difference between the nightmares of Ms X, which are personal, and the nightmares of (for instance) survivors of the Holocaust, which are collective.

Current research in Israel indicates that those survivors who remember no nightmares make better lives for themselves than those who do. This is scarcely surprising, though it must be cold comfort for those who cannot escape their dreams. From this evidence, however, it is neither a logical step, nor necessarily a wise one, to assume that those who do suffer nightmares would be better off if their nightmares were artificially prevented access to consciousness.

If it is conceded that some purposeful wisdom in our nature with a range of vision greater than our conscious viewpoint manifests itself in dreams, then nightmares too should share in this recognition. The fact that they are so distressing that they cannot be ignored, and that their very persistence demands an expansion in consciousness, only increases the importance of recognizing them. Attempts to block this process where it naturally occurs may bring a short-term gain in material well-being, but the cost might very well be a long-term loss in more intangible measures of well-being such as soul, spirit, and meaning. When people with 'personal' nightmares have them blotted out by drugs or ECT,* the cost to the personality is palpable to themselves and to those who know them. There is a shallowness of emotional response, a tendency to rigidity, both physically and mentally, and a poverty of creativity, in an ego which has to be artificially protected from its own matrix of unconscious.

Between 'personal' and 'collective' nightmares there exists a difference in scale: Ms X experienced her early world of the family as persecutory

*Electro-convulsive therapy.

because it failed certain of her essential needs; many millions of Jews in the Second World War similarly experienced their environment as cruelly persecutory.

In both instances the core sense of there being a goodness to life and existence comes under threat, and life is all but intolerable without this. The task of digesting the evil experiences of one's life seems as if it might be easier if the scale is smaller; even the child actively tortured and sexually abused has some chance of recognizing that his or her misfortune is sporadic and that the evil incarnate in their tormenter may not destroy all hope or faith in goodness because others with whom they come in contact may show concern or even kindness.

But for the Jew in a Nazi concentration camp or the Australian Aborigine being hunted like an animal by settlers from Britain, the evil is not sporadic; it is systematic and collective; simply because he is what he is, a whole nation of people wishes him ill, and acts upon that wish. In situations so comprehensively hostile it must be desperately hard to keep alive the certainty of goodness and love.

Some survivors of these experiences of life's potential for collective evil are not troubled by recurrent nightmares. They do not have the task of conscious assimilation laid upon them. But those who *are* confronted by a nightmarish psyche are forced to face a colossal task indeed. To face up to evil on so huge a collective scale is to have to go beyond the integration of personal evil; it is to stare right through the individual shadow and out beyond it into the darkness that is Satan; it is to have to know in utter reality that Kali tramples through life, her skulls clashing, the blood and guts and shattered limbs dribbling from her lips.

GOOD AND EVIL: LOVE AND HATE

We saw that, in the course of Ms X's assimilation of her nightmare evil, she dreamed of a swarm of bees; poison was brought together with honey, pain brought together with love.

The experience of evil, when it remains undigested by psyche, lies like a stain in the soul, poisons and darkens the heart. This sickness of the soul flares itself across the inner vision of consciousness in the nightmare, demanding to be digested.

Consciousness, fearing eternal and irretrievable engulfment by the powers of darkness, can only flee until it has strength enough to face, to see, and to know. The strength to do that can come from no other source than the experience, faith, or hope, that there is a goodness to match the evil, a creativity to match the destruction, a love to match the hate.

166

Ms X found enough of goodness, creativity, and love in her analyst for her to dare to realize 'her' evil. As she did so, she confirmed through real personal knowledge that a matching goodness, creativity, and love were in her too. Once it had all been *digested* and processed by her conscious psyche, the 'good' and 'evil' (loving and hating energies) were transformed within her soul; they had become known and natural; they were no longer the stain and the weight she had dragged through her years as an attachment extruded from her image of herself; they now felt like potent energies that belonged to her and enriched her.

But for those whose nightmares begin after experiences of massive and systematic external persecution, the task of conscious processing is daunting. They have known an evil reality that is truly there in life, and the knowledge cannot be undone altogether. Where can they find a power of love to match that evil? Can there be no outcome but wrecked lives, suicides, or nightmares silenced by drugs?

Each individual who conquers the panic of nightmare, who faces up to the terror of evil, and thereby discovers a goodness which heals and cannot be destroyed, brings fresh love into the world. The deepening of their capacity for love will first heal their own soul, and then go further; it will spread its gentle influence upon and into those around in family and friends.

When the scale is magnified to one of collective evil it seems likely that those who do suffer recurrent nightmares do so because they are the very ones in whom there is a possibility of finding a goodness comparable to the evil.

FURTHER READING

Hadfield, J.A., *Dreams and Nightmares*, London: Pelican.
Huysmans, J.K., *Down There*, London: Sphere Books.
Roscher, Wilhelm Heinrich and Hillman, James, *Pan and the Nightmare: Two Essays*, Dallas, Texas: Spring Publications Inc.

Twelve

ANXIETY DREAMS

IF THE DREAMING '*I*' feels particularly anxious, then one can call the dream an 'anxiety dream'. It is a common-enough term but rather vague in its boundaries. At the one extreme, anxiety overwhelms the dream-ego, which collapses into panic and the dream becomes more aptly described as a nightmare; at the other extreme anxiety may be so faint or fleeting that it is no longer sensible to characterize the whole dream by its presence.

Between these extremes it is certainly true that anxiety dreams are very common: but they are also a very mixed bag. Anxiety is the term we use to mean the psycho-physical state accompanying insecurity of the ego, and a variety of underlying states may make the ego feel insecure.

That the dream-ego is anxious is an immediate datum of experience; it begs the more important question, What is making the dream-ego anxious? Often enough, this may be perfectly obvious; life is full of anxieties and if, for instance, a woman dreams anxiously about getting pregnant, or a man dreams of losing his job, one may need to look no further than the current realities of circumstance. But it is far from unusual for anxiety dreams to have *no* obvious links with the waking situation; even when they do, and immediate causes of anxiety appear self-evident, there is often more around than meets the eye.

When anxiety dreams are not fairly obvious manifestations of a realistic outer threat, one has to look more deeply. It can be helpful to have in mind some of the root causes of anxiety. Usually they are one or another (or a combination) of these emotional states:

Falling short of expectations and/or duty failed
Guilt
Shame
Loss and abandonment (including being lost)
Fear of engulfment and/or disintegration (including the fear of madness)
Aggression, envy, and jealousy (including fear of one's own aggression
    and fear of retaliatory aggression).

FAILING IN DUTY AND EXPECTATIONS

I am at the office. I have this terrible feeling of work undone, of things I must do, of having been lazy and frightened and not having done what I should. All around the others are busily engaged in their work, but I can't even think where I'm meant to be or what exactly it is I'm meant to be doing. Disapproval gathers around me like an atmosphere; sooner or later the axe will fall.

The business executive who dreamed this was uncommonly conscientious; her annual assessments were good and the dream situation seemed to have little correspondence with waking reality except that she often did feel daunted and over-anxious inside, and always felt she could or should have done more.

I'm driving a big powerful car, but trying to drive it from the back seat; it's an immense struggle to reach the controls and there seems to be something wrong with the gears so I'm never sure what will happen when I change gear. There's a man in the passenger seat watching me coldly and critically like a Test examiner. I get more and more upset because I know he's failing me. Eventually he gets out and walks away without saying anything.

The dreamer was a young woman in her first week at college. Her immediate thoughts on waking were to link the dream with her anxiety at not being up to the intellectual demands ahead of her. Her family had moved frequently and her schooling had been disrupted; her exam results had not reflected her real intelligence and her father, who was often away on business, had been critical and dismissive when he did appear, telling her she must have 'got her brains from her mother'. The result was a disabling lack of confidence in her intellectual powers, which, as the dream shows, were actually powerful. But she felt scrutinized so unsympathetically that she hadn't the faith to come 'up front' and take control of her powers.

THE EXAMINATION

One may find oneself being tested, asked questions, scrutinized in an infinite variety of ways, both to do with the state of one's soul and the state of one's social performance;* however varied the specific situation, the

---

*The dreams of Catholics sometimes involve the confessional, clearly showing that the examination is related to God; but Protestants, whose confessions are typically made alone and within, or those without any particular religious beliefs, have no such ready-made symbol to distinguish secular from sacred examinations.

theme of *being examined* is easily recognizable and almost always accompanied by anxiety.

Actual examinations are common enough, of course, especially during the first half of life, and such dreams may well come about because all the anxiety and feelings of being unprepared for a forthcoming examination have been kept below the surface of consciousness (often down in the belly region, where they may be causing discomfort). The dream then serves to make the feelings conscious, which may spur the individual on to greater efforts.

But it is a fact that many anxiety-ridden dreams of being examined come without there being any obvious external, or public, examination around at the time. We have an examiner within us which goes by various names such as conscience, superego, God, or self (not all exactly the same thing, but nor can they be sharply separated).

GOD AND THE PARENTS IN EARLY LIFE

The experience of being critically scrutinized, of one's performance and/or very nature being examined and evaluated and perhaps found wanting, begins very early in life. It begins at a time when the enormously powerful but wordless experiences of what may later come to be called God* are not yet distinguished from experiences of the parents.

How, you may wonder, can such a thing be known? Both Jungian and Freudian analysts, from work both with young children and adults in regression, are in broad agreement that this is so. Furthermore, it may be inferred from that later stage when little children begin to ask all sorts of questions about what God is, and where he or she lives;† attentive and unprejudiced parents may easily recognize that their child is sorting out this mysterious higher agency called God from the still nearly all-powerful figures of mother and father.

Within the eyes of the parents (and thus within the eyes of these two opposite halves of God) there exists not only the loving and all-accepting glance, there is also the hard look, the glint of disapproval, the frown of censure, and sometimes far worse. These outer communications join up with the primitive God-experiences innate to the infant.

*Attempts to speak of babies and their experience of God are beset with verbal difficulties. It is more than usually important to bear in mind that we do not know all of what God is, and also to recognize that notions about God, images of God, and so on, all undergo change in the developing individual, just as they do in the development of whole cultures.

†Some children first refer to God as 'she'; if they do so from inner experience they are slow to make the change to 'he'.

Unfortunate combinations of nature and nurture can result in very profound and powerful feelings of judgement by a harsh and condemning God. Altogether, the God-experience of early individual life seems to be more like the God-experience of earlier cultures, so that what we are calling 'God' for the baby may be thought of as more like the Old Testament Jahweh than the psychologically more 'humane' God of the New Testament.*

It may happen that these very early and inevitable experiences of examination and condemnation remain unmodified by consciousness in the course of development; instead, and usually *because* they have been so terrible, they remain buried in the unconscious where nothing can change their quality of absolute severity. If this has happened it leads to a deep and inexplicable sense of being no good, worthless, damned. If circumstances arise to make these buried feelings approach close to the ego, that ego will suddenly feel weak, shaky, without ground to stand upon. The anxiety can easily mount to panic.

Even modified as it usually is, so that the God-image becomes a more loving, tolerant and accepting presence, traces of the earlier appalling absoluteness will linger in the depths of the mind, often so deeply below consciousness that they are better thought of as 'body memories'. When dreams are charged with deep anxiety they are likely to be touching these depths where, or when, a small and weak ego felt threatened with rejection or annihilation by an all-powerful merciless God.

The same essential interweaving of outer human experience and inner God-experience continues to exist in the examinations to which we are subject outside the parental home. Before long other people are judging us with their hard critical looks; adults outside the family, teachers at school, university boards, interviewing employers, peer groups, and, hugely, public opinion.

The realistic and outward experience of being scrutinized bears a relationship to, but is not identical with, the inner spectres that have taken up residence within us and make us go hot and cold all over as we lie in our private beds and imagine what public opinion is saying about us.

GUILT

In every life there are but a few days of extraordinary moment; days when one's life turns, when a span of years seems to reach its summation and a

---

*The very name 'Jahweh' contains a sense of becoming, and suggests the evolving of God. Whatever one's faith may be concerning the existence or evolution of God, it remains a psychological fact that our notions, images, and understanding, of God certainly do evolve.

171

new direction begins. But most days seem to be much like any other, just adding their little bit in the general direction one is already going.

Dreams are much the same. Most dreams add their little bit to the moment; only rarely do they lay bare a complete and satisfying understanding of a lifelong theme. Like the days, we have to know them in regular succession, each bringing its own contribution, another brick being laid in the construction of a building we can only half-imagine.

Often this feels tantalizing, as it does in the dreams of guilt which follow. The whole story cannot be seen through the single dream, yet each dream brings a contribution towards a complete understanding:

> I am with Jung and two others; following Jung we climb a stairway or a path which goes up through darkness inside the mountain, eventually emerging through a tunnel onto the summit. Then we are on the top, sitting in a boat, gazing over the peaks in the light of the sun. Jung is sitting with his back to me; I want to hug him but wonder if the others would not like it, or perhaps he would think it wrong. But I do put my arms round him and hug him anyway, and it is alright. Then he gives me a fishing rod and tells me to fish. I cast and to my surprise catch a fish almost immediately; I don't like the idea of taking the hook out of its mouth, and am not sure I'll be able to do it, but in fact it happens easily. Then we are going down again; just near the beginning of the tunnel I realize I have left the hook all bloody and I think it's his and feel bad about him coming to use it and finding blood on it. So I hurry back to the hut where I left it, but now it's locked and I haven't got time so I leave it and catch them up.

A couple of nights later, this middle-aged therapist, who was in analysis, dreamed:

> Two of us have been condemned to die, but each for a different crime. I am to be hanged for murder − although I have not murdered anyone in reality. The other person is female, I think, but I don't know what she's done. The person I am convicted of murdering is unclear ... a woman perhaps, a sort of partner; if I weren't a woman myself, I would say she was my wife. I want to be with the other condemned woman because I feel only she would understand. I am to be hanged at 1 p.m.; it is up to me to get myself to the place of execution, which means taking several buses. I go some of the way but then stop off and go upstairs into a dark café with a friendly woman. I tell her about it and she's comforting; I try to pray but it's arid and dead; I think there will be a chaplain and wonder if I will be able to have a Catholic priest because

172

I want to confess before I die. The woman tells me to stay, asking me why it matters if I'm late.

There was anxiety in the first dream, but not very much; it was attached to the wish to hug Jung, and around the blood on the hook. The second dream, however, was laden with anxiety; she described it as close to a nightmare, although she did not wake in panic.

Among her associations to the first dream she said that Jung was a man extraordinarily open to ideas, and yet also a very feeling man, and an earthy one; he was rounded, complete. This all-roundedness finds an echo in the journey from the dark roots of the mountain right up to the spiritual heights; as well as low and high, dark and light, there is also a marked inclusion of all the elements, earth (the mountain), air (at the summit view), fire (the sun), and water (in which she fished). With a view to the following dream it is important to note her anxious doubt about embracing such completeness. The way she felt about the blood on the hook reminded her of her feelings about menstrual blood; a mixture of shame and guilt.

Her first association to the second dream was that she had recently read about the people who were hanged because they conspired to assassinate Hitler. The implication, of course, was that the person she'd murdered was Hitler. This seemed incomprehensible at first sight, but she went on to say that she thought of Hitler as one who was obsessed with a single idea, closed and impermeable to anything else. She had not been thinking of it when she said this, but the moment I remarked that her view of Hitler was the very opposite of her view of Jung, she agreed instantly.

Why, then, did the dream itself contain the idea that the person she had murdered (or not, as she was sure she hadn't) was like a wife? Over the past weeks she had been increasingly troubled by guilt: she felt she had become more self-centred, less generous, less charitably selfless.

She had previously been excessively charitable; she had, for instance, always given to *everyone* who asked, which is scarcely a feasible proposition in today's world. But we began to see that her guilt in the dream was because she had 'murdered' this 'wife-like' part of herself, characterized by generosity, charity and selflessness.

This certainly made sense; but what on earth did it have to do with Hitler? How could her victim appear to have two such opposite sides?

She was, or had been, a Catholic; her schooling had been under nuns, and their belief systems had got right into her. So it was with considerable difficulty that she now admitted some of her secret doubts about it. She said that the Catholicism she had known had focused entirely on God being 'out there', and had stressed the importance of never-flagging acts of selflessness and charity *directed outwards* to others. There had been no sense

173

of *God within*. In her heart of hearts she had long felt there was something closed and obsessional in this outwardly directed Catholicism. It seemed to her that it sprang from a fear of what was within, as if the inside of man was believed to be bad and any looking within would only bring one face to face with the devil. This is how the dream drew together the two faces of her old faith: on the one hand selfless feminine charity; on the other obsessional, domineering, closed.

By now we had a greater understanding of these two dreams. By choosing to commit herself into a Jungian analysis, with its ideas of embracing the wholeness of oneself and finding a way to the knowledge of God within, she inevitably experienced herself as turning away from the teachings of goodness she had grown up with. Hence the accusation that she has murdered this part of herself, although the dream also contains the knowing that she has not truly murdered it.

Nevertheless, her intuition that she had *not* murdered this part of herself was not enough; she did feel guilty; hence the death sentence. The ultimate severity of the punishment derived from her own earlier God-image, reinforced by all the various priests and members of her family who believed so strongly in this outwardly-directed Catholicism. Her guilt was strong enough to make her move towards her own death sentence, but not to reach it. Truly to change from one vision of what is divine and right to another vision, is a change laden with anxiety; and this was what she was going through.

A couple of final remarks are worth making: first, that the fish is an ancient, traditional, and widespread symbol of Christ, hinting that embracing the way of wholeness would enable her to draw Christ up from her deep blue sea and into the light of conscious knowledge; and secondly, that the association between the blood on the hook and her menstrual blood hints that her female sexuality, the very thing regarded with maximum suspicion, frequently connected with the Devil, and laden with guilt and shame by her Catholic upbringing, was to be essentially involved in hooking the fish into the light.

SHAME

It is said that the culture of the West has been shaped by *guilt*, while that of the East has been shaped by *shame*, but anxious dreams to do with the fear of something shameful being discovered to other people are common enough in the West.

Shame, or the anxious fear of being shamed, is usually to do with the shadow. It is the fear that some shady part of oneself, which one knows about and tries to keep secret, has become visible to others and that they will think less of one as a consequence. Stealing seems to be the commonest cause of shame in the dreams of both men and women.

> I'm visiting Anne. I go to her bedroom and get into her bed. The bed is double but there is a crack in the middle and I can feel something in it. There's lots of money. I take a handful and am just about to put it in my bag when Anne comes in, sits on the bed and chats to me. I feel very anxious. I tell her I'm not feeling very well so I want to stay in bed, but really it's because I can't face bringing my hand out of the covers and her seeing that I've stolen from her.

The dreamer was in her late teens. She was not short of money, but she had, years before, stolen some money from Anne, whose happier family life she envied. She still felt guilty about it and would have liked to confess, but was too ashamed to do so.

LOSS AND ABANDONMENT

Love and need are not the same thing; one can love someone without needing them, and vice versa. Nevertheless, attempts to distinguish between need and love exercise us all from time to time. The further one goes towards their roots, the harder they become to separate. More often than not, and especially as children, we love the ones we need and need the ones we love. They seem like a part of us and the fear of losing them is also the fear of losing a part of ourself.

> I'm climbing a mountain; B [the dreamer's son who is two years old] is up ahead of me. He loses his grip and falls, sliding past me down a gully. I feel so sick with anxious fear that I nearly faint and fall myself.
> In London; B has been kidnapped; I find him in the top floor of a partly built house; I rescue him and arrest the criminals.

We tend to think more readily of children needing grown-ups. But because our need for people is just as much a question of their 'being a part of us' for the time being, as it is of them being able to look after our practical or bodily needs, grown-ups can need children just as much as children need grown-ups.

In this dream the anxiety is for the threatened loss of his son. Outer and inner circumstances both, as always, were playing a part; the outer fact was that his boy was not well at the time (though not seriously ill) and, worrying about his health, he was prey to those deadly irrational fears which beset all parents who love and need their children.

175

The inner circumstances were, as usual, less easy to know. Parents may need their children in a variety of ways, good and ill; among these needs, the one most relevant for this dreamer was that the existence and presence of his son was enabling him to get in touch with his own infancy. This he very much wanted and needed to do. In this way he *needed* his son.

Having children has this effect, more or less, in everyone: this strange little bundle of soul and matter, half-made out of one's own soul and matter, automatically evokes echoes from the time when one was little oneself. Hence the global and absolute quality of the states of joy and anguish that parents can find flooding through them; the littleness, weakness, and liability to flooding of the infant's ego becomes once again a part of their own self-experience. To parent little children is to have another chance to integrate unprocessed bits of one's own infancy.

A dream from a few days later made him realize that the 'kidnappers' were the intolerant and angry outbursts at the children that occasionally erupted from him. He tried to be the good, reliable and reasonable parent, but there were times when the 'child within him' took over and he exploded.

He described how he came home from work one day to find that his daughter and the Nanny had somehow broken his son's toy plane. He (the father) found himself extraordinarily upset for his son, more deeply than seemed appropriate, almost 'an end of the world feeling', he said. A bit later on the little boy pestered his father for crayons. Suddenly, 'I felt unbearably pestered; I lost my temper with both of them and harshly sent them to bed'. Later, when he had cooled down, he felt remorseful and guilty, again in a way that seemed 'too huge and unbearable'. That night he dreamed:

> I'm walking with my children along a narrow mountain path towards a cave. Then, an abrupt change, we have been kidnapped and we're in the back of a van. I pretend to hold a gun against the driver's head, take the keys, open the back and release my family from this violent bad man; I hurt him, immobilize him, and poke his eyes out with a stick, before getting into the driving seat myself and driving them home.

How savagely he punishes his own 'kidnapper'!

The feeling of being utterly and helplessly abandoned is one that most of us may remember from moments in childhood; it is a huge inner experiential state that can engulf one, bringing anxiety or panic, and despair. As the ego grows stronger, and as the protective powers initially experienced in the outer parents are taken inwards by the maturing person, the vulnerability to experience abandonment seems almost to disappear.

But anything which strips the ego of its adult powers, states of regression for instance, may bring it back with appalling suddenness. This is especially so if some little 'pocket' of the personality, buried and unconscious but nonetheless present, is brought together with the ego:

21.11.76

(a) I'm sick in bed and caressing W's vulva which is very juicy; I ask Ralph, Rachel, D and S if they have been in my bed with me while I was fuddled with fever. Under my severe gaze Rachel stammers and her face distorts as if she's unable to deny it.

(b) There is a carefree adventurer doctor; some moments I am him and see through his eyes; at others I see him as separate. He bursts into a dormitory of three monks, all of them pale with strain and worry. One says, 'All is hopeless — God doesn't care!' But the others say, 'We must hang on — God will remember'. There is a bust of a monk's head, strained upwards with desperate longing; it expresses their terrible agony of feeling abandoned.

The dreamer was not only ill in the dream — he was ill in fact. W is his wife, whom he can caress legitimately; but D and S are his children, and Rachel is his sister. He is evidently anxious that there has been sexual incest while his conscious policing was knocked out by illness, and it seems there has, at least in the dreamworld. In the second dream two very different parts of himself, the carefree adventurer and the godforsaken monk, make very dramatic contact with each other.

From the dream series as a whole we know that 'the God who had abandoned his monks' was, in human terms, the mother who had abandoned her son. As is so often the case when anxiety characterizes a dream, we see the presence of that childlike state of the ego for which God and parental imagos are intermingled.

ENGULFMENT AND DISINTEGRATION

When the ego is threatened with the end, or seeming end, of its existence, anxiety is likely to approach nightmare levels. A man in his forties remembered a recurrent dream from his early childhood. He could definitely trace it back to the age of three, and felt fairly sure it had begun before then, during that uncharted time when the ego has not yet matured sufficiently for memories to be linked and related chronologically.*

*That time, as Jung's metaphor has it, when ego consciousness is no more than a number of tiny islands just breaking through the surface of the great ocean unconscious, not yet grown into the continent it may become if all goes well enough.

I am a minute thing, no bigger than a speck of dust. I am resting on an absolutely flat surface like a plain of rock which stretches to infinity. The surface itself exists in the infinite, scarcely illuminated grey vastness of the cosmos which yet seems as if it might be the beginning of a great dawn. Nothing moves, nothing changes.

Then something begins which is hard to describe. It is both silent and yet a grinding sliding sound which reverberates through all the universe. Another plain of smooth rock, exactly like the one upon which I rest and from which I cannot move, is sliding across the surface of the lower one. There is not the slightest possibility of escape. I must be ground into extinction.

He remembered vividly how he used to wake from these dreams in extreme anxiety and dread. It says something about feeling threatened by annihilation; but the images are so 'cosmic' that it is hard to know where to go from there.

It seems clear that the speck of dust was his infantile and still fragile dependent ego; perhaps it is resting upon his mother, represented by the lower 'surface', and the upper 'surface', which ground so closely upon the lower that even a speck would be annihilated, was his father. This would be the personal or parental level of interpretation, and it would lead into various of his concerns at that time about his parents.

But the indistinguishability of God-images and parent-images in very early life is surely in the dream. There is also an apprehension (in both senses of the word) of existence which employs imagery beyond the human level of experience, and this must be taken into account. The two infinite solidities in an infinite emptiness represent *the great opposites* between which all life exists, and by which all life will be returned to death. By thinking of them as the opposites of masculine and feminine, the father and mother of all things, one can bring together the cosmic inscape with the humanly personal.

The dream illustrates the difficulty of speaking about the God-experience of infancy. There is no 'familiar' image of God in the dream, any more than there is a familiar image of the parents; but the vastness, the sombre grandeur, the experience of infinity, the purpose, unstoppable and incomprehensible and apparently merciless as it may be, of the grinding opposites, the smallness and unutterable vulnerability of the 'I', all constitute a relatively early, psychologically primitive but nevertheless immensely powerful and shaping experience of the sort we later associate with the word 'God'.

When a more adult ego dreams of the threat of engulfment or disintegration the dream imagery is naturally more differentiated because

178

the inner stock of sensate imagery has grown immensely. The feelings and the invisible reality behind the images may still be much the same, but consciousness has more to work with:

26.4.77

(a) I am standing with my wife very close to a tremendous drop of sheer cliffs; I want to look over but have to ask her to hold me tightly because the abyss is tugging me to throw myself into its terrifying and yet fascinating depth so powerfully that I am shaken half to bits with vertigo. She holds my hand; but this is not enough, the pull is too strong and I fall. Then find myself standing on a ledge halfway down, still with a mighty drop to the plain below. Desperately holding myself together I manage to climb back up.

(b) I am Frodo the Hobbit walking with others along a road of rock carved out of the mountain which is itself all harsh bare rock. We come to a primitive settlement of animal-like men in caves; they growl out that we must wait for Rabbit to decide; I laugh. (The dreamer's prep-school nickname was 'Rabbit'.) A change of scene: I have been suspended in a vacuum which I somehow know is in the roots of mountains and valleys. The knowledge comes to me that deeper still under the mountains a 'pocket' of red dust is shaking and starting to move out. This has significance for the whole world. I cannot tell if all will be destroyed, or it will be shaped anew.

Vertigo is a very common experience in dreams; it is a particular form of anxiety, and is felt when the ego experiences the threat of engulfment, the devouring pull of the abyss. If felt very powerfully (awake or asleep), it is interesting to note, the sickeningly painful pull is distinctly focused on the lower pole of the testicles or ovaries.

What is the abyss, and why does it pull at us? We all know what it feels like to stand at the edge of a cliff or on the parapet of a tall building, but what is that feeling about? Evidently we do not wholly trust ourselves not to go over; a part of us, more in some than others, feels drawn to let go and fall. Why?

In that mysterious place where psyche and nature are one and the same, in that awe-full place where symbols merge endlessly one into another, one might say that the abyss is the mother; within the deepest roots of our psyche-experience it is the personal mother and, without differentiation, Mother Nature, the Great Mother; it is the source and the cradle below us; it is the unconscious, the sea of Oneness. Ego, once born, rises out of this sea of Oneness and reaches further and further into the realm of *separate things*, division, conflict, disharmony. It suffers the dismembered state of

179

knowing existence. Always some part of it yearns to return, and there are times when it more-than-half longs to throw itself back into that deep where all is one and one is all.

At the time when the young doctor dreamed this (above), his unconscious was very active. Lots of dreams were pouring into his consciousness, and he was fascinated by them. At the same time as going about his business and daily life, half of himself was gazing downwards and inwards. He sensed an enormous importance for himself in all that was happening and 'gave himself' up to the process as much as he dared. The dream-image for this is his position at the edge of the abyss, and the dream shows that he was being supported by his wife, as much as was possible.

Whenever the pull of the abyss is very powerful there must be a doubt whether it will lead to a tragedy in outward terms, i.e. a catastrophic regression, or madness, or suicide. But there is an alternative possibility: descent into the abyss, and return from it, will lead to a growth and enrichment of the personality. From this first part of the dream alone it would be hard to tell whether his fear/desire of the abyss was a regressive suicidal urge, a wish to fight no more; or whether he would be able to descend however far he had to go into the depths in order to return with whatever is necessary for his further growth.

The second part of the dream strongly suggests the latter, which indeed turned out to be the case.

The theme in the second part is essentially the same, but its exposition is now mythic rather than personal. The dream-ego is no longer the same as the waking ego; it is now Frodo (the hobbit hero from *The Lord of the Rings*). In other words the dreamer's ego has identified with the hero archetype. Being Frodo, specifically, means that the character and quality of the hero for this man is shown to be like 'Frodo'. His task, we may safely assume, is essentially the same as Frodo's.*

The descent into the abyss, the journey into danger, *has to be made.* But in the first part of the dream, when the dream-ego was himself in his own body, the ego's anxiety was too great for him to let go completely. When his ego is symbolically merged with Frodo, however, it becomes possible to go further. Inasmuch as dissolution into the abyss *is* the end of the world for the ego, the uncertainty concerning the approaching fate of the world

---

*Dreams often weave in literary or theatrical stories. A rather delightful example is:

13.3.77

(a) I wake up in Molly Bloom's spare bedroom; Stephen Dedalus and she bring me breakfast; Leopold, who is beside me, gets nothing.

In the never-easy task of unpacking dreams for conscious assimilation, full advantage should be taken of these easy amplifications.

shows what high stakes are involved, and why his ego is so anxious. It fears the end of its existence.

AGGRESSION

Very many people are frightened by their own aggressive potential. Often it has been more or less repressed, and if something happens to make it begin to boil up, people may begin to shake uncontrollably; they 'go to pieces'; there is a high anxiety about things getting out of control, a dread of killing and/or being killed.

Women often dream that they are being chased by an ill-defined group of angry men; far and away most often, this does not reflect an outer or realistic anxiety to do with the streets; the dreams come when the woman's own repressed anger has been roused; the angry men are the portrayal of that woman's own pent-up aggression. The equivalent dream for men is more likely to be a single, large, fairly well-defined, brutal man, or an ape or beast-man.

In analysis, where aggression can be explored gradually and reliably, it usually turns out that its repression began in early infancy. Even with satisfactory parenting the infant does not find it easy to distinguish between the limited realities of its aggression and the inner fantasies, which may be all-destroying. When these confusions are seen in conjunction with fears of retaliation, and the anxiety of destroying the very thing (or person) upon whom one depends, and last but not least the demands for control of aggression in modern civilized life, the forces tending to bottle up aggression can be seen to be huge.

Women, traditionally expected to be gentle and kind, have particular difficulties over the exhibition of their aggression, a fact which may regularly be seen from their dreams. This is especially marked around the whole area of mothering. Those about to become mothers for the first time often have dreams which deal with their anxious fear of damaging their own baby:

> I am pounding cassavas, working hard at it so as to make sure all the poison is beaten out and they will be good to eat.

This was dreamed by a rather fiery woman about six or seven months pregnant; she had travelled in the tropics and knew how the village women pounded the cassavas by the banks of the stream, soaking the mush in the flowing water so that the poison would be washed away. Cassavas are breast-shaped, and she readily understood that she was — metaphorically — making her breast milk nourishing and safe for her baby. Psychologically, this would mean that the maternal soul-food which the baby drinks in with its eyes at the same time as it feeds at the breast, was having as much as possible of the poisonous aggression towards the baby, pounded out of it.

Another woman, who had felt very doubtful about her ability to be a good mother, had the following dream shortly after her delivery:

> I am in a house with many women, all with babies. At first I don't think I have a baby, then remember I do and go anxiously from room to room searching. I come into a room where babies are in steam baths and see a coffin-shaped steam bath on a table. I know my baby is in there. I open it and see my baby all steamed, red and swollen. The other women do nothing to help.

Her anxieties about her burning and deadly destructiveness were very exaggerated, the explanation for which lay in her own infancy. She mothered her baby well.

ENVY AND JEALOUSY

Envy, once known as one of the seven deadly sins and more recently elucidated with fine understanding by Melanie Klein, is often described as a 'two-person' state of experience, whereas jealousy necessarily involves a third. I envy you when you seem to me to have something which I myself seem not to have, and I cannot stand this because it makes me feel empty and worthless; if I'm feeling really mean I'll do everything I can to spoil what you've got so then it won't be any good for you either. But I'm jealous over you because you want (or might want) someone else and I can't be content unless I have you all to myself; if I'm jealous enough I may even kill you or the other person, so they can't have you.

Aggression, in fact, is intrinsic to envy and jealousy; they are states in which there must be fear of attacking and fear of being attacked.

Because we know first the two-person relationship, and only later the three-person relationship, envy tends to have roots reaching very far back. If it so happened that it was experienced very powerfully in those early months, the chances are that it will continue to lie around the very foundations of the ego, constantly emptying satisfactions and emanating destructive impulses.

Those afflicted in such a way, usually by a mother herself damaged who needed to provoke envy in her baby, may sometimes limp their way unaided through life, half-crippled by the envy itself and their defences against it, but will usually need psychological help because the tasks of dis-covering, repairing, and then re-growing are truly huge.

To give examples of single dreams in which anxiety is rooted in unconscious envy is not easy without bringing in an unwieldy mass of supporting information. By the time envy has become more conscious, and therefore more clearly visible in the dream, the anxiety will have diminished.

An example of envy becoming realized through a dream appears in Ch.9, p.133; the same woman, over the previous three years, had had many very anxious dreams, almost all of them concerning envy, although she could not let herself know this and any attempt to tell her so was met with furious rebuttal. In one of them:

> She was toiling up a hill, looking at the comfortable homes which lined both sides of the road. Suddenly a swarm of wasps buzzed round her head and snaky things crawled around her feet. Then she had entered a house; it was her analyst's house although not the same; she saw a woman in mid-air, being drawn by some weird invisible force which pulled all the hairs of her head straight out; she was being drawn horizontally down into the basement. Watching this, with her heart in her mouth, she suddenly *knew* that her analyst was down in the basement having breakfast with his family, a breakfast which was also a communion.

She couldn't see much sense in the dream at the time; it was just another of her anxiety dreams. It went by and was not referred to again. But in the light of the terrible envy she later came to realize, it cannot be far out to guess that the snakes and wasps were symbols of her poisonously envious feelings towards those comfortable homes. These generalized homes then condense into the single comfortable home of her analyst, which she enters. Now it is revealed that the envy is more particularly to do with eating and communion, i.e. a togetherness not only of body and physical food, but also of mind. The striking image of the woman being drawn through the air shows how immensely powerful is the attraction of this feeding togetherness. One can also see from the dream that it is not yet experienced by her ego; the 'other woman', which is a part of her not yet experienced as 'I', is pulled with a weird and magical strength which frightens the 'observer her'.

Dreams in which anxiety is founded upon jealousy are usually more recognizable to the ego. They involve three persons; often the traces of the old rivalry with the parent of the same sex over the opposite-sex parent may be discerned behind the present situation.

I'm in the house of a couple I know, kissing the husband when his wife suddenly appears with a snake in her hand with which she tries to kill me. Then a long pursuit ending up in a graveyard with the woman, now wearing a dress my mother used to wear, rushing at me with a big knife, like in *Psycho*.

This midde-aged woman had had many boyfriends, nearly all of them married men, but she had never married. All her life she had felt her mother came between her and her father; the fear of that jealousy had remained unchanged all these years.

FURTHER READING

Jones, E., 'Freud's Theory of Dreams', in *Papers on Psychoanalysis,* London: Ballière.

Jung, C.G., 'A Psychological View of Conscience', in *The Collected Works*, vol. 10, London: Routledge & Kegan Paul.

Klein, Melanie, *Love, Guilt and Reparation*, London: The Hogarth Press.

Klein, Melanie, *Envy and Gratitude*, London: The Hogarth Press.

Thirteen
EROTIC DREAMS

P‌ROBABLY NOTHING IS better known about Freud than that he believed sex was at the bottom of everything. Such a simplification of his beliefs necessarily conceals many subtleties, but it remains true that he understood both dreams and neuroses mainly in terms of the difficulties arising between sexual energy or *libido* and the requirements of civilized society. This view was not shared by all at the time, and many psychologists, Freudians among them, have introduced wider perspectives. Perhaps, in the time and place where Freud saw his patients, there was a great deal more repressed sexuality than there is today.

LIBIDO

Libido is, near enough, our experience of instinctual energy, and often refers particularly to the *appetitus sexualis*.

Attempts to describe it often make use of metaphorical images of water or electricity. 'Whatever turns you on', we say; pointing to images like turning on the tap, or switching on the power, the juice.

Our instinctual nature *is* experienced exactly like this: turned off − and we feel deadness in our glands and hormones and autonomic nervous system; nothing moving, no juice, no charge, no buzz, only an empty cut-off dissatisfaction; turned on − and it's all there, flowing and coiling, that old serpent within us, tightening our bellies, stirring our groin, urging, swelling, liquefying ... immensely precious to us because it is the very sensation of life being alive within us.

MALE AND FEMALE

More obviously than in any other type of dream, the sex, and the sexual identity (which is not always the same thing), of the dreamer takes centre stage in erotic dreams. It goes without saying that the great majority of female erotic dreams involve the male, and vice versa. But are there characteristic differences in the style of eroticism? If one sees the experience of love as a journey which gradually involves more and more of the whole person, there is some truth in the saying that a man's love begins in his senses and slowly makes its way towards his heart, while a woman's love begins in her heart and slowly makes its way to her senses.

Girls have more dreams of romantic love while boys of the same age are dreaming of physically sexual love. The two converge as the years pass, but remain as a characteristic difference between the sexes throughout reproductive life and beyond, a bone of contention that is familiar enough in the marriages of most couples.

THE YOUNG

When it comes to sexual libido, none experience it more tensely than the adolescent. Their sexuality, whatever it may or may not have been in their infancy, has now become a physiological reality. Mind and matter are one: as the hormones seep into the blind bloodstream, they simultaneously portray themselves to the mind's eye in the shape of sexual images, cascades of erotic dreams.

Having worked quite hard to be the sex they are, which has usually involved some contempt for and avoidance of the opposite sex, nature suddenly demands of teenagers that they begin to engage sexually with the other sex, which is no easy matter.

Somehow boys and girls have to begin to see each other in a new light. To a very large extent, this new light is brought about through erotic dreams (which do not have to be remembered to be effective, though many are). Filled to overflowing with beckoning desire, their inner world is so highly charged that it suffuses outwards and lends a new bloom to members of the opposite sex who might have been regarded with relative disinterest only months before.

Erotic dreams *pull* boy and girl together, overwhelming their shy reserve, drawing them into the sexual adventure. The best and oldest educator for sex is ... the dream. Wet dreams initiate boy and girl into manhood and womanhood; teach them the new functions of their strangely changed organs, and bring a new depth of mystery to the dizzying new consciousness of love.

THE LONELY

Teenagers are not the only ones who need to be drawn into sexual relationship. A wide variety of difficulties, both psychological and circumstantial, can prevent adolescents from negotiating the successful transition to sexual mating. The years pass and they remain isolated and lonely. Others may have found sexual relationship but somehow lost it.

Erotic Dreams

Alone and lonely, fantasies and dream-life will tend to fill the void. Without a sexual partner, without a real-life love, erotic dreams continue, or come again, as if one were still an adolescent. The instinctual desires shape themselves into the dream-images of union, togetherness, intercourse, still trying to prod the dreamer into the relationships they lack.

A business woman in her late thirties was still single and for some years she had had no affairs. She had always prized her freedom most of all, but recently she had begun to wonder if she hadn't missed the boat and whether a lonely old age stretched ahead of her. Still, though, she could not imagine sacrificing her precious freedom. She dreamed:

It's the middle of the night, pitch dark. I have been working late somewhere and I come out onto the street and look for a taxi. The street is deserted and poorly lit so I walk towards some lights. As I get closer I see they are actually lights on a ship and realize I must be by the docks. I begin to feel alarmed; it's a rough area.

Three men come running out of a warehouse. I throw my briefcase at them and run for my life, going through all sorts of alleys and muddy paths over waste ground; but I can't get away. I expect to be killed but they throw a thick rope net over me and carry me away, bumping on the back of a donkey-jacket.

Then I'm in a very elegant and sumptuous room with silk carpets and soft lights. I'm alone and think I must escape but, ridiculously, find myself looking at the hems of the curtains, admiring the stitching. A tall man comes in, rather dark, perhaps Lebanese or something. He is beautifully dressed and looks a gentleman, though his eyebrows are very slanted. He asks if I would like to have a bath.

Then I'm in a bath, being washed by an oriental woman without any clothes. I watch her and suddenly realize she is preparing my body with perfumed oils. Now I see! This is his harem. I lie still as if I haven't guessed. She leaves the room and I open the window and climb out. It's a big garden with a high wall all around. There are flowers everywhere and the scent is almost overpowering. I see a little arched wooden door in the wall. To my relief it opens.

But I've been tricked. The man catches me the moment I go through. I see the sun rising with a strange fateful feeling, as if it's the last sunrise I shall ever see. My strength falls away from me and I become like jelly. He carries me into a lake or a large swimming pool and we sink underwater. His mouth opens very wide, like a snake, and with a shock of horror I see his tongue is black and shiny and very very long. It slips through my lips and I feel it flickering and darting from side to side as it goes down and down until it touches my womb.

187

Something happens – I can't describe it – inside me and outside me at the same moment. Everything changes. I want him to hold me for ever.

I woke up and found I was 'going at it'.

This dream virtually demolished her insistence upon freedom. Almost overnight her views changed; she realized she had been running from her own longing to be held, and even overpowered.

THE ADULT

But it is not only teenagers who dream erotic dreams; nor is it only the lonely who dream of love and lust for images whose substance they live without. We all, most of our adult lives, have occasional erotic dreams, usually because our erotic reality leaves something to be desired.

It is not hard to understand why. To live out fully in waking reality 'whatever turns you on' is simply not a practical proposition.

It might have been thought to be so before Freud. But once he'd held before us that mirror within which we've seen not only our social mores and consciously careful attitudes, but also those less-than-fully-conscious desires whose existence within us manifests in our dreams, it became clear that sexual acts in waking reality are, for most people, a compromise between fantasies of 'whatever turns me on' and just how acceptable or unacceptable I and other people (especially my partner) find these libidinal imaginings.

At the simplest level it is obvious that many erotic dreams in sexually active adults involve feelings and desires which were not or could not be realized. Refusing to disappear, they seek satisfaction in our dreams, and perhaps urge us to try to make them real.

In our dreams we may find ourselves fulfilling urges we have wanted to explore with our partner, but been inhibited from doing through shame or fear of rejection. Or we may find ourselves in relationships, sexual and romantic, with no end of 'objects' which have inflamed a momentary desire: friends, partners of friends, colleagues, bosses, subordinates, prostitutes, children of our own or others, parents, members of either sex, film stars, animals, inanimate objects, even religious images such as Christ and the Virgin Mary.

THE ORGASM

Some sexy dreams reach orgasm, which may be extraordinarily satisfying in the young and in those without a sexual partner. As one gets older though, and especially if one has a real person with whom to make love, dream-orgasms may begin well, but tend to end in disappointment as the dreamer wakes at the crucial moment, as if no longer allowed to spend this physical reality within the dream state.

I'm in bed with a plump unattractive girl who is a sex priestess. She intones instructions 'devaricate the thighs ... isolate the button of joy ... and caress ...' I carry out her instructions upon my wife, who is annoyingly slow to respond. Another girl comes in, lies on the bed and wriggles her skirt up and round her waist, showing me her black silk panties; I get very excited because she's a stranger. I turn them both over on their knees so their bottoms are sticking up and gaze with fascination at their anuses. I wonder if either would let me in there. With two fingers in the stranger's vagina, I enter my wife's vagina. An intruder comes in via back door just as I reach the point of orgasm.

I woke up as the first spurt came; the rest felt dry and dead.

I'm holding a rifle with telescopic sights; I want to shoot at some targets but notice they are dangerously close to a derelict house in which I now catch sight of several half-dressed females. Instantly excited, I watch them through my telescopic sight. Two begin to swing on ropes, their skirts falling back and their black silk panties stretched so tight I can see the shape of their vulvas.

Again I woke in the throes of orgasm.

These two dreams were separated by about a week. The dreamer, a research-scientist of about thirty, had a very active sexual relationship with his wife. Why does he have these dreams?

Seeing held a particular fascination for him. He had chosen a line of work which meant that most of the day he gazed down a microscope and saw into the hidden mysteries of matter. The particular fascination which appears in the first dream is to do with *seeing* and exploring the back entrance into woman, the forbidden and private way in. Hence his orgasm coming just as the intruder enters the back door.

He was perfectly conscious of this desire, but although it tugged at him with enormous power, he felt ashamed of it and had not even spoken about it with his wife. He recognized too that the very same desire to *see* right inside mother nature also came out in this sexual form with actual individual women. He found it very hard to be shut out of any part of that enticingly hot rich feminine darkness.

In the second dream he is once again *seeing* into somewhere private, this specifically visual quality of experience being emphasized by the telescopic sights which lend magical power to his natural vision, enabling him to peep from afar, to see without being seen.

While it is obviously true that the rifle in this dream could be called a phallic symbol, it would be absurd (in the light of the previous dream) to think that it appears as a rifle rather than his penis in order to disguise the fact from his conscious ego.

On the contrary, the symbol of the rifle and its telescopic sight *helped* the dreamer to understand himself better. The tremendous emphasis upon *seeing* led him to reflect on seeing in the sense of understanding ('Oh! I *see*'), and he began to *see* that he might be trying to understand the feminine, to *know* her. And he recognized a wish to be in control, to wield power which can act at a distance, and a hint of a sadistic wish to hurt. All of which were better conveyed by a penis/rifle than a penis alone.

THE TWO LOVES

Sexy dreams, with or without orgasm, are not the only erotic dreams we have. It would be wrong to think of erotic dreams as nothing but sexual. The word 'erotic', nowadays, is usually taken to mean sexual but, looking back to the Greek god Eros, we are reminded that erotic does not necessarily mean overtly sexual in the genital sense. The fact is that the whole spectrum of love appears in dreams, from the darkest of earthy lusts to the most unearthly of sublime radiances. To recognize the full spectrum of Eros can lead us into a deeper appreciation of erotic dreams than the recognitions of unlived-out sexuality.

A woman in her late twenties, isolated and unhappy, wary of men after a very destructive experience with a scoundrel, had many 'Cinderella dreams' as she called them, in which she met her prince:

It's night, very dark; I'm in South America. We've been struggling through jungle, me and another woman ... a vague figure but she's old and helps me. We see a circle of women, very short black women, leaning together over a fire. The woman tells me they are making love [this did not mean having sex − it meant *creating or invoking love*].

Then it's morning ... sun shining on a mountain. A prince comes down the mountain, the sun glinting from his golden hairs. I can see he is strong in mind and body, he can take on anything. I admire him intensely, and feel a rush of gratitude when he notices me.

The feelings for the man were for him as a young god, a hero, a prince. They were not sexual, and when she had fantasies about him they were of a destined love that involved them in journeys to distant lands, adventure, song and poetry − for he was spiritual as well as noble.

190

But interspersed with these dreams of noble love there came occasional dreams of sexual love; many, like this one, were as 'low' as the former were 'high':

> I'm walking along a street in north London. It's dark. A man comes towards me with his dog. The dog pushes its head up inside my skirt and begins to lick me. I look at the man expecting him to pull his dog away but he stares away disinterestedly. I feel helpless, afraid if I push it away it will bite me. It makes me excited even while I hate it. I orgasm.

Although the divide between higher and lower love was quite extreme in this woman at this time, it is nevertheless a division one may expect to find in everyone, man and woman. It was a major theme for Dr M and a closer look at it helps to understand an immensely important stage in the psychological development of both men and women.

THE TWO WOMEN

Two women, W (his wife) and Beatrice, appeared many hundreds of times in Dr M's dreams, far more often than any other individuals.

A soulful and rather unearthly love regularly accompanies the dream-Beatrice:

3.6.76
> I am in a meadow, near a little arched bridge over a river. I think it is evening because the air seems misty and somewhat dark. Beatrice, dressed in a long white gown, is walking under low trees on the other side of the bridge, her head bowed as if sadly. I can only see her dimly but my heart yearns with unbearable love and helpless loss. I have lost her, she is gone, and all I can do is grieve over what might have been. She is my very soul. I weep bitter tears of nostalgic longing.

By contrast, the sexuality gathered around the figure of his wife is irresistible, like a compelling earthbound magnetism:

19.2.77
> Through an open door I see W sitting on a chair and exposing her fanny to a handsome Chinese man. I am tremendously excited and jealous at the same time.

22.2.77
> We are watching a show. Suddenly I become aware that Andy and Rick both have their hands up W's skirt and she is panting heavily. I become excited and orgasm just as she does.

191

The spirituality of his love for Beatrice quite often seems to be struggling to maintain its unsullied purity:

8.10.76
(a) I'm eating in a Chinese restaurant; there's a metal screen beside me and I peep through the holes and see four Chinese, two Chinese men and two women, eating at a table. But under the table there are another four, who are naked. While the ones above eat their food, the ones below lick and suck at their genitals. Watching a man licking the vulva of the girl whose dress is around her waist I get so excited I orgasm.
(b) I'm at L.House with Beatrice after a long absence; we are on my bed, passionately caressing. But they are caresses of pure love-joy, not sexual. 3.30 am, and my father comes in and says we must stop.
(c) In a busy street with D; she is running ahead through people and I keep losing sight of her; I feel very anxious about her getting lost or taken by someone bad.
(d) Walking naked in front of my hospital; a paralysed woman, who looks like my mother, says it makes her better to see me naked. She gets up and walks; I understand that her illness has made her resent all deceptions. She half-falls downstairs while I look on, feeling I should help. Then we're in a bus and she sits like waxwork, perhaps she's paralyzed again because I am dressed and acting a part again.

Much in these dreams points back to early infantile and oedipal fantasies: satisfying the hunger drive by eating food is woven together with analogous satisfactions which go on at the lower genital level, in which he can only participate by peeping; his father puts a stop to his 'pure caresses' with Beatrice; and his mother, he thinks, needs his naked body to animate her.

Particularly centering around W but often, as in the above dreams and the following one, involving his daughter and his mother, many of his dreams portray a combination of jealousy, forbidden seeing, and extreme sexual arousal:

8.11.76
I'm wandering through a girls' school, excited by seeing under their tiny skirts as they play netball and by glimpses of them undressing in their rooms.

Then I'm in USA with a girl who tells me how last night she was in a street famous for glamour and vice.

Sitting in the back seat of a car with her, being driven along this street; I realize I know her and keep glancing across at her as we swoop up and down as if riding a switchback. At one moment she looks like an old photo of Mummy, at another like D (dreamer's daughter); when her eyes meet mine for an instant they remind me of me. All around are neon signs in garish burning colours, and a never-ending kaleidoscope of breasts, thighs and bottoms, all brilliantly lit like pornographic magazines. Cosy and excited, I begin to feel inside her clothes; feel her breasts, her nipples, between her thighs. We are both aroused but suddenly I become aware of another man on the other side of her, a babyish-looking but older man; I hear him telling her he is in 'the million-dollar business'; a pang of jealousy pierces me as I suspect she is letting him have her too.

The theme of incest is unmistakable now and his feeling of lovelorn separation from the dream-Beatrice can easily be connected with separation from his mother who has died (crossed the bridge). And one can guess that the claim of purely spiritual love for Beatrice has links with the father's sexual ownership of the mother — a mystery of physical union into which he can only peep and imagine.

Naturally, this all points backwards to his early life and involves the still-echoing presence of feelings he once felt in relation to his mother and father.

But while this is true, and as important for this dreamer as it is for everyone, it is not the whole story. The sexual woman-image is *also* clearly rooted in his mother, so these spiritual feelings for Beatrice cannot be explained simply by the need to deny sexual involvement.

The fact is that themes of incest also point forwards because the universal and taboo-shrouded urge to unite sexually with blood-relatives of the opposite sex, as divinities and royal dynasties used to do, is also a manifestation of the urge towards wholeness. The opposites of masculine and feminine within the one nature do not only fight; they love too, and are drawn together.

A few people (although we are now beginning to realize just how many) act out these urges in waking life and sexually abuse their own children. But for the vast majority it is a drama enacted through imagos of the psyche upon the inner stage.

The thing to grasp is that these female figures in Dr M's dreams do not simply refer outwards to the actual persons; they are the mother-sister-daughter within his psyche, the personified images of the female and feminine *within his own self*. They are archetypal images of his anima.

The relationship between a man's ego and his anima is enormously important and influences the whole course of his life and relationships, just as a woman's ego relationship to her animus is equally important for her. These contrasexual figures within the psyche of both men and women are typically polarized, as Dr M's anima is, between a spiritual pole and a sexual pole.

The vivid and highly charged sexuality of the sexual anima/animus makes for the majority of erotic-sexual dreams, and these are the dreams most readily thought of as erotic. But dreams involving the spiritual anima/animus are actually no less erotic – it is the same love and attraction, but known through the spirit.

Beatrice and W, more often than not, happen to be the actual women whose images appear in his dreams. This is because they provide a visibility together with a ready-made tapestry of emotional associations, through which he can become conscious of his own feminine in 'her' sexual and spiritual energies.

In the following dream, from some months later, Dr M's continuing struggle to harmonize, or at least bring closer together, the sexual and spiritual components of his soul, can be seen to have advanced:

4.4.77

A strangely fascinating and powerful-eyed artist is taking me to meet the very great and very strange woman who lives in a remote and wonderful castle made out of black jet on the outermost rocks of all land, where they finger out to sea. Many others want to see her and have to wait. A servant asks me to come up; I drive along the causeway past a guardhouse where space is so narrow that I can only get in by scraping the sides of the car. Then I'm in a huge baronial kitchen with a sexy looking blonde girl who says we were once lovers; I can't remember but pretend I do; then I feel a powerful presence and turn to see a beautiful dark-haired woman; I know she is the wiser twin sister of the blonde woman.

This is no ordinary woman and she lives in no ordinary place. One can sense how the dreamer struggled to make words convey how impressive it all was to him. The dream is more archetypal than personal; he had, as one might guess, few personal associations to the images. This means that he cannot yet do very much to connect it all up with his individual and daily life, but it promises well.

The castle of the feminine (his anima), he is shown, is to be found at the outermost extremity of land, virtually surrounded by the sea. Translating this into conceptual and psychological language, the place where she exists is on the very boundary between the firm land of his ego-consciousness and the seamless ocean of the collective unconscious. The way he can get in touch with her is through the artist in himself, which is to say that his creativity *is itself* like a road or track connecting ego and anima. She herself, his anima-soul, is still divided; but, as twin sisters, the split seems reduced to a minimum.

KEEPING EROS IN THE DARK

Compared with nightmares and anxiety dreams, the great majority of erotic dreams tend privately to be welcomed — but they are usually kept private too. Not only the earthy end of this great realm of Eros in dreams, but the purest and highest extreme too, tends to be concealed from all but the most deeply trusted; for many this means that erotic dreams are concealed from everyone: a lonely state.

Why should this be so, in our sexually liberal society? Freud's wisdom, rigorous striving for truth, and immense personal courage, played a major part in changing our attitudes towards human sexuality from the guilt and shame-ridden hypocrisy of the nineteenth century into a greater openness, curiosity, and understanding. But changes in *conscious* attitudes can often leap ahead of *unconscious* or *semi-conscious* attitudes which have deep roots and change more slowly.

The detail in which Dr M recorded his erotic dreams is quite uncommon, and requires a sort of courage; he does not conceal everything under some blanket term like 'we made love'. Many people present a bold and rather swaggering ease with sexuality ... until it comes to the intimate reality of their own desires, imaginings, and acts:

A boyish man of nearly forty, a writer, began his analysis with, so it seemed, no particular problem; he just thought it would be a good idea, he said. Perhaps good for his work. He clearly felt he was quite a man for the women and believed himself open-minded and unshockable so far as sex was concerned. The first thing to emerge from this 'regular guy' image was that he actually felt no satisfaction in his many conquests; his erection felt half-hearted and he had to work hard for an orgasm which was a non-event when it came (not with a bang but a whimper).

He was, in fact, largely cut off from his own juiciness so that sex was split into body happenings he could hardly feel and mental experiences of frustration and chagrin.

He remembered no dreams for several months, but then began to dream virtually the same dream over and over again (a dream of a woman who shone like the sun, for whom he felt pure worship). A few months later there came a deluge of dreams, but try as he might he could not tell me them. Weeks went by before he overcame the resistance.

There were dreams in which he was tied on the floor while a cleaning-woman penetrated his anus with the nozzle of her vacuum-cleaner;

dreams in which he was a boy or man dressed up in women's clothes and being sodomized or sucking a man's penis; dreams in which he was a beautiful woman being raped by a huge god-like man with an immense penis.

He was both horrified and delighted by these dreams: horrified because they were perverted, 'unnatural', homosexual, and a shocking confrontation with a part of himself which he refused at first to admit could really be him; and yet delighted because within the dreams he participated in his own sexual arousal and his experiences of orgasm were 'cosmic' in their intensity and completeness.

This man's encounter with his erotic dreams was delayed, dramatic and extreme. A disturbed and sometimes brutal father had made it difficult for him to see any value in men. He had tried to do all the manly things, but without any satisfaction because all his self-worth lay not in his masculine self-image but in his anima, which first appeared in her extreme pole of spirituality.

His sexual imaginings, when they did come, were still centred in his femininity, but they gradually changed and became those of a young boy, part of himself which had seemingly lain buried and unaltered all these years. 'He', this boy-part, grew up surprisingly quickly after coming to light.

SEX AND RELIGION

For most of us erotic dreams come as less of a shock ... but frequently still shocking enough to be kept to ourselves. Sexuality is a wild urge and many of the ways in which it seeks expression are in conflict with civilized and socialized consciousness. In sleep the repressions and prohibitions upon sexual urges are less powerful. Dreams of sexual encounters with people other than one's partner are almost routine. Dreams of sex involving three or four or many people, are quite common, often with some emphasis on seeing one's own partner making love with someone else. Particularly upsetting for many are dreams of incest; mother and daughter are the commonest objects of incestuous desire for men, while sex with father, brother, and mother, appears most often in the dreams of women; but any blood relative, of either sex, may be involved.

Sexual dreams quite commonly involve a lover who is primitive in some way, as if the animal in the human is being emphasized; often they are dark-skinned and extraordinary in their vitality. Dreams of sex with animals are a further extension of this theme. Sexual acts, longings, and satisfactions appear in endless combinations with lavatories, underclothes, excreta, and assorted 'dirtiness'. Heterosexuals find themselves aroused in dreams of homosexuality and vice versa. Fetishes festoon the private chambers of dream; sadism and masochism abound, and so do the secretive delights of voyeurism.

Dreams can bring us all the forbidden fruit from that steamy jungle where every conceivable possibility can take shape and bring pleasure.

Even in the well-boundaried and well-trusted analytic relationship I regularly see reluctance to describe fully the intimate details of erotic dreams. A number of difficulties enter into this reluctance.

For more than a thousand years before modern science began, generations of our ancestors were shaped by the great religions of Judaism and Christianity, both of which regarded sexuality with peculiar suspicion, often verging on open hostility. Despite all the openness Freud helped to bring, such a psychic background does not fade away within two generations. Every culture, past or present, has been and is shaped by its collective beliefs, ultimately by its myths.

Each has its own particular attitudes concerning sexuality so that, for example, what one might call the distortions peculiar to Christianity are noticeably different from the distortions peculiar to Islam. When Freud first began to confront Western man with the sexuality rampant in his unconscious, he was received with extreme hostility; now, however, it is more fashionably liberal to criticize *the Church* for its repression and suppression of sexuality, which may have some justification but may also be short-sighted.

No informed person can doubt the enormous role of sexuality in the overall economy of the psyche and the tendency of the world's major religions to have been hostile towards sexuality is, in a way, reactive acknowledgement of this fact. It is worth remembering that sex is so powerful a numen that it always threatens to be the central sacred experience. What would be wrong with that, you might ask?

In the times and places where this has happened, the consequences have been seen to be so disruptive for human society that sacred sexual cults have either burned themselves out or been stamped out.

The point is that unbridled sexuality tends to transect all developments of spiritual and whole person love by creating mobile sexual liaisons, together with an increasing acting-out of sexual fantasies which often become destructive. There is no getting away from the fact that Mount Venus begins to smoulder very easily, and the Old Cock, who raises his crest at his own will, is not slow to action either. When both have free reign, the changes in sexual partnerships inevitably spin webs of jealousy and hatred.

The spiritual components of love, which are there from the beginning but undoubtedly need time commitment and trust to flower fully, have little

197

chance to grow. Furthermore the stability needed for the parenting of the new generation is threatened. How many marriages would last, and how much sexual attraction would have the chance to mature into deep love if the religions abandoned their age-long cautioning against sexual licence?

So fear of adverse judgement by religious orthodoxy combines with a deep intuitive, and often unconscious, knowledge of the dangers of unbridled sexuality, to make people reluctant to share with others their inner eroticism, or to face it honestly themselves.

Even when the religious values of a particular culture have been taken into account, however, there remains an essential privacy surrounding sexuality which is universal and guarded by shame. Freud and Kinsey have made it possible, for instance, for us to acknowledge that nearly everyone masturbates; that knowledge is now sufficiently in the collective consciousness for every adult to have some idea of it, but the curious thing is that it tends to be accompanied by the notion that simply because we now know it, we should no longer feel any shame when we masturbate.

Why not? Some sense of shame simply does accompany masturbation; that too is a fact and equally deserves acknowledgement, otherwise we start feeling guilty because we are not free enough from hang-ups to feel no shame! Certain ritual acts and abnormal mental conditions aside, no peoples anywhere in the wide world masturbate shamelessly (i.e. with no attempt to conceal the act from others).

All in all one must acknowledge the existence of a natural modesty and need for privacy around our sexual life. To do so makes it easier to look honestly into our erotic dreams, whether they bring us experiences of true love, spiritual and heart-rending, or of physical acts of lust we might prefer to ignore. In their very different ways, both are extremely intimate, revealing vulnerabilities that should, quite rightly, be protected from ribald jokes or unconsidered disapproval.

Eros was the god of love; love may find expression in dreams in an endless variety of ways, some of them seemingly bizarre or ugly or unrealistic or dirty or even evil; but so long as they are to do with the loving potential of that dreamer, they concern something of the utmost importance for that individual. Life is scarcely worth the living without love.

FURTHER READING

Freud, S., *Three Essays on the Theory of Sexuality*, London: Imago Publishing Co.

Jung, C.G., part 2 of 'Symbols of Transformation', in *The Collected Works*, vol. 4, London: Routledge & Kegan Paul.

Jung, C.G., 'Psychological Aspects of the Mother Archetype', in *The Collected Works*, vol. 9, part 1, London: Routledge & Kegan Paul.

Jung, C.G., 'The Syzygy: Anima and Animus', in *The Collected Works*, vol. 9, part 2, London: Routledge & Kegan Paul.

Monick, Eugene, *Phallos: Sacred Image of the Masculine*, Toronto: Inner City Books.

Storr, Anthony, *Sexual Deviation*, London: Penguin.

Fourteen

DREAMS, DAYDREAMS, FANTASIES AND VISIONS

A WOMAN ARRIVED a few minutes early for the second appointment of her analysis and while she was waiting she had a vivid fantasy:

> She was in the room behind my consulting room together with my father who was dressed in a Chinese robe; gravely and wisely he told her, 'My son will help you'.

The following day she had a similar experience:

> This time, again in his Chinese robe, he was taking boxes of rubbish from her and pushing them out to sea.

I was powerfully impressed by these fantasies which seemed to have come with the unexpectedness and clarity almost of visions. Having met for no more than one hour we knew very little of each other at a conscious level; certainly we had not spoken of my father, and yet elements of her vision were uncannily appropriate.

At the time when these events took place he had been dead for more than a decade, but for the last twenty years of his life he had immersed himself in Chinese language, art, philosophy and religion. He had possessed a very special mandarin's robe which he kept in his study; this robe came to me after his death but mysteriously vanished some years later.

The room behind my consulting room is used as a waiting room and she was in there for the first time when she had this fantasy; it contains a number of Chinese ornaments which doubtless provided clues for her imagination. Inasmuch as the waiting room is the room *behind* our own conscious meeting place, I also took its fantasy representation to symbolize

200

the 'room of the unconscious'; rather like the Indonesian puppets whose shadow-play upon the screen reveals the archetypal realm at work behind our manifest world so the room behind the consulting room was being used as a screen for the visualization of archetypal presences behind our conscious and material encounter.

I noted also that the prognostication seemed very favourable, that a kindly and wise father was involved, and that she was evidently laden with unwanted stuff ('rubbish') which needed to be returned into the collective unconscious ('the sea'). Beyond these reflections, I simply wondered and waited. In due time I came to know firstly that she had been profoundly wounded by her father and secondly that she was unusually intuitive, almost mediumistic.

About a year later she appeared in my remembered dreams for the first time:

> I was in my old bedroom in my father's house; there was a double bed there and J (this woman) was in the bed, pulling the bedclothes about her to warm herself up. I was looking through my clothes in the wardrobe, and getting out a green jacket.

The following day when she came for her appointment she told me she had woken during the night feeling very cold (at this point I had not told her of my dream, but we subsequently worked out that the times must have roughly coincided); while trying to get warm she had another fantasy, seeing a figure which now combined me and 'my father' in the one person, again wearing the robe (which I now learned for the first time was of green silk), holding a box labelled BOX which contained rubbish.

Almost immediately after telling me this, and before I had said anything to her, she regressed into the child within her, vividly re-experiencing terror and extreme distress to do with her father beating her and, even more distressingly to her, beating her twin brother.

In this session she did indeed clear out of her system and hand to me a great lump of her 'rubbish'. After the pain had surfaced she gradually recovered her adult self and I then told her my dream, feeling I owed it to her because I could not believe it belonged to me alone. She was touched and grateful, and wondered as I did at the rationally inexplicable and mysterious connectedness of the psyche's imagination.

IMAGINATION

Imagination is a highly prized quality and yet, like fire, it can be a deadly enemy as well as a wonderful servant. It does not, of course, confine its manifestations to the dreams of the night. The waking mind is continuously imaginative and some of its products are not dissimilar to dreams. Daydreams for instance, like night dreams, spontaneously and naturally come to everyone, although some people contrive to remain unaware of them. In point of fact it takes a very considerable effort for consciousness to direct itself in an *unimaginative* way, to think entirely rationally and logically; any relaxation in effort, and imagination will instantly drift in, weaving hopes and fears, possibilities and probabilities.

As I write these words my own* imagination throws an image before me: ego consciousness, like a ball-shaped flickering cluster of lights, floats or hovers above the restless contents of a cauldron; fumes and vapours rise from within the cauldron and coil round and about and through the ego. When ego consciousness is wide awake and full of energy, it both burns more brightly and also rises higher above the cauldron of the unconscious so that the fumes and wraiths which steal through it and coil caressingly about it, become almost transparent in the light of its brilliance. In this energetically charged state the ego possesses vigour enough to rise up above the cauldron's rim and gaze briefly at the outside world — to see, to wonder, and to think.

So much energy is thus consumed, however, that it tires quickly, dims, and sinks that little bit, allowing once again the fumes and vapours to drift their imaginings through its sunlight. In the state of sleep, so much energy is withdrawn from the ego that it subsides deeply and involuntarily into the vapours and on through them down into the cauldron's brew where its now-dimmed lantern wanders the corridors of dream.

Directed attention, focussed concentration, application to and judgement of reality, are efforts for the ego; always, immediately below, the imagination is ceaselessly active and ready to swallow one up. Think of times when you have been tired but in a situation not permitting sleep; driving late at night perhaps; one moment you are squeezing your eyes, trying to maintain focussed concentration on the road, the next you find yourself jerking abruptly out of a stream of fantasy into which you had fallen. It may have taken no more than a split second in 'real' time, but a whole drama, existing in unguessable time, may have enveloped you in that moment.

Such commonplace experiences enable the reflective person to know that the imaginal realm is ever-present; if we are unconscious of it, it is only by

---

*As becomes clear shortly, 'my own' imagination does not mean the imagination that 'I' possess; imagination is not an ego possession; at most the ego has some control over imagination in that it can sometimes shut it out or allow it in at will.

virtue of a minute quantum of energy toning the ego. Moments of 'sleep while awake', though, while useful in reminding us how easy it is for focussed attention to be utterly dissolved, are no more than dramatic extremes. Less dramatic, more part of the normal daily fabric, is the way we relax into imagination after an hour's hard work at the desk; sitting back, removing our eyes from the printed word, gazing out of the window, drifting off into daydream.

Little if anything can be gained by attempting the rigorous definition and separation of daydreams, fantasies, and visions. They are loose and overlapping terms, and better left that way. All of them refer to the influence of the imagination upon consciousness.

It is worth noting that the 'images' of the imagination are not necessarily visual, in fact frequently they are not; daydreams especially, and to a lesser extent fantasies, often come to one as *thought images* which have not yet shaped themselves into words. It seems rather absurd to suggest that visions may not be visual, but it is a fact that people whose imagination does not come to them in clear visual imagery may have experiences which are essentially visionary without there being 'optical' imagery. Having said this, it remains true that visions are typically *visual*.

DAYDREAM

My impression is that most people use the word 'daydream' to refer to wish-fulfilling imaginings, usually involving love-life or ambitions for power, wealth, or recognition — fame and fortune. For instance:

A woman daydreamed while she ate her breakfast: I was sitting on top of a hill looking down at one of those old mills nestling deep in the Yorkshire valleys. I own it. Smoke is rising from the two tall chimneys; the factory is working, steadily, calmly, continuously, making me money. Everything feels secure and stable and I feel relaxed and happy.

Because daydreams belong to the waking state, people have a tendency to believe *they* have *made them up*, and to devalue them for this reason. Only a deeper knowledge of the psyche enables one to realize that daydreams are truly not made up by the ego; rather, they are *made up* in the unconscious and *made known* to the ego when it relaxes focus and allows them in.

Their value should not be underestimated; they are the very shapes of our desires, although, like dreams of the night, they may need to be understood symbolically rather than literally. Whether we know them or not their subliminal but constant presence influences all that we are trying to realize in actual life; all the time we are indeed trying to 'make our dreams come true'.

Those who devalue daydreams can point to some people who, daunted by the challenges of the outside world, give up their attempt to forge their dreams into the flesh and blood and gold and bricks and mortar of reality, and turn hopelessly inwards to live more and more *within* their daydreams, feeding only upon their imaginations. Of course this is failure, and futile, but the failure of some individuals should not make us condemn the creative process of daydream as a whole.

Daydreams reveal to us what we want, and thereby give us direction and purpose so that we can set about the task of getting it, or as close as possible to it, in reality. That is why it is better to be consciously aware of one's daydreams; if they remain unconscious we are even more like moles than we have to be, scrabbling through the darkness to make real an unknown desire; by knowing them we know somewhat more clearly what it is we want and this can help us to make it real.

FANTASY

When ordinary people refer to their fantasies they are usually describing a quite well-defined inner experience of imagination which feels more autonomous than a daydream, and often not so clearly wish-fulfilling. Whereas daydreams are usually drifted into quite voluntarily, with pleasure, fantasies may come upon one quite suddenly and unexpectedly.

Not long after beginning her analysis a woman who was really struggling to keep going despite feelings of worthlessness, found this fantasy coming of its own accord and appearing before her mind's eye:

She saw herself as a gigantic, world-sized snake, coiled into the shape of a cornucopia-like woman; the skin of the snake was richly patterned and although it had no legs, little scarlet toe-nails peeped out at the tip of the tail. The face of the serpent woman, which was swayed to one side of the topmost coil, had long dark lashes, bewitchingly slanted eyes, huge luscious red-painted lips, a tongue ending not in a fork but in a triangle like the devil's tail, and wore a wide hat with a feather boa. Be-ribboned and gift-wrapped presents cascaded from the dark vortex within her spiralling coils.

This fantasy is clearly primitive, in the sense of belonging to an early stage of her feminine development, as if it might have been an unconscious fantasy image from the age of three or four perhaps. It is an image from the collective unconscious and therefore best understood by turning to collective mythic imagery for amplification. Many paintings of Adam and Eve in Paradise show the serpent with the self-same face as Eve. Not only does her fantasy thus link her with the Eve, the 'first woman', whose temptation was irresistible to man, but the link between Eve and the serpent itself points back to the earlier worship of the Earth Goddess, which was supplanted by the later worship of the masculine Sky God.

At the time, she probably knew nothing of the paintings depicting Eve and the snake with the same face, nor knew anything of the history of religions; when she was three or four she would certainly have had no conscious knowledge of all this. But lack of learning made no difference to the intrinsic power of the image, which was charged with immediate meaning. The fantasy brought back to her an image and a feeling of her worth − grossly exaggerated and absurd from the adult point of view of course, but that was not the point. What mattered was that it reconnected her with the time when she *had* felt herself rich with gifts.

But fantasies may look to the future no less than the past. A woman wanting to get to sleep but gripped by obsessional thoughts about a particular person, tried to clear her brain by half-imagining, half-remembering a long walk down an icy mountainside. At first she was trying, creating the images by an act of will; but gradually they came more autonomously. Suddenly she came upon a little old brown man sitting on a rock. He made quite an impression on her: she *knew,* firstly, that he had been through all the passions of life − he'd seen and known and felt it all, so that nothing in her could harm him; she could be, do, and say, whatever she was. Secondly, she *knew* that he could do without people; he no longer minded what they thought of him. This was in stark contrast to her own endless preoccupation with her effect upon others. To have encountered this figure within herself was bound to lead to changes in that direction within her.

Using my image of the ball-of-light ego floating above the fuming cauldron, daydreams might be imagined as a relaxing and dimming of the ego as it allows itself to be aware of the fumes wreathing through it, while fantasies (never forgetting that these two overlap) are more like an unusually potent vapour which envelopes the luminous consciousness by virtue of its own potency.

The contents of fantasies may, like the dreams of sleep, be anything at all: they may be erotic, terrifying, anxious, violent, repulsive, satisfying, instructive. Sometimes, as for instance if one has just been insulted or attacked and then has a fantasy in which one says all the clever and cutting retorts one wished one had said at the time, the connection between fantasy and present mood and circumstances is obvious. But this is not always so; they may just as readily appear to be shockingly incongruous with the consciousness of the moment.

A young social worker, brilliant but undermined by deprivations in his childhood, and now in quite a precarious state of mind, dreamed:

I am sitting at a table and eating with Dad; through the semi-opaque glass door I see a black dog, a bitch, and I feel sexually excited. She comes in, turns into a woman and says, 'I am the Whore; you are going to Hell.' Dad waves his arms about in a feeble way. I try to protect myself by intellectualizing about the forgiveness of sins.

Following this dream, insecure anxiety, never far off anyway, began to mount. Black dogs began to appear in his life at every turn, in outer reality no less than inner imagination. A couple of nights later he dreamed:

I and a number of others are in the service of Omar Sharif (this was a clear link with a prior dream in which he was in the service of an evil king). One of us is a spy who wants to blow up Omar with explosive one-pound coins; somehow the spy is tricked by the others so that what gets blown up is actually a soft round full-fat cheese which is exploded into white fat fragments which fly everywhere.

Clearly there is a sense of danger in the presence of an evil wicked power, but it is far from clear whose wickedness it is. The cheese was a symbol which referred, amongst other things, to the breast, and these dreams had powerful links with his earliest years and the rage aroused in him by privation and subsequent deprivation.

At this primitive level of ego development, to have exploded the good, rich, nourishing breast-mother is bound to be accompanied by extreme anxiety. Words cannot really convey what is pre-verbal, but one might say it is both the fear of being unable to survive without it and also the fear of its retaliation. It is, in effect, being in hell, so long as one understands that 'hell' is initially an experiential state which only later acquires a name and a traditionally based metaphysical elaboration.

The following day growing anxiety began to get out of hand and turn into ungovernable trembling fear, despite his feverish intellectual attempts to convince himself that the eternal damnation of the lost soul was not inevitable because of the forgiveness of sins. At the same time, trying to come at the problem from a different angle, he also noticed his thoughts running over the necessity of evil and sexuality as the initiator(s) of all knowledge.

He knew from previous experience what he had to do to discharge this unmanageable fear; he had to allow a fantasy to surface. He was, quite precisely, caught between the devil and the deep blue sea because fear of

206

the devil drove him to face his fantasies, but the loss of control involved in allowing the fantasy to surface was itself like the fear of drowning. On top of that he knew that the fantasies were usually very disturbing, but that he would have to think about them, try to decipher them, and digest them. There was no choice really, so he went to his room, lay down, and let it in:

There's a big black dog/gorilla with a huge penis under a tree. The Dog explodes into a thousand stars which come down and enter E through his anus and root of his penis; they go up through him and come out of his mouth as ducks which fly off, looking like migrating ducks in early winter, but dropping golden eggs as they fly. The eggs turn into trees with lots of different-coloured flowers on them. Then his mother is lying asleep among the roots of the tree and his father is in the branches; he slithers down like a serpent, though in human form, and offers her a golden apple; she hesitates in taking it and because of her hesitation the serpent-father begins to turn into the dog/gorilla again, so she takes the apple. As she eats it he enters her mouth as a snake and goes into her belly, writhing about inside her in a combination of ecstasy and pain. Now E can 'see' not only the outside form of his mother but her insides too. He sees the serpent-father coil himself around and up her spine in such a way that spine and serpent appear like copulating snakes twined about each other.

At this point the fantasy ended and E found his nervousness was much less but still there. He chose to let more fantasy come up:

He is having sex with a girl (seen at a party the night before); the sex is brutal and defiant and blasphemous (like the couple on the altar).*

Almost immediately this was followed by a further fantasy:

The black dog is lying before him, cut open; it says to him, 'Take any part of me you want.' E takes its kidneys and eats them. Then the snake (dog has become snake) offers him its heart; E holds it, it is as big as a human heart; he eats it; then the snake is entwined with his own spine.

It may not be transparently obvious, but it is possible to see that the same themes of the imagination are appearing in both his dreams and his fantasies, and, although not shown here, they appeared in his daydreams

*This is a reference to a vision he had had about a year previously; it is described on p.209 of this chapter.

too. E guarded these fantasies jealously, both wanting to examine them with me, probe them, and understand them, but also anxiously afraid that any comments I might make would threaten them as if with a butcher's knife. He held all products of his imagination and protected them as if each were a precious divine child.

The content of his fantasy is clearly concerned with the sexuality of the parents, which is portrayed through the medium of Judeo-Christian mythic imagery with all the attendant allusions to good and evil and knowledge.

As happens so very often, the mythic collective imagery of the psyche illuminates and offers a depth of understanding to the vicissitudes and mysteriously painful complexities of personal development.

No less important therapeutically than the content, however, was his attitude towards it and me. I could know from his attitude how much the adults who parented him had failed to value, or had even butchered, his imagination, which was exceptionally vivid and strong, and hence one of his 'treasures'.*

Fantasies tend to be visual more often than daydreams, although this distinction is almost obscured by the differences existing between individuals. People vary greatly in how visible they find their imaginative process; some almost always see in pictures, some 'see' in pre-verbal thought-images, some 'see' in body postures and movements. From the point of view of the purpose of imagination, it really does not matter which it is and those who do not naturally see pictures are wasting their energy if they strive to do so. The thought-images of their imagination have exactly the same value and meaning as more visual images would in someone with a visual imagination.

It also tends to be true, as illustrated by E's fantasies, that fantasies are organized with more complexity and with more distinct elaboration than most of the dreams of sleep. On the other hand they are less 'flexible' than most daydreams, which is to say that ego consciousness plays a greater part in the daydream choices.

VISIONS

Visions are generally understood to be more autonomous than fantasies which, in turn, are more autonomous than daydreams.

Visions flood the waking ego consciousness, coming quite unexpectedly and often shockingly. At times when someone is having numbers of visions it is quite common for their dreams to show inundations by one or other

*This was why the explosive device was 'money'; his valuable imagination, being unappreciated, became explosive.

of the elements, most often water in the form of a tidal wave sweeping across the land, but sometimes a violent wind which flings open a door and blows the dreamer off his feet, or, less commonly still, a fire which erupts, a volcano for instance, or a forest fire.

Visions may be momentary and fragmentary, or they may be extremely long, lasting for hours, and very organized, complex, and 'complete'. They may be experienced as remote, in the sense of having no apparent connection with one's life or meaning; or they may, like Saul/Paul's vision, be the realization of truth, meaning and destiny, so profound that the course of life is changed once and for all.

Visions are feared and desired in equal measure; modern anthropological research has underlined how universal is the desire to induce states of trance and vision, and discovered the commonality of the entoptic patterns which manifest in early stages of trance vision. Although these lines and dots of light are more noticeable in deliberate trance inductions, they are quite often noticed beforehand by those about to experience spontaneous visions. Visions may also be regarded as more likely to obliterate outer perceptual reality than fantasies; this clearly verges on another overlapping term — hallucination.

E's fantasy (see above) made reference to a vision he had had about a year previously, before he began his analysis. It had frightened him a lot and probably played a part in his decision to enter analysis.

Many years of struggle against a despair close below the surface, and an unwelcome but unrelenting awareness of the evil of the world, had led him to a puritanical attitude. He had begun seriously to consider leaving University and going East to become a Buddhist monk. No more than dimly conscious at that time, perhaps, but retrospectively realized in the course of his analysis, there existed within him an enormous rage at the absent father/god, and omnipotent fantasies involving the destruction of his parents which, though unconscious in the main, nevertheless lay coiled around the roots of his being and were the source of his massive insecurity and anxiety.

He was alone one day in his room at University, feeling uneasy and restless, when with shocking suddenness he saw a vision of a man and a woman having sex upon a church altar. Their intercourse was brutal, animal, unbridled lust; but he could see in their facial expressions that their souls were far from absent; they were deliberately, defiantly, rebelliously, flinging the act into God's face; a chosen blasphemy.

E fled the room, very shaken, fearing madness and fearing to return to his room as if the evil madness might still be clinging to its very walls; he walked for hours before he returned.

Many find themselves considering the monastic life from time to time, and most know that they would never really do it; they are simply toying with the momentarily attractive idea of a retreat from the world when everything feels too messy and difficult. Among those few who actually do try to enter monastic life there are some who are seeking escape from psychological problems rather than following their vocation. Some of these are redirected towards more appropriate help before they enter monastic life; some get through, only to break down sooner or later and then leave, usually in a terrible mess; and some, like E, are warned beforehand from within. His vision was compensatory to his conscious desire to live in obedient chastity; it confronted him with another and hitherto less conscious part of himself which he could not ignore. The intention to become a monk faded away, and not so very long after he began analysis.

E's vision, though powerful, lasted only a few moments and did not take over his ego consciousness completely. By contrast the following vision, experienced by a middle-aged woman, lasted most of a day in the sense that she had no awareness of her surroundings for many hours.

Although in many ways a sophisticated and cosmopolitan woman, and a loving mother, there continued to exist within her an undeveloped part of herself which could not tolerate separation; this manifested in obsessive jealousy and a tendency to violent outbursts. The vision was triggered when a man with whom she had recently fallen in love rejected her. The moment he spoke of his intention to leave she turned from him and ran headlong into a forest, crashing through the undergrowth until she was exhausted and flung herself to the ground:

> The next thing she knew she was in a cathedral. She was moving through it, possessed by cold fury, smashing it up methodically. When she broke the cross, blood came foaming from its shattered parts. Then gouts of blood began to spurt from her mouth, thrown up violently by her stomach. Now the cathedral was gone; she was lying on the forest floor, blood about and beneath her. All around her black men stood in a silent circle; she noticed that they, and she too, were transparent. Again blood began to gush from her stomach out of her mouth, but now it was black.

Her sense of time and everyday reality did not return to her until near evening. She could not tell whether the vision had lasted all the time or whether she had fallen unconscious after it. So vivid was her recounting of the vision that I had to ask whether she really had found herself in blood when she came to.

The same destructive passion which appears in this vision also brought about a termination of her analysis not long after (although she resumed it about a year later), and exploration of its meaning for her remained incomplete. But it is nevertheless clear* that uncontrollable fury makes her smash the very symbols of goodness, the containing Mother Church and the redemptive Cross of Christ. That she does this to herself, or within herself, is shown by the bleeding cross becoming her own bleeding stomach. It is followed by black despair.

During the course of the three-month sequence of dreams we followed in Chapters six and seven, Dr M had a number of fantasies and visions. To understand them best they should be read in conjunction with his dreams and the accompanying comments; but it is also interesting to see them on their own, unfolding in chronological order:

8.10.76   Woke with surging and very vivid memories of home when I was young.

9.10.76   Fantasy/memories of early childhood; father killing a chicken; mother catching a fish in her hand; grass snakes and grasshoppers.

16.10.76   Remarkably vivid and totally unexpected image, clear as a vision, of a green snake coiled round a large black egg. I haven't the faintest idea what to make of it.

17.10.76   More startling images, which came at sunset: a furnace door, closed, but bulging with the heat inside; volcanic lava; fire.

25.10.76   Late evening: began as memory and then took on life of its own; half-known half-seen but very strong impression that I am in the nave of Westminster Abbey; shaft of light comes vertically from above; then walking north transcept and see fiery triangle.

26.10.76   Waking fantasy with thought/image mixtures of new moon and Venus; in one I breathed out a moonbeam; in another I climbed a moonshine ladder into Heaven.

28.10.76   Waking visual fantasy: I am in vast dark sphere, or castle or cathedral; scraping away black gravel to find a burning triangle on a white background.

2.11.76   Vivid thoughts/images of church, cross, Jesus, cross within circle; realization that Jesus, living within me, can actually turn his eye, which is his seeing-heart, upon me as individual.

7.11.76   Fantasy of being in dark cathedral; find huge grey stone column, tie myself to it with long rope, then explore and find little blind-ended grey stone chamber; inside I find a red triangle on wall, smoking and glowing.

*She was a Catholic.

23.11.76   While reflecting on Christ and the cross, a sudden image of black sun as *the source of darkness* which has knowing in it.

FURTHER READING

Jung, C.G., 'The Transcendent Function', in *The Collected Works*, vol. 8, London: Routledge & Kegan Paul.

Jung, C.G., 'The Undiscovered Self (present and future)', in *The Collected Works*, vol. 10, London: Routledge & Kegan Paul.

Meyrink, Gustav, *The Golem*, London: Dedalus European Classics.

Fifteen

COMMON TO ALL

DREAMS DO FOR US what all the rest of our life-experience does for us too: they knit together in the most seamless way the *uniquely individual* and the *common-to-all*.

In all the previous chapters I have placed emphasis on the importance of *personal* associations, the links that engage the dream with the unique individuality and day-to-day life of the dreamer.

I have had good reason to do so. If people are not in therapy, and are not deeply versed in dreams, they tend quite naturally to look for ready-made interpretations. When these are found − in symbol dictionaries or magazines or teletext interpreters − they cannot possibly take account of the personal threads; they may be accurate, and they may be interesting, but they must be operating at the collective level, the common-to-all.

If one does not sniff out and follow through the personal connections, a dream-understanding based in the collective remains detached from life as it is actually lived. It is like seeing something through the wrong end of a telescope: far-off and like another world.

But the collective aspect of dreams is no less important in dreams than it is in the rest of life. My mother may be *my* mother, towards whom I have all my uniquely personal feelings; but these would have no context for meaning whatever were she not also *a* mother, more or less like all the mothers there have ever been. We have a collective attitude towards *the mother* and it may be valuable for me to compare *my* attitude towards *my* mother with this huge collective attitude to *the* mother which has formed over aeons.

This final chapter, then, explores those ingredients of dreams where meanings are not personal but are common-to-all. Usually this constitutes the background against which the dreamer as an individual acts and reacts in the foreground. But this is not always so, as we shall see; some dreams are so filled with the collective that the dreamer is speechless when it comes to finding links with his own personal life.

THE FOUR ELEMENTS

Human consciousness, as Jung has pointed out, has a distinct tendency to grapple with allness, everythingness, by dividing it into four, quartering the circle. The four points of the compass, the four winds, and the four elements are obvious examples.

Being primary divisions of all-oneness into only four conscious distinctions, each of the four must necessarily be subtle and many-sided enough to represent one quarter of all possible experience. Earth, air, fire, and water, the four elements, were for millennia among the few fundamental conceptual bases upon which human consciousness struggled to develop conscious orientation out of the all-in-oneness of unconscious experience.

This might seem irrelevant for today's consciousness; not many of us continue to make conscious use of the four elements as a divisionary structure for understanding. But our dream symbolism arises from our unconscious, and down there the ways of the past still exist in the present.*

Water

I'm standing on the deck of a boat looking down into the strange sea; I'm fascinated by the water; I see the pale shapes of innumerable fish and know the sea is exceptionally full of life. Then a strange wave forms itself on the surface, much bigger than others and moving as if with a will of its own; I know somehow that this is a round sea, and now it is hollowing itself out at the centre like an immense whirlpool. My boat is drawn into it and moves round and round the walls; through the glassy surface the moving water is filled with wild, turbulent, beautiful shapes; the textures and colours of this rotating wall of water are both frozen static and also full of life and movement.

The woman who dreamed this was a doctor in a London hospital. She had not even seen the sea for years, let alone been on a boat. She truly had no personal associations at all. But she had certain feelings and intuitions. She felt excited and rather nervous, like someone approaching a big event. She

---

*Psyche, no less than body, is *evolved*; behind its 'state of the art' presentness lies the unconscious wisdom-from-experience of all evolution. Exploration of the psyche, just like exploration of the body, reveals that psyche and soma both operate from bases so ancient that even the recorded history of our species is no more than a superficial layer.

had the sense, she said, that she was being drawn inexorably into a state of fascination by the depths of the human mind, or soul.

She was using her innate understanding of dream symbolism, and using it well. She did not have to have learned that the ocean symbolizes the mind, and more specifically the collective unconscious — she *intuited and felt* it. Some time later she changed the direction of her career and began to work with the human soul.

The joy and reverence of her dream-ego for the life-filled depths of this self-willed sea, showed that the descent of her ego into the unconscious is not a catastrophe but a true development of her self.

Earth

3.2.77 A difficult dream to describe; I am both in a house and also seeing it from outside; it is both my house and my father's house; there comes a moment of pregnant terrible stillness and then an earthquake splits the house into quarter and three-quarters.

A few more personal links come into this dream than the previous one, but the main event is the earthquake which is at a different level altogether.

We know from the sequence of dreams in Chapters 6 and 7 that the dreamer was involved in separating psychologically from an identification with his father. In this dream we see that a division takes place, but the earthquake symbolizes how deep in the collective ground of his being this event has to be.

Separating from archetypal identifications cannot be brought about by conscious will alone; something deep in our collective nature has to act too. In the months and years after this dream he did indeed become more 'his own man'.

Fire

I am alone upon a great plain, feeling very remote from everyone and everything, walking endlessly though I don't know where. Far away ahead of me a volcano erupts. I see plumes of black ash and red fire cascading, but feel nothing where I am. Now I know where I am going.

The dreamer was an artist who had isolated himself for months while he worked with a growing sense of desolation upon his paintings. Some six months after this dream he began analysis and within days an uprush of rage-filled images poured out in dreams and fantasies.

Air

I enter a room, crawling like a child; the room has only three walls, the fourth side open to the world. My mother is lying on a couch, ill or damaged badly. I feel terrible. I manage to stand up and lean against a wall but then a mighty cold wind blows. With the missing wall there is no protection from it.

The dreamer was a young man who had had to drop out of University because he had begun to fear for his sanity and could no longer study.

The dream shows that his resources at present are those of a young child. There is no help to be had from his mother; quite the reverse; her condition causes him terrible concern.

But these predominantly personal symbols are presented within a context of collective symbols which tell more about the dreadful state he is in. The room has only three walls, the fourth side being open to the world. This means that the boundary separating his personal ego from the collective is partially missing. Between the house, or room, and the world at large there should be doors which can be opened and closed at will.

Then there is the wind: a mighty cold wind from which he has no protection because of the missing wall. Wind symbolizes collective spirit and intellect, the coldness indicating that it is devoid of feeling, remote from any living worldliness.

And this was exactly the case for him. At one and the same time he was both a child in desperate need of holding and loving understanding, and an impersonal, extraordinarily brilliant philosopher/theologian because he had become a mouthpiece for collective spirit. Philosophical and religious ideas of a completely collective nature were streaming into his consciousness without his being able to shut them out when he'd had enough, or digest them into his own personal context.

He was losing *his* mind and being taken over by *collective* mind. Had he not found help he might well have gone irretrievably mad.

Each of these dreams has illustrated a dream-ego experiencing some movement in their collective psyche, which has found symbolic portrayal as an elemental force. But ocean is not the one and only form taken by the *water*, nor is volcano the only form of *fire*, and so on.

Earth, air, fire and water can each manifest in an infinite variety of forms: water in the form of a scalding geyser will not symbolize the same thing as water as whirlpool or water as snow. But we all possess some capacity to sense the inner common-to-all meaning being represented by every different form; each according to our gifts, we can feel and intuit our way down and into the natural world and *know* what psyche means by clothing its invisibility in this or that particular shape of nature.

When finding one's way into the meaning of the elements, it is worth considering the following general points:

Water

symbolizes psyche, predominantly unconscious, in its fluid, mobile and life-generating aspects, with a particular aptitude to represent *as-yet unconscious feelings* and emotions. Water in its solid form − ice − is the cold hard feeling one may see in an icy look, or the frozen emotions that may make a mask of the face.

One should consider whether a dream shows there is too little water (I'm in a parched land; nothing is growing; my mouth is dry'), or too much ('There's been a flood and it threatens my house'). And what is the dream-ego's attitude towards the water? If there's too little, does it know it wants more? If there's too much, does it fear inundation, drowning, suffocation, or being swept away? Or does it seem to be unaware?

Is the water pure, or mixed with another element? Naturally enough, the elements are often admixed one with another: water and fire, for instance, might appear as dream images of hot water e.g. hot pissing or hot tears or steam; water and earth might appear in dream images of swamps, bogs, with the fear of being sucked in.

Earth

being the most clotted, thick, dense and dark of the four elements, is all too easily regarded as the least 'psychic'. It is the element hardest to understand, especially because our so-called materialistic society is actually quite hostile to matter. Earth does not symbolize matter as opposed to psyche, it symbolizes *psyche as matter*, and many people seem constantly to be trying to get away from this, trying to escape it because it is seen as dirty, binding, limiting, heavy.

Earth and air, being the two elements upon which we are most immediately dependent, naturally appear in almost every dream in the most literal sense of there being ground and solid objects and air to breathe, but at this level elemental interpretations, although they might be philosophically relevant, would fail to take account of the point of the dream from a psychological perspective.

Earth only becomes relevant for elemental interpretation when the dream focus is on the substance itself as, for example, when the earth itself moves in an earthquake or avalanche, or when the dream-ego struggles through sand, or handles clay, or faeces, or when it goes below

217

ground as in dreams of tunnels, caves, basements, graves, etc. so that the dream-ego is then inside the earth.

When psyche clothes itself in the element earth it is representing that part of itself which is usually deeply unconscious, wholly dark, slow to change, in which things may be buried, but from which things may grow.

The earth element appears a lot in the dreams of those who suffer psychosomatic illness. A woman with various disorders recognized to be psychosomatic, for instance, dreamed repeatedly of uncovering things (such as a bird and a little girl) from the earth in which they had been buried.

Air

symbolizes psyche at its most mobile, most free. In the greater sense it is psyche as spirit which 'bloweth where it listeth'; in the more limited sense it is psyche as ideas and intellect with their winged quality, darting hither and thither, rising high above, then swooping down.

This is what our society truly values; our 'materialism' is not really a love of matter, it is more correctly a delight in 'mind over matter', and so, just as there is a wish to escape the earth element, there is also a marked tendency to take to the air element (e.g. dreams of flying or climbing high places until one reaches the summit where the ground beneath one's feet is minimal and airy height is all around).

As with all the elements, admixtures are important to note: air, still or active, may be hot or cold, mixed with water as rain, or with earth as blown dust, etc.

Strong winds in dreams mean the ego is exposed to fierce movements of the spirit; whether exhilarating or terrifying they will affect conscious balance. If blown off one's feet by a dream-wind there will be a risk of waking manic behaviour.

Fire

symbolizes psyche as passion and imagination, ever-hungry, devouring, dangerously quick to get out of control and highly liable to destroy, but, if only it can be sufficiently controlled, purifying, creative, bringing warmth and illumination to the ego.

Fire is the only element which, in its pure form, has no living creatures natural to it. From the point of view of dream symbolism the creatures proper to each element may be regarded as more differentiated and specific symbols for that element.

[Fishes, sharks, crabs, octopi, for example, *mean* water and water means them, so that catching and eating a fish means an integration of something from the watery element, while threat from a shark means danger of some (or all) ego being engulfed by the watery element.

To the air belongs the birds like winged thought* (of which the eagle is the commonest representative in dreams), and to the earth the worms, insects, beetles, and snakes (the last being the commonest in dreams).†]

But fire has only imaginal creatures such as dragon, phoenix, and salamander. And indeed fire is, in a sense, the most unhuman of the elements, the most holy or unholy. It is the nearest to pure energy, the least material in itself.

If a dream shows fire breaking out on any sizeable scale one may be sure that a passion has been inflamed, that imagination is getting out of control, whether this is conscious or not. Conversely, control and management of fire in dreams, indicates the harnessing of raw passion and imagination.

In either case it is worth remembering that passions, once they have been brought to life, govern an individual more than anything else.

When the elements appear in huge or overwhelming form in dreams, especially in a natural and collective setting, the main difficulty lies in integrating their meaning into personal life. But when, as is far more common, dreams portray situations and events which are predominantly personal the difficulty lies more in noticing the meaningful presence of the elements *at all* because they appear in ways which are so familiar to us that we take them for granted. We may notice the swimming pool, for instance, or the mountain in the distance, or the fire in the drawing room, or the wind howling outside the house, and yet not pause to consider the meaning for us of these collective elements.

Such apparently routine relations with the elements do not demand interpretation with the same urgency as dreams like the four above; but it can nevertheless be extraordinarily useful to consider them. They offer a fundamental sense of orientation in self-understanding.

POINTS OF THE COMPASS

The four directions — North, South, East, and West — are another four-fold orientation of consciousness as ancient as ancient can be. They

---

*See dream of seagulls below, under 'animals' heading.
†All the living things that walk as we do upon the surface of the earth, and participate as we do in all the elements, are thereby closer to us and we can identify with them more readily than we can with creatures belonging to one element alone.

divide all-in-oneness into 'whereness' in the same way as the elements divide all-in-oneness into 'whatness'.

Both are such ancient, primary, and simple divisions of consciousness that there is naturally considerable overlap and much that has been said in general terms about the four elements applies also to the four directions. Points of the compass appear quite often in dreams, though not as often as the elements.

A woman, in analysis, whose sexuality was blocked by some involuntary inhibition had turned most of her conscious energies towards mysticism. At a time when she was trying to decide whether to give up the attempt to free her sexuality, she dreamed:

> I am trying to catch a train North to Scotland but when the train has started I discover I've got on the wrong one; this one is going South to Venice. I keep trying to get North, but every time I find the same thing has happened again and I'm going South. Eventually I think, Maybe I'm meant to go to Venice. Then I begin to like the idea.

This same theme was repeated in several dreams, sometimes involving planes or cars instead of trains. Her personal associations to Scotland and Venice corresponded perfectly with the collective associations for North and South (see below), and she decided she had to continue her attempt to recover her sexuality.

In the northern hemisphere, at least, the collective meanings of the points of the compass may be summarized as follows:

> **North** as mystical, blue, ascetic, cold, bleak, empty, uncivilized and wild.
> **South** as sensual, sexual, red, warm, teeming with life.
> **East** as place of sunrise, beginnings, new hope, secret possibilities and things yet unknown.
> **West** as place of sunset, the beautiful tragic death, the end, the long journey home, things known and done.*

*The cross formed by the four directions also has resonances with the cross of Christianity: the vertical axis (North/South) holds a tension of opposites such as asceticism/sensuality, spirit/matter, good/evil, mysticism/sexuality, which are essentially not temporal but eternal.

It is cut across by the horizontal axis (East/West) which stands for the temporal, the day by day, year by year, the journey of life from beginning to end, the world as it is, the incarnated individual.

To see oneself as crucified upon the cross of the four directions may provide a valuable access to the inner Christ.

The points of the compass actually participate in more dreams than it might seem. Having no visual presence they tend to be an invisible and often unremarked background knowledge. But, if they ask themselves, a lot of people discover they do have a distinct sense of orientation throughout the dream, even though they had not thought about it; they find themselves able to say, for instance: 'Yes, the road was running north, and so when I took the right turning I must have been going east.'

TIME

As the four elements deal with the whatness, and the four directions with the whereness, so time deals with the when-ness of the 'all-in-one'.

In the four seasons we see the same tendency for consciousness to divide wholeness into four, multiples of which also appear in the twenty-four-hour clock and the twelve months.

In one way or another time is woven into every dream although, as anyone with the slightest familiarity with their inner world must know, our inner experiences of time, timelessness, eternity, and simultaneity, are bewilderingly subtle and complex and not at all ruled by the linear time sense of alert intellectual consciousness. The following dream rather sums up the ego's nightly journeys into the unconscious:

14.2.77 I'm with a mysterious older man/girl; he/she takes me into silver rocket which transcends space/time; this is how he/she can appear anytime anywhere, and different places at the same time.

Very specific clock times (e.g. I arrived at Alice's house at ten past three) often come into dreams. Usually the associations to them are personal, although they sometimes remain a mystery. Sometimes they are collective, as when the hours of the day are linked with the journey of the sun which is linked in turn with the course of one's life.*

The same is true for the year; describing a complete circle around the sun it can also symbolize a complete lifetime; a man of thirty-five dreamed:

It is high summer and the sun is blazing down on me; I feel weak and listless. An old woman is sitting in the shade of a tree with a baby by her side; somehow she shows me I am wearing a crown, but it is made of tin or paper; she says the baby was born in January and gives me a meaningful look which I understand and don't understand at the same time.

*e.g. the dream in Ch.5, p.63.

Discussing it later this man felt the old woman was telling him to 'remember' or go back to January, i.e. the beginning of his life, because the crown he was still wearing had something to do with his own (inner) baby.

The four seasons have meanings which overlap with the four elements and the four directions e.g. spring/air/east; summer/fire/south; autumn/ water/west; winter/earth/north. The dream-seasons often refer to the seasons of life (e.g. 'in the winter of his life').

Dreams referring to specific years, or set either in the future or in the past, usually have a combination of personal associations and collective associations which are historically familiar to collective consciousness* or arise from popular collective fantasies about the future.

Rather less easily recognized is *mythic time*. It has to be understood that our linear reckoning of time is itself contained within mythic aeons. When a new myth grips a people they feel as if time has begun anew and they start a new reckoning of the years, e.g. time BC and then time AD.

Conscious appreciation of the supraordinate importance of mythic over linear time may be rather hazy for most individuals, but it is nevertheless 'understood' in the collective unconscious and certainly features in dreams:

> 29.11.76 I arrive back home and find many people there. Then my home and L.House are confused; Daddy is in the family-room, which is thick with dust and insect-ridden; his fire is nearly out so I add more fuel. I go upstairs and find all in decay; Justin and his father are there but their room is so decayed it needs fumigation — if savable at all.
>
> Then with W in our bedroom, which seems OK except for some smoke coming through from the kitchen despite a hairy partition.
>
> Then back again with Daddy who's sitting in a strange old chair made out of a cow-bones and cow-hide; all around him are his stones and military medals, his microscope and books; everything is getting old and dusty. I'm forced to realize his time is nearly done.

We know he has been struggling to separate himself from his unconscious identity with the traditional paternal god-image. In this dream the old myth is shown to be on its last legs, its fire almost dead, its substance being

---

*A true instance, although it sounds like a cartoon cliché, was a man fascinated by Napoleon: shortly before a mental breakdown he dreamed he came to a door with the number 1815 upon it!

returned to dust by the deconstructive work of insects, its symbols of power old and disused.

The final death of the old myth may be understood to have happened at the time of the earthquake dream (see p.215), which split the house that had been both his and his father's.

The new myth, which does not appear in this dream but glints here and there through many others we have seen, involves a higher valuation of the feminine, ultimately involving her inclusion into his god-image.

People often feel anxious about the prophetic possibilities of dreams. If I'm planning to take my children to a fair and then dream my daughter has fallen from a roller-coaster and died, does this mean she is going to die? Or that I should not go to the fair?

This sort of direct foretelling of the future is extremely uncommon, although something quite like it does occasionally happen:

> Just as I was falling asleep I distinctly heard my father's voice, as if from far away, calling my name. It woke me wide awake and I had to stare around the room although I knew perfectly well he was not there.
>
> In a dream that night I was told that he had died.

The dreamer was in America and had been out of touch with her father for a long time. She telephoned and discovered he was not dead, but had fallen ill. He died some six months later.

Although no more than a tiny minority of dreams are prophetic in any literal sense, all dreams are concerned with the future in the sense that they deal with the unfolding of the self, the realizing of innate possibilities. Many of the dreams used as illustrations throughout this book have pointed the way ahead in terms of developments to come (see, e.g., the first 'overture' dream in Ch.6, p.75).

COLOURS

Colour symbolism is very common in dreams. Everyone has their own personal associations to colours and these are often more immediately relevant. But there are collective associations to colours, which tend to be quite well known, and therefore easily considered.

The spectrum runs from ultra-violet to infra-red. The two extremes, being invisible, may be understood to symbolize on the one hand that essential spirit which is unknowable-in-itself, and on the other that essential instinct which is unknowable-in-itself.

Between these invisible poles lie the visible colours: blue symbolizing

223

mind, perceivable expressions of spirit and intellect, cool and calm. Red is blood passion, perceivable arousals of instinct, hot, dangerous, exciting. Green is life. Purple is imperial. Brown is earthy. Yellow and orange are to do with light and fire. Black, being the absence of all colour is death, depression, ignorance, frightening, unknown, impure, evil. White, being all colours, is life, joy, knowledge, safety, goodness, purity.

The two main polar opposites, most collective and most often carrying meaning in dreams, are white/black, and blue/red. Other colours tend to be more influenced by personal meanings.

OVERWORLD, WORLD, UNDERWORLD

All mythologies divide the all-in-oneness into a number of realms which were perhaps believed literally when what we now call myths were still living religions. No longer literally and consciously believed, these realms nevertheless still mean something to us, and dream-allusions to them are commonplace.

The arrangement, broadly speaking, consists of an upper realm of supernal gods associated with light, spirit, and good, a middle realm of mankind, and a lower realm of infernal gods associated with darkness, materialism, and evil. To hold awareness of these collective insights while working with one's dreams can be valuable. Obviously enough, the better one knows the myths the more they will amplify and illuminate the dream images.

14.10.76
(a) I'm sharing an hotel bedroom with an American man who is reading a book on spiritualism; we both smoke cigars; I notice the book has an erotic picture of two girls on the cover. He tells me he gets nervous with any girl but his wife; consent is necessary.
(b) In St Tropez with W and kids. I climb up a brightly coloured path like a rainbow that rises, unsupported, high in the air. Soon the world is far below; I get dizzy, nearly fall. See old Chinese woman with three daughters; she falls.

On the ground again. She has hurt her hip; then she vanishes. Using magic power I summon her return out of the sky. Now at their home, but she is gone again. I realize I love a different one of her daughters and kiss her, then say I must get the old woman's belt to bring her back. We find a black silk belt with ABRAXAS stitched in gold; we walk through the garden until I can see the sun; I seem to see two suns, but my girl tells me the other is not a sun but the Moon or Star. We hold the belt out and I invoke ABRAXAS. Instantly a huge Negro boxer bursts out from house outraged by the invocation.

(c) On St Tropez beach; thousands, of all ages, all in vast sexual game;
I see only a writhing mass of breasts, buttocks, thighs, genitals, mouths.
I'm excited and disgusted.

He is caught between spirit and sex. Somewhat like Icarus, his spirit chafes
at the gravitational (and specifically sexual) pull of the material world. He
tried to rise above it, but humans are not designed to walk on rainbows. He
falls back to earth. So he cannot be an angel. Fair enough, but what can
he do about this pull of opposites, from which he has not escaped? Through
the feminine, the old woman and her daugther, he invokes Abraxas, an
ancient god reputed to contain and reconcile the Godly and the Satanic.

In ordinary personal terms this would mean something like coming to
terms with the conflicts between noble ideals and physical appetites;
accepting that both were in him, and he could not get rid of the 'Old
Adam'. But these dilemmas are never just 'simply personal'. They are
archetypal and universal; consciously or unconsciously the 'gods' are
involved.

Some of the commonest ways in which the yearnings of the spirit take the
dream-ego towards the overworld are dreams of flying (especially
'unassisted' flying, but also flying in planes and rockets, etc.), or being on
top of very high places and looking down, or sometimes a rising up above
the world, as if carried straight up by an invisible elevator.

Such dream elevations may follow, or be accompanied by, dream flights
of brilliant talking, soaring ideas, lofty insights. Often they are
accompanied by vertigo as the earth element pulls ever more strongly,
attempting to maintain the correct human level which necessarily has its
space between the overworld and underworld, with part of its nature in
each.

When the dream-ego is down in the underworld it tends to feel trapped,
suffocated, entombed, dirtied, etc. But there is a redeeming feature.
Material treasures are to be found in the underworld; Pluto was the 'Rich
One'. Gold, gems, oil, coal.

The underworld can be divided into two: the earth element underworld
(of e.g. Pluto) and the water element underworld (of e.g. Poseidon).
Common instances of the former are travelling in the Underground, being
in basements, entering caves, tunnels, graves and tombs; while the latter are
partial or total immersion in water. In either case it is now the air element
which exerts an upward pull:

I'm strolling through Windsor, feeling happy and carefree; I fancy some
coffee and apple-pie. In a square I do not know an attractive woman says

she can give me the best apple-pie. Then I'm in a dingy cellar surrounded by half-dead men whose faces are smeared with pale paint – zombies. The owner is a huge swarthy man. He questions me as if I'm a drug-addict. I try to argue but feel my will draining away and my thoughts drying up. I begin to feel paralyzed, rooted to the spot. I need air but can't see the way out.*

'Out of the world' dreams of a rather different kind may represent the ego's experience of alienation:

I am clinging onto a some sort of metal scaffolding in cold dark of outer space.

This was dreamed by a middle-aged woman who had broken off relationships all through her life and, at the time of the dream, had lived in complete emotional isolation for years. She could remember almost nothing of her childhood; she felt nothing but an unassuagable craving for warmth and connection. All the circumstantial evidence suggested her mother had been depressed when she was born and she (the mother) had died a few years later.

Such dreams do still find amplification in the myths (not that it makes the slightest difference to a dreamer in such a condition), but one has to look back into the earliest cycle, the creation myths. In the Greek myths, for instance, this dream would relate to the cold darkness of Uranus *before* he united with Gaia, the earth goddess, and began the generations of gods, mortals, and all life.

In human terms the suffering of such states, the anguish of unrelatedness and not belonging, is quite terrible.

SUPERNATURAL

Gods, devils, angels, demons, ghosts, witches, wizards, sorcerers, and all varieties of magical happenings may appear before us in our dreams:

A young prostitute dreamed: I am staying in a house run by a couple. I keep getting lost in the corridors as if the house changes shape whenever I try to get somewhere. In the night I pass a door and see the man with

*Homer's descriptions of the 'shades' in the underworld of Hades has remarkable similarities: loss of courage, will, memory, and thought; also the tendency to become stuck in the place. These mythological and dream images are easy to link with states we now call depression (which also involves the image of an ego *pressed down*).

his back to me. He is holding a wand; I realize he is a black magician. Then I'm waking up to find his witch wife menacing me.

A supernatural quality always indicates an archetypal, hence collective, component to the image.

The archetypes are the eternal, collective, innate structures of the psyche. Invisible and unknowable in themselves, their existence can be inferred, and known as far as it can be known, by sensing the commonality within swarms of archetypal images which cluster into groups. At the invisible centre of each group, as it were, lies the archetype itself.

Study of them, albeit indirect, reveals that we apprehend the archetypes in terms of two characteristic pairs of opposites:

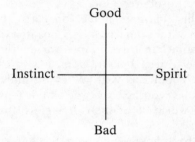

The archetype of the father, for instance, may be inferred to lie at the core of a swarm of images all characterizing aspects of 'fatherliness'. Behind or within all the various images lies his central and invisible mystery within which are contained the tension of both pairs of opposites: 'he' is good and bad, instinctual and spiritual.

Each actual image, however, tends to represent one or two aspects only. If the 'bad' father, for instance, is allied with the 'spirit' father, then the actual image could be some sort of devil, or black magician. Or if the 'good' father is combined with the 'spirit' father, the image might be God the Father-like, or good wizard-like, and so on.

Because the spirit component of the archetype *does* transcend the natural world of matter, it is, in this sense, 'supernatural' and most definitely belongs to the collective unconscious, not the personal. It is a disaster if the ego becomes overwhelmed by their power.

But if the ego can become strong and self-knowing enough to cope with the natural fear of their uncanny power, it is possible to establish relationship between ego and archetype via the image. To do so is to add an unusual, powerful, enriching depth to the personality.

Extreme caution is needed however. The task for a still weak and defensive ego is quite simply not to be overcome by the archetypal powers.

HOME

Home is a word, the meaning of which seems obvious at first, but the more one tries to catch the heart of the meaning, the more it recedes before one.

Ultimately, 'home' seems to connote *a state of experience* in which one feels one belongs, has security, there is absence of conflict, and everything needful is provided; *'home is where the heart is'*.

Nostalgia — which literally means 'home-pain' — may appear in the first instance as longings to return to one's country of origin, or parental home, or sweetly remembered situations in past experience; but at its core lies the universal longing to return to the golden age, to paradise, to the time and place of harmony, where discord and sin are not, where man has not fallen because he has not yet disobeyed God.

We cannot find this 'ultimate home' on earth, but we all have the archetypal image of it within ourselves — hence its expression in all myths everywhere. When 'home' features in our dreams there are bound to be many personal associations, but it is always worth considering this collective meaning of 'home' as well. When an individual feels sick and tired of seemingly endless conflict, struggle and difficulty of life, there will tend to be dreams in which he or she is 'trying to find their way home':

> I am trying to get back home but I seem to be in some foreign land, in a city torn apart by war. All around there are flattened buildings, piles of rubble, dead and wounded, and gun-fire. I slip into the shell of a building to hide. I seem to fall asleep there because I'm suddenly woken by a man trying to strangle me.

The dreamer actually awoke to find his own left hand gripping his throat, making the inner conflict painfully obvious. Recently, although religion had never before played any apparent part in his life, he had felt so troubled that he had taken to visiting churches where, if he was lucky, he felt tranquillity envelop him for a while. These moments were like a respite from his inner war. He used to say, 'I feel at home with myself then.'

THE ROYAL FAMILY

Kings and queens were once experienced as gods and goddesses. Time went by and psyche as human consciousness began to divide the realms — kings and queens became representatives of divinity rather than the actual divinities. Over the last few centuries many peoples have got rid of their royalty altogether, making all on earth earthly and all divinity supramundane.

228

In psychological language the members of the Royal Family act as collective symbols of the divine self central to every one of us. They are living incarnated images of the archetype of divinity, the crown being the sun rays of the sun-god, less effulgent versions of which appear in the hats of commoners.

Hence the fascination with the Royal Family, and hence the continuing sense that they exist at the centre and apex of the nation. To make one's way closer and closer to the royal circles is to live out in action (rather than in ever-deepening consciousness of self) the powerful archetypally-rooted urge to make one's way closer and closer to one's divine self. Anti-royalists, sadly, seem unaware of the Royal Family's role as psychological resource for us all.

While the 'royal' is in general terms an archetypal image for the mystery of the divine-and-yet-human self, the way that kings, queens, princes and princesses actually appear in dreams naturally varies according to the dreamer's stage of development in the relations between ego and self.

For example: a child, boy or girl, passes through a stage in which it is important for the development of the 'father-figure' within them, that they see their dad as wonderful, all-powerful, king-like. If he is such a shit that they just cannot manage this, then dreams will supply archetypal images of the king-like father, which appear 'in loco parentis'. How can the 'dream-maker' convey the royal quality? It can use imaginary pictures from films or books of course, but there is an added advantage in using the likeness of Prince Charles or the Duke of Edinburgh because they are also real people. Many children with an inadequate parent have pictures of the Royals stuck inside their toy cupboard.

FORESTS AND ANIMALS

Whenever the hero or heroine goes 'into the forest' we know something is going to happen; something strange, often magical, and important. Forests in dreams are just the same. Plants are alive, but the life is still deeply unconscious, seemingly fast asleep from the perspective of our human consciousness. Dream-forests symbolize a dark and drowsy level of psychic life.

Another term for the autonomic (self-regulating) nervous system is the *vegetative nervous system*. This metaphor gives some sense of the level of psyche symbolized by vegetation: the vegetative nervous system basically regulates our being at a level of blood flow, heart rate, respiratory rate, glandular productions.

229

20.12.76

(b) I'm with a small group beside a thick dark forest; we enter it and follow a path into the darkest and oldest part. The path lies alongside a fast brown river. In a clearing I find an old black car with a flat tyre. With Anna's help I fix it, but it's no good because then the whole back of the car collapses. A cow/dog with 8 teats approaches me because it has a wounded, blinded right eye; I treat it and feel sad and sorrowful.

The 'cow/dog' he tried to treat symbolized the mother, and so did the car he tried to repair because it was like the car his mother drove just after the war, when he was still very young. The dreamer, as we know, already had some consciousness about needing to make better some damage to the mother-imago. Why then does it need to be set 'within the forest'?

In part it is to do with showing him that his struggle is not his alone; that it is a collective common-to-all struggle. And in part it is to do with a very deep experience of *feelings*. Repairing wrongs within our psyche is not so much a matter of *doing* things; it is a matter of *feeling* the wrongness all the way through. That is the only way it can be dissolved and redeemed.

But this is easier said than done. The deepest guilts are the most deeply and darkly buried because to know them would mean great anguish. If one is to find them one will have to go into 'the darkest and oldest part of the forest'. There one may experience the *knowing-feeling of the emotions themselves*. This is deeper than, and usually precedes, conceptualization.

With animal symbols we leap a great step higher in the levels of psyche.

Cat and dog, often known intimately from infancy onwards, make apt symbols for the already felt and known animal and instinctual parts of one's self. Similarly, we find it easy to identify with farm animals and many well-known wild animals, and effortlessly understand them as symbols at the collective as well as the personal level.

The following dream shows how both personal and collective associations can contribute in reaching a satisfying understanding:

I am close to a single-roomed chalet-like house on stilts, high up, near cliffs; thousands of seagulls are screeching and whirling, trying to get into the room. One smashes a window; another, with prodigious strength and alarming instinctual cunning uses its beak to try to lever up the latch of the door while I fight to stop it.

This was dreamed by a brilliant and powerful young man who was unusually susceptible to woundings of his self-esteem. Until quite recently (he was in analysis), whenever he had felt wounded he would hit back with extreme ferocity, mainly in words which bit and tore at whoever had hurt him; this had tended to destroy his relationships, especially with women. Now, however, he was striving to bring these savage attacks under control.

His own associations were (1) a walk that day in a quiet valley where he had disturbed nesting birds and been mobbed by them. (2) Hitchcock's *The Birds* film. (3) The huge muscularity and tearing hunger of herring gulls.

To our work with these I added the following collective associations, which he had a gift for understanding: birds, being air-element creatures, symbolize psyche as thoughts, ideas, words, speech, while simultaneously demonstrating their unconscious and instinctual origin.

Putting personal and collective together − instinctual energies of hunger and aggression are shown in the dream to be giving direction and aim to thoughts, ideas and speech which are therefore hungry and attacking.

He understood the room to represent his nest, his place of security. Given this, I felt unsure whether the seagulls represented attacks he experienced from others which threatened his inner sanctum, or his own scarcely controllable aggression which equally threatened the loving relationships he needed. He, however, was clear about it: the seagulls were his own tearing and attacking thoughts and words which he had to fight with in order to stop them from wrecking what was precious to him.

The imaginal beasts and beings such as unicorn, phoenix, salamander, mermaid, etc., symbolize certain realities of the psyche which cannot find adequate portrayal in naturally existing creatures. It is not at all uncommon to see natural images modified or combined in dreams, the better for psyche to represent something about itself (e.g. a cat with the hands of a woman), but the imaginal creatures are so universally known that they clearly represent universals within the human psyche which need just these images to become visible. This process is beautifully described in a poem of Rainer Maria Rilke (in which 'they' are we, each and every one of us):*

> Oh, this is the animal that never was.
> They did not know it and, for all of that,
> they loved his neck and posture, and his gait,
> clean to the great eyes with their tranquil gaze.
>
> Really it *was* not. Of their love they made it,
> this pure creature. And they left a space
> always, till in this clear uncluttered place
> lightly he raised his head and scarcely needed

*From *The Sonnets to Orpheus*: Second Part. English translation by C.F. MacIntyre, University of California Press, 1960.

231

to be. They did not feed him any corn,
only the possibility he might
exist, which gave the beast such strength, he bore

a horn upon the forehead. Just one horn.
Unto a virgin he appeared, all white,
and was in the silver mirror and in her.

DRESS AND UNDRESS

Not infrequently the dream-ego becomes aware of what it is wearing or, more embarrassingly, *not wearing*. Inappropriate clothes, missing clothes, other people's shoes, masks, suits of armour — most are fairly readily understandable as portrayals of the state of the persona, that interface between our naked self and society.

If the dream is one of partial nakedness it is important to note which part of the body is exposed (usually the genitals or bottom), and to whom, or where, one is exposed (most often at work or before members of the opposite sex). This will help one to realize where one is being so self-revealing that shame, embarrassment, or fear, are being experienced, all of which may well have been unconscious, or momentarily conscious but then ignored.

Armour, masks, helmets, etc. all show extra-ordinary states of defence, sometimes shown to be stuck on, unremovable. A young woman, a business executive, was very vulnerable to criticism but she had learned to keep it hidden. Others usually saw her as brisk, efficient, a little prickly perhaps, but seemingly invulnerable. Quite often she dreamed she was wearing many layers of clothes, or supple vests of chain-mail. In one dream:

I have a sudden sharp pain in my side. Looking to see what has caused it I find I have some sort of snakeskin or crocodile skin over my left breast. I peel it off with difficulty and see a little red mark inside. It looks and feels like a bee sting.

The dream came the night after a party during which a young man had teased her. She had taken it as hostile and felt wounded (and hidden it as usual), but the dream suggests that she had unconsciously recognized an erotic component in the tease. This turned out to be right and they later became lovers.

Wearing someone else's clothes, e.g. a woman wearing her mother's blouse, suggests that some part of the persona has been taken over from that other person — a state of affairs that can usually be improved upon.

232

THE WOUND

None of us grow without receiving wounds to the body, and this fact of nature is no less true for the psyche. Most are healed in time, leaving nothing more than a scar which does not disturb function (although it may turn out to be the Achilles heel in times of later trouble).

But many of us have a wound somewhere which is still not healed. These wounds appear in our dreams, both bringing them to a painful consciousness but also helping them to heal:

7.11.76a) I arrive at L.House carrying a little gazelle I have found; I tell Daddy I want to show it to S, he agrees. I lay it on the floor by the black cupboard, close to Rachel. Mrs P carelessly breaks its leg with a chair. Very upset, I examine it; there is a *small puncture wound to the right forefoot and right shoulder*. I try to staunch the bleeding but it dies. Then I see it lying underwater except for its head. Sad.
b) I have a little car; I have to take it to Soho for servicing.

23.12.76b) I'm with a group in a car; I see a big spider on a branch and ask if it's poisonous. As if in answer it jumps onto my left shoulder, runs across my back, and *bites my right shoulder and right hand*. I kill it and examine its head and fangs with anxious interest.

13.2.77a) At the hospital; Regina incises my *right hand and shoulder* to let out poison; bright blood fountains out and I dance in it so it makes beautiful traceries over my body. N (a surgeon) stitches me up. Then I make love with Regina, feeling my penis big and strong in her, although her vagina seems to be an external pouch/purse.

Note the considerable intervals between the dreams.

THE WAY

We speak of 'finding my way', 'things getting in my way', 'everything going my way', 'doing it my way', 'having my way with you', or 'so-and-so having a way about him'.

We do try to have our 'way', and, as these sayings show, this usually means things fitting in with our conscious intentions, ambitions and desires. This way, as we know all too well, is frequently frustrated by the irritating and sometimes maddening reluctance of the outside world to fit in with what we want.

But the obstacles we experience in other people and the world of outer objects are not the only ones nor even, in the last analysis, the most impossible to overcome. There exists another 'way' within us, which is the way of our *self* and this is like the 'way' as it is meant in the *Tao*.*

To be in conflict with the Tao, the way of the self, is to suffer. How can we learn and accept the way of the self, so that we may suffer less?

In every aspect of an attentively lived life we may see the way of the self at work, but our dreams can help us in an exceptional way: not only do they draw upon a wisdom beyond our conscious ken, they are also tuned uniquely to each of us as an individual in a way that no outer communication can ever be.

When the way of our ego is in conflict with the way of the self, our dreams can help us to know it, and often help us to see something more about the way of the self which makes it easier to swallow. Living with dreams is a way to know and accept the way of the self.

Most of the dreams sprinkled throughout this book have shown one or another aspect of clashes taking place between the way of the ego and the way of the self. So very often dreams describe these clashes in the context of a journey: 'I am with so and so; we are trying to get to somewhere, but such and such happens.' Up mountains, through valleys, over bridges, down rivers, across oceans, within cities, towns, villages, into forests, swamps and bogs; on foot, in cars, boats, buses, trains and planes – the dream-ego is on the move, caught up in some way, impelled into some journey, engaged upon some endeavour which is rarely clear and never uncomplicated.

It seems appropriate to end the book with one last dream of Dr M's, in which his dream ego is trying to reach 'home', running into difficulties, but coming to understand, dimly, that he is following some deeper way:

20.1.77 A woman very close to me is driving me towards L.House, but taking some strange way which seems to involve going round in a triangle.

Then I'm driving her through a swamp with thick hairy trees; the track is flimsily made out of trunks tied lengthways with lianas; it has sharp turns and huge steps and drops; I feel very anxious.

The way gets harder and harder and eventually I come up against an impossible step.

A man comes out of the jungle and tells me we might manage because deep down the spires of churches are providing support. As he says this I somehow see what's happened in the past: long ago there was a flood on an immense scale; down below us, under all this swamp, is the real

*See the *Tao-te-Ching*, the fundamental text of Taoist mysticism and one of the fundamental texts at the roots of Zen Buddhism.

Indian Highway and this is what I have actually been going along, but without knowing it.

Nevertheless I feel doubtful about trusting to the support of occasional church spires. But then I hear the flood is subsiding. Now I know I can make it although there is still danger because it has left very thick silt.

The way seems strange to him; difficult, dangerous, impossible at times. The man who comes from the jungle is a personification of some unconscious wisdom, an inner teacher. He communicates three things: firstly, that it may be possible; secondly, that although everything seems swampy, there are holy aspirations deep within it, and they give support; and thirdly, that whatever it might seem like at the moment, the dreamer is actually following the Real Indian Highway.

Dr M understood the 'Real Indian Highway' to refer to the 'High Way of India' rather than some specific road. And for him, the High Way of India meant the tradition and the urge towards wholeness of self-knowledge; an exploration of the self that embraces the light and the dark, the masculine and the feminine. The dream itself was a reassurance that his way of living with his dreams was not just a futile swamp, but a real way.

* * *

LIVING WITH DREAMS

The journey towards self-knowledge associated with the East holds allure for many Westerners; but the way is hard and it is neither appropriate nor enough simply to copy ancient oriental techniques. Learning rituals, ways of breathing or sitting, and copying styles of dress, may easily be no more than a Westerner trying to become an Easterner, a rather futile enterprise.

Deep self-knowledge that goes beyond the commonplace understandings of the conscious personality, always has been and still is quite a rare phenomenon. *Know thyself* is both very simple and very difficult. All it involves is looking at and into oneself and *seeing whatever is there*, be it inane, wise, painful, beautiful, dirty, stupid ... or whatever. And, if one is a Westerner, this means knowing oneself *as the Westerner one is*.

Although the urge towards wholeness is in itself the same everywhere, the journey into which it propels the Westerner is not the same as that known to the East because the religions that have shaped our entire Western culture have been very different from those of the Orient. The myths of East and West, although they may have had common roots in a far-distant past, have grown in different ways and the psychic contents of twentieth-century Western man, with two thousand years of Christianity behind him, are not the same as those of a fifteenth-century Indian.

We have few truly relevant texts to help us. But we need some guide, something that can reflect to us what we are. Everyone who needs to will stumble across the occasional outside source that helps their self-understanding. They will know it when it comes because it feels as if it meets something already unconsciously 'known' inside. It comes with a sense of re-cognition, a re-membering.

Ultimately, as this sense of re-membering shows, the guide is always within; and it is constantly at work in our dreams.

They are not always easy to understand, for all the reasons we have seen; and they are not always welcome, because we do not always like what we really are. They are certainly not always profound, wise and holy, because nor are we. Often enough they seem to deal with tiresome minutiae, although there is usually more than meets the eye.

But they are the simplest of our natural treasures, easily scorned because they are not exclusive. Everyone, rich and poor, clever and stupid, good and bad, has them for free. They come from a depth within our psyche where our nature is still one with all nature, and they come to each one of us uniquely, making each of our existences a matter of real consequence in all existence. Logic finds it hard to comprehend that every single soul is the most important one to God, but one can come to know what this actually *feels* like through the simple complexity, the easy hardship, of living with one's dreams.

FURTHER READING

Hillman, James, *The Dream and the Underworld*, London: Harper & Row.
Jung, C.G., 'Paracelsus the Physician', in *The Collective Works*, vol. 15, London: Routledge & Kegan Paul.
Tao-te-Ching (trans. by Chù Ta-Kao), London: George Allen & Unwin Ltd.

INDEX